The Last Ferry Home

LaVonne Chastain

NEWMAN SPRINGS PUBLISHING
320 Broad Street
Red Bank, NJ 07701

First originally published by Newman Springs Publishing 2020

ISBN 978-1-64801-938-8 (Paperback)
ISBN 978-1-64801-939-5 (Digital)

Printed in the United States of America

To my beloved Lexi and Stan.

The Fairy Tale, Utopia, and Small Town, USA

My childhood was as close to a fairy tale as you could possibly get. Between the best parents you could possibly ever get and the idyllic woodsy setting of where I grew up for most of my school years, well, who could ask for more?

I lived in a big house in a lovely neighborhood with my mom and dad and my grandma and grandpa (my dad's parents) who were right upstairs—convenient to dash up the stairs if I was in need of spoiling. And spoiled I was… My grandma called me "precious, precious." Yes, two preciouses.

My mother would tell the story of making me something for breakfast, and when she turned for a split second, *poof!* I was gone! Up the stairs I went because I knew I'd get a half grapefruit with mountains of sugar on top, specially prepared by my dear Grandma Lilian.

Grandma was the cutest, sweetest, cutest Grandma ever. She was like a fairy-tale grandma rather like a grandma gnome. She was gentle, quite proper, and very loving. Grandpa Edwin was also a quiet person, and I always believed that he was quite a smart man. Daily, I could hear the *click-click-click* of his typewriter. Don't really know what all that typing was about, but he seemed most content clicking away in his upstairs office.

One night, something terrible happened. I didn't know what was happening, but I knew something bad and confusing was taking place. I was standing at the top of the stairs and could see down to the bottom, out onto the street—sporadic red lights flashing in that odd out of sync way that makes you feel sick to your stomach. It looked so eerie all the way down those stairs. People I didn't know were dashing around me. I could only see lots of legs running by. Being only about three years old at the time, it was like a terrifying nightmare—so much confusion and a sense of chaotic hysteria. Grandpa had died.

I didn't even know still what had happened till sometime later when Grandma moved into an apartment...without Grandpa. That was the first traumatic thing I had ever witnessed, and it stayed with me for a very long time.

Life went on, and it was good. One of my favorite things to do in that big old house was to get on my tricycle on the big sun-porch and go around in circles. Funny, I didn't fall off that trike going around and around for what seemed like hours on end. My mom probably thought, *Oh, good, that'll keep her busy, and she won't be bugging me for a while.* I was an impy kid and always dreaming up my next adventure or scheming up something to get in to. Just like the time I disappeared.

I was three or four, and I took off. My mom was beside herself with worry because at that time of day, everyone who worked at one of the factories in town was heading home from working that particular shift. She searched everywhere. Then the phone rang. It was the man who owned the grocery store, saying, "I've got your little girl here."

My mom said, "Oh, thank God, is she okay?"

He replied, "Yes, yes, everything is fine. I'll just keep feeding her candy till you get here."

So I knew where the sugar was! Again with the sugar. And it was quite a hike to the grocery store for a tiny tot to find her way. I probably chanted to myself all the way there, "Su-gar! Su-gar! Su-gar!"

My mom was such a sweet and loving person, and I loved her with my whole little heart. She was there to scoop me up and to wipe my tears with a beautiful sympathetic smile. And little did I know as a small child, she had diabetes to the worst degree. She never let on and would tell me some years later that she was lucky to be alive because they had just discovered insulin shortly before she was diagnosed. I think she was eight when they gave her the news that she would have the disease for the rest of her life. And she had a dreadful time of it from there on out.

I always felt bad for her because of her condition and would see her at times giving herself the shot, pinching her thigh, and putting that big needle in. And when she would go to the doctor, she'd come out crying, saying the doctor had harshly scolded her for her sugar levels not being what they should be. She had always watched every morsel she put into her mouth! But I must say, if you didn't know about her medical problems, you would've never guessed what her day-in, day-out life was like. She had a wonderful sense of humor and was so understanding of others. She was everything to me, and as the years went on, she would become my best friend.

Both my brother, Vance, and I were adopted due to the fact that my mom was advised not to have children of her own because of the diabetes. I can't imagine my mom being the person she was and not having kids. She had so much love to give. And I've thanked my lucky stars always for having been chosen by my mom and my dad.

My baby brother, Vance, appeared, and I do mean appeared. Normally, your mom would go through a whole pregnancy, get bigger and bigger, and head off to the hospital and then return with a new sibling.

So I would imagine on first viewing this tiny human being magically appearing, I must've thought, *Who are you and where did you come from?* Darn it, my days of being the "big cheese" were over. Still precious-precious, but now there was another one who was also precious.

Daddy was a good, kind man who no one ever could say a bad word about. He also had a funny sense of humor and always was spouting off crazy sayings. So much so that truthfully, we got sick of hearing all those sayings. His all-time favorite was, "Did you know blackberries are red when they're green?" or "She sneezed in her tomato soup, and everyone thought she had the measles." See what I mean? He was always so fair and treated everyone equally. I used to love horsey-back rides from him or going fishing with him. Just Daddy and me. I truly loved him and all his antics.

But don't piss him off. I was supposed to be getting ready for Sunday school one Sunday morning, and I did not want to go for whatever reason. I was sort of dancing around in my bedroom, repeating the words over and over in a sing-song way, "I don't want to go to Punday Pool, I don't want to go to Punday Pool." Suddenly the bedroom door opened, and it was Daddy. I wasn't ready at all. He was mad, and I most likely said something "smartie," and I got a spankin' on the bare butt! Bet I got ready in a big hurry for Punday Pool after that.

That was the one and only spanking I ever got (and later, in my teens, a slap across the face—not bad for all those growing up years). I still believe that when nothing else works, a spanking doesn't hurt anyone. Experts will now say it harms a child's self-esteem. I think not. There's a big difference between beating a child and giving a spanking or a slap. I feel in no way did that punishment change me nor harm me for the rest of my life, and I still loved my dad just as much.

As I mentioned, the town I lived in when I was small had two factories, and the whole town was built around those factories for the people who worked in them. My dad, my uncle, and Grandpa—and just about everyone we knew—worked in one of those two factories.

Someone had a vision of a small utopia which would provide all you would want all in one spot in Utopia-town. There was my favorite grocery store, of course (Su-gar! Su-gar!), post office, bank, hardware, school, playground areas, and my two all-time very favorites: the drugstore and the AMAZING clubhouse.

The drugstore was (well, it was the '50s) just what you'd imagine for that era, and all the kids were in heaven the minute we came through the door. Right off the bat was the giant candy counter (Get 'em as they come in the door!). The rest of the place held all sorts of goods and sundries. The pharmacy was in the back, and they had those large, mysterious, glass, scientific-looking decanters of colored water up high where you could see them clearly, even if you were short. I was sure they contained some exotic elixir that could cure the worst of ailments. They always looked like something in a Frankenstein laboratory. Fascinating.

But the primo attraction at the drugstore was the soda fountain. When we did have money (usually not), we would have a cherry coke, root beer float, or maybe a hot fudge sundae. That was all good and well, but even better, the soda fountain had the twirly stools to sit on. More like spin on. That was so much fun. And how many times were we told off for spinning? Plenty. Then why have seats that spin?

The AMAZING clubhouse: I get a shiver of excitement even now just recalling it to mind. The building itself had a beautiful facade. A lot of the rooms in it housed offices for the factories I mentioned. Come take a tour with me:

You always entered through the back of the building on a rather grand staircase. Straight ahead, through the doors, was the auditorium, a large room with wooden floors and a stage at the far end. Chairs would be lined up around the walls for dances held there, or chairs would be set up in rows if there was some sort of show taking place on the stage. I danced my way to "stardom" on that stage quite a few times during my childhood in various dance recitals. Off to the side of the auditorium, behind a door, was a steep staircase, quite narrow, and it struck me as a bit creepy. It was dimly lit. But the minute you hit the bottom stair, turned left, and opened another door, there it was—a large blue sparkling pool. Beautiful. Carry on past the pool, through another door, and on your right was a huge basketball court which had a running track at the top in a circle up by the ceiling. Straight ahead was a ping-pong table. Look to your right again, and there you have it—a mini bowling alley!

Keep going, and there were two pool tables, and last but not least, a sunken handball courtroom that had a viewing window so you could watch the people down in there playing a game. What a place! Talk about a kid's paradise!

Lots of times, we'd visit everyone in Utopia, and lots of times, we'd stay overnight with my mom's mom and dad—Grandma Inga and Grandpa Sam—and Auntie Shirley too. Shirley still lived at home, the youngest of my mom's siblings. Shirley was just five years older than me, and I wanted to be her. My mom's younger brother had left home and was in the service. My mom's other sister, Auntie

Lovey (a lot of my relatives had cute little nicknames like that) lived in Utopia too along with her husband and their six kids and counting. Sometimes me and Vance would stay with Auntie Lovey, Uncle Chum, and all the kids. Wild times and always so much fun.

Now Grandma Inga (Swedish roots) was very glamorous. Think of Joan Crawford. She was skinny as a stick, wore tons of makeup, and always dressed "to the nines," even for one of the kid's birthday parties! Actually, from now on, I'll just call her Glam-Gram (a.k.a. Glama). It wasn't till years later that it dawned on me just how glamorous she was. She was always just Grandma to me.

Her day pretty much consisted of sitting on the couch, watching TV, drinking coffee, smoking, and chatting on the phone. Many times on the phone, she was ordering groceries to be delivered. The good old days. She was very particular and wanted what she wanted. She would say, "I want the large size of the canned tomatoes, don't give me the small one, I want the large one. I'd like some nice bananas, not brown, I want nice yellow ones. Give me two pounds of your good ground beef, the good pink stuff." And on and on it went till at last she hung up the phone. About an hour later, there was a knock on the back door, and the groceries (all the good ones) would be handed through in a kind of assembly line to the kitchen.

Glam-Gram was a character in her own right and was full of fun, a quirky sort who was full of surprises too. Always when I would ask for a glass of water, she would ask me, "In you or on you?"

I always said, "In me."

She'd promptly give me the water I'd asked for.

One day, I decided I'd call her bluff. I said in a determined voice, "On me."

She took the biggest damn glass she could find, filled it to the top, and poured it over my head! I was shocked but shouldn't have been because that was Grandma.

Grandpa Sam was a quiet man who worked a lot, and when he wasn't at work, he sat back and let the world carry on. When all the kids were around, he was the quietest person in the room. He was kind and gentle...until he was fighting with Grandma. It was the age-old saying that applied to Grandma and Grandpa., "You can't live with 'em, you can't live without 'em."

Oh, how they fought. Grandpa would be upstairs, Grandma downstairs, and they would swear and holler till the air turned blue. All the kids in the family knew every swear word in the book from a very young age. Since this was a common occurrence, we just ignored it and carried on with whatever we were doing. Poor Grandpa Sam, he didn't have a chance because how it came across to me, Grandma was quite demanding, and Grandpa would just reach his threshold of Grandma's rants, and the air turned blue again. Then indigo, purple, dark purple, and then black as if an indoor storm was about to take place. That's how bad it really was.

Auntie Shirley was a character too. Well, growing up with such colorful parents, what choice did she have? For the most part, she and I were great pals. But she had a habit of making up fantastical stories to freak me out or just plain scare me. She told them to me as if they were the God's truth. Here's one:

There was a girl sitting under a tree, reading a book in the park. She fell asleep. Later, when the girl was sitting at the dinner table, her nose started itching. It was tickling and itching so bad she took her fork to scratch it. Soon she was raking at her nose and digging at it with the fork. She ended up tearing part of her nose off, and millions of ants came pouring out. Honestly, where did Shirley come up with that stuff?

It was after one of these "lovely" stories she told that I sent a Valentine card. My mom bought a card for me to sign and send to Auntie Shirley. I was still mad about the evil story she had told, so I quickly signed the card, writing, "Dear Auntie Shirley, you are a brat. Love, Me" (I still wrote "Love, Me" like that would smooth it over). I quickly shoved it in the envelope and gave it to my mom to send. Ooh, I got in big fat trouble for that. To this day, I still think Auntie Shirley had it coming.

When Vance and I stayed overnight at Glam-Gram's, we ate treats and watched *The Twilight Zone.*

Then off to bed. Grandma would stay up, maybe all night, doing her usual: watching TV, drinking coffee, smoking, and chatting on the phone. Shirley and I would go upstairs to the bed she and Grandma shared. Grandpa had his own room, and Vance would sleep in Grandpa's bed. Grandpa, most times, was off working the midnight shift.

Shirley and I would crawl into bed, Shirley having turned on the radio quietly to the most popular station/music of the times. Since she was just that much older than me, now in her teenage years, she couldn't live without the music. The radio played softly, and I lay there, thinking about what I had just seen on *The Twilight Zone*. It never scared me, just scrambled my brain a bit. I would try to decipher and analyze it till I had an idea of what the show meant before I could settle myself enough to try for sleep. Thank you, Rod Serling…

Lying there, I could smell the coal burning downstairs in the old furnace. I liked the feel of the nubbly bedspread with all the little fabric balls on it. And an ethereal orangey hue was cast into the room from the streetlight outside. The light shone through the worn shade that covered the window at the foot of the bed. All these things were comforting in an abstract way, and I felt happy and loved being at Grandma's. As I drifted off, the music softly playing, I'd hear my favorite song come on, "Ferry Cross the Mersey." What a perfect way to fall asleep, hearing my favorite song.

As we both got older, and Shirley quit making up those horrifying tales, I envied Auntie Shirley. She was older, witty, funny, and wore the coolest, latest, most up-to-date fashionable clothes. When she went to the prom, in my eyes, she looked like Cinderella. Sabrina (my cousin) and I were allowed to go to the prom's Grand March. I didn't know what a Grand March was.

My mom, Grandma Inga, Sabrina, and I arrived at the high school gymnasium. Some grand music began to play (it was the Grand March, after all), and all of the prom-goers came out onto the floor in formation. What a beautiful procession it was! All the girls in their magnificent dresses and the handsome boys in their suits. Who cares about the boys, just look at those gorgeous girls! They gracefully glided around the floor, never breaking formation. Had they practiced that? To a young girl as I was at the time, it was one of the most breathtaking things I had ever seen.

The times Vance and I had at Auntie Lovey's were some of the best. We might have gone ice-skating in the winter or go play at the playground at the school right across from their house. Or we might have gone to the AMAZING clubhouse. By now, there were eight kids and still counting. There would be ten kids altogether by the time Auntie Lovey became too worn out to have any more.

Auntie Lovey was a nice congenial sort, always smiling and willing to listen, even with all those kids! The volume of food she made round the clock was astounding, but she just got on with it. Sometimes Auntie Lovey would make her famous chocolate sauce to put on top of ice cream. She made everyone's favorite sauce by blending baking cocoa and some sugar, a bit of water, and butter into a saucepan. The best was when she had marshmallows and would throw a few in for extra goo. YUM. She had to be creative with all those kids.

Uncle Chum was a jokester, always coming up with something clever to say. He was what you would describe as jolly. I overheard an amusing comment one day when he was speaking to one of my elder boy cousins. My cousin was scolding Uncle Chum in a teasing way about not attending church. Ever. Uncle Chum spoke right up and said, "What are you talking about? I went to church twice today! First time I went, I dropped your mother off, and the second time, I went and picked her up!"

Chum was witty and he was an artist. He could draw cartoon characters of people he knew and would make a neat card for someone with a caricature of that person on the front. Along with his quirky sense of humor and his talent for drawing and painting, I always felt he had missed his calling.

Mom and Dad, having gone out for an evening, would leave Vance and I in the care of Lovey and Chum. When it was bedtime, all the girls would head up to the girls' room, all the boys to the boys' room. There were a few sets of bunk beds in both bedrooms. In total, there were only three bedrooms for that big family. Of course, one of those rooms belonged to Auntie Lovey and Uncle Chum. No one minded being a bit crammed, and that's just the way it was—pillows, blankets, and clothes everywhere. No getting around it with a pile of kids.

All us girls would find a spot in the beds and wiggle in together. Just as we got settled, Uncle Chum would come through the door. He would say, "Who's first?"

Someone would call out their name. Then he would write that person's name in the dark with the glowing tip of his cigarette, high enough for all to see. What a hoot! When everyone's name had been written as only Uncle Chum could do, he bid us good night and left the room. Now the real party began!

Now was the time for telling spooky stories and dirty ones too. Now by dirty, I mean to a kid dirty. And you think as a kid it's the dirtiest thing you've ever heard. All quite innocent but at the time...

The one that was the funniest and dirtiest went like this: There was a three-story apartment building. A man lived on the top floor. One day, he was shaving, and he dropped his electric razor, and by God, it chopped his wiener off! Somehow there was a hole in the floor, and the wiener in question fell right through that hole. At the same time, the person on the story below was fitting a new light fixture in their ceiling, leaving a hole for the wiener to fall through. Of course, that person had a mysterious hole in their floor too, and there went the wiener on its travels to the bottom floor.

A lady lived in that bottom apartment and was busy canning pickles that day. She turned her back for a minute, and the wiener fell...*kerplop*! Right into a jar of pickles! Imagine that! We screamed and laughed, and someone fell onto the floor from laughing so hard, all because of the disgusting and hilarious tale!

The tribe of cousins I had, belonging to Lovey and Chum, ranged in age from Don who was four years older than me all the way down to the newest baby. Auntie Lovey liked to add a "y" to all of their names if they weren't already named with a name ending in "y." As follows: Don (Donny), Louis (Louey), Josh (Joshy), Sabrina, Matt (Matty), Gwen (Gwenny), Barrett (Barry), Eileen, Wanda, and Tina (Trixy). That's all ten of 'em.

Donny, Louey, and Joshy—the oldest three—had a habit of punching everyone in the shoulder; not too hard, but just to be cool, I guess. It got old, fast. Most times, I liked them, though, just fine. Sabrina was a year younger than me, so we did things together when our families gathered for holidays, birthdays, and picnics. Matty was a fun-loving kid with a good sense of humor. Gwenny was a pretty little girl that liked to tag around with me and Sabrina but didn't bug us too much. Barry was a cute little boy, smallish and adorable with brown eyes. Eileen was a quiet little one, and Wanda was a tiny girl who had lovely red hair and could be described as a peanut. At the bottom of the totem pole was Trixy, a smiley baby who got her nickname from Uncle Chum. They all had such different personalities, and I loved each one of them just the way they were (and are today). Still do.

It Was Only a Dream

At Auntie Lovey's, there were always so many people around—her own large family, visitors, relatives, neighbors, and because of the volume of people, there was always a new baby on show.

Everyone had gathered in the dining room as was the custom at Auntie Lovey's. They were all oohing and ahh-ing at the newest bundle of joy I assumed must've been seated in his or her little carrier seat on the dining room table. There was a large crowd around the table, but I managed to squeeze myself toward the front of the group in order to see this adorable new baby they had been gushing over.

It was just the head of a baby! The head was as small as a baseball perched atop a small Styrofoam coffee cup! The head had a face and a smile and was saying, "Goo-goo, ga-ga" as babies do…but it was just a head the size of a baseball!

Our Big House in Our Small Town

When I was about five, we moved to our new house around twenty miles away from Utopia, another paradise for kids. The town was beautiful and wonderful and very small. So small that people would say, "Blink your eyes and you'll miss it." It was nothing but a dot the size of a period on the map. "Downtown" consisted of a small grocery store, a gas station, a post office, a nice-sized co-op, the elementary school, high school, another teeny candy-cum-sundries shop, and a couple of churches. But the best two places were Bob's Beef Drive-in and the Dairy Freeze. The town also had a real dairy with all sorts of cows just down the road, a short way from our new house—nice fresh dairy products for all the people who lived in Small Town, USA.

The brand-new freshly built house we moved into was on a dirt road with one other house at the very end of the road. There were lots of trees and fields, and we had a huge backyard. Also, at the end of the road was a river we would spend a lot of time at when Vance and I got a bit older. It was quiet and safe there, and our whole family settled right in.

I started kindergarten there, close enough to walk, but I rode the bus, mostly because of my age…can't have the wee ones go astray in the "booming metropolis."

It Was Only a Dream

I was a rosebud in the dream. That was me. A teeny tiny pink rosebud. I was floating on a breeze over the front yard of our house. The breeze would whoosh me up a bit, and then I'd gently decline. I was sailing around, having a wonderful time just lilting around, little rosebud me. I looked over, and there on the road in front of me, I saw the school bus driving by. I called out in my dainty rosebud voice, "Ha ha, you have to go to school, and I don't."

*****

I started dance classes at a very young age. Most of the time, I enjoyed it but found out after a year or two I did not enjoy tap dancing. Too much slapping around in those noisy shoes. I was taught a sampling of each form of dance: ballet, acrobatics, and the dreaded tap. Since the three oldest girls in the family were involved with dance classes, Glam-Gram was an excellent seamstress and made costumes for me, Sabrina, and Auntie Shirley. With stars in their eyes, I guess Mom, Glama, and Auntie Lovey wanted their girls to, in fact, be little stars. We had some beautiful costumes, and I remember Glama swearing as she sat at her sewing machine, all the intricate and lavish details she tried to get near perfect.

Once we were dressed as ballerinas atop music boxes. Each little dancer had a circular platform to dance upon that was decorated in powder blue and light pink to match our costumes of the same colors. We wore huge baby doll hats, blue trimmed in pink.

We had another number which was a bit more jazzy, probably a tap number. My dance class was on the stage at the clubhouse this particular time. We were lined up, tallest in the middle, shortest on the ends. We were giving it our all. At one point as the music played, we were all to turn to our left. I guess some thought left, others thought right. A girl in the middle thought she knew for sure and started pulling the arms of those on either side of her to get them going in the direction she believed was correct. So the whole dance line was going in opposite directions. Some followed the girl who thought she knew the way, and others were doing their own thing. The parents and other people in the audience must've gotten a real hoot out of the whole production. Once we had lost our way, I heard lots of raucous laughter coming from the darkness, those faceless people in the audience.

17

I once did a solo when I was about seven. This would be considered too sexist nowadays. The tune I tumbled to (an acrobatic number; I was limber as a small piece of rubber) was "Itsy Bitsy Teeny-Weeny Yellow Polka Dot Bikini." I came out in an old-fashioned swimsuit—one-piece, flouncy sleeves, flouncy pantaloon-type bloomers, and a matching poofy hat with a ruffly brim. Sometime after the "Teeny-Weeny" part of the verse, I peeled apart the Velcro which held the front of the costume together, stepped out of the old-fashioned monstrosity, and finished the tumbling in the teeny-weeny bikini. Really? What they used to talk me into...

Later, after the show, I got all kinds of praise for my limberness. That almost made it worthwhile after I had felt pretty close to naked doing all my stunts.

For first, second, and third grade, I rode the bus out to the countryside. That was a neat old school that sort of looked like it was painted into its surroundings, *Little House on the Prairie*-ish.

First grade was exciting, and all the girls in my class, including me, were all fond of our teacher, Mrs. McKinnon. In order to learn about money and the counting of it, sometimes Mrs. McKinnon would pull out a cardboard storefront to the front of the room. We loved playing store. Someone would stand behind the window of the store, and another kid would approach the window and fake-purchase an item with real money. There were items such as an apple, a ruler, a hammer, a small rubber ball—just little stuff like that. One day, after we were done purchasing items and were putting the goods away, Mrs. McKinnon climbed on a chair to put some items on the roof of the store. Suddenly, one of the items fell. It was the hammer, and it clunked poor Mrs. McKinnon on the head! She fell to the floor! Oh no! All the little girls started crying! We were sure she was dead! But no, she got up, a bit dazed, but she would live! What a relief!

Around about second grade, something fabulous happened: The Beatles had their premiere performance on *The Ed Sullivan Show*. All the girls in my class were buzzing in school the next day after the glorious TV event. Everyone had a favorite, and we were actually in a big debate on which one of the Fab Four was the cutest. Little did we know how famous and everlasting they would be in years to come.

The Little Girl Down the Road, My Bestest Friend

Right before the next new school year started, my mom told me a new little girl my age had moved into the neighborhood right down at the end of the road. Mom said, "Honey, why don't you ride your bike down there and say hi?"

Didn't have to tell me twice. There were no girls my age in the neighborhood, even though the area had a few more houses since we had moved in a few years back. My mom described the house to me. I got on my bike, got to the house, and went to the back door where the new girl lived. A nice dark-haired lady came to the door, and I asked if she had a girl about my age.

"Do you mean Ally?"

I nodded my head yes, hoping she would be the girl I was looking for.

Then Ally timidly appeared at the door. I told her my name and asked her if she wanted to come to my house. From there on out, we were best friends and were inseparable for many years. Little did I know we'd be lifelong friends, and I treasure her to this day more than words can say. If anyone gets me, it's Ally. And I've always adored her mother too as if she were my own.

When Ally and I had become better acquainted, I told her that I had been adopted. She asked, "Who's your real mom?"

I replied, "You know, that lady I live with down the road in the yellow house. The one I call Mom."

Both Vance and I had been told from the time we could understand words that we had been adopted. Our parents put it across as, "A wonderful lady had you and couldn't keep you, so she gave you to us."

We said, "Okay."

That's what you do as an adoptive parent. It's the right thing to do. You do not keep that information from a child. Because sooner or later, that child finds out, maybe years down the road, and then it stings like the worst betrayal. I've known a few people in my lifetime that this has happened to, and it was confusing and shocking when they finally heard the truth.

I'd never had a burning desire to know who my birth parents were. Sometimes I'd seen a show on TV about someone searching for their mother or father, and they were completely obsessed and thought of it every day. Some of the adoptees felt left out, abandoned, or just plain bewildered, wanting to know and yearning with all their soul to locate their missing parent(s).

I credit my feelings on the subject to my wonderful adoptive parents who couldn't have loved me more. I felt their love every single day and was told I was loved every single day. This is so very important. Some kids are never told these important words from their parents. Some are never kissed or hugged. That is unbelievable to me. I feel sad for those kids, now adults, who didn't have outward expressions of love conveyed to them on a regular basis. Is it karma passed on from a previous life? In mystical writings, it's said you actually choose your parents. If that's true, then I chose very well to be so well taken care of and truly loved.

Others who've been adopted were maybe adopted for the wrong reasons, and it hasn't worked out well for them. That's unbelievable to me too. If a couple wants a child so much as to go through the whole process, the hoping and the waiting, then wouldn't they be so thankful and delighted to finally have a child that they would be like my mom and dad and love that child to pieces? All those children and then adults have a place in my heart for not being loved to pieces.

Reading, Writing, 'Rithmetic,
and Assorted Antics

When I reached third grade, everyone got a classroom on the third floor. Why that was such a thrill, I don't know. Maybe we felt we were moving up in the world.

Enter "Danny the Manny." He was a funny, mischievous kid who would entertain us at lunchtime by flipping his eyelids inside out. Ooh, how utterly gross and awesome at the same time. You could see the meaty insides of his eyelids, and I think it hurt his eyes a bit afterward, but that got him all the attention, so he was always game. I adored him as much as a third-grade girl could. He got trapped in his locker one day. Me and a few other kids walked by his locker. We heard a muffled, "Help…help." *Danny.* We finally realized where the "Help, help" was coming from, and the janitor was summoned to dig him out of there. Danny was always up to his tricks.

Also in the third grade, our class put on a play. The play was *Cinderella,* and the little girl who was picked for the lead part was taller than most and had the longest hair. Her name was Faith. All the little girls wanted to have the coveted role of Cinderella, and we were all green with envy when we found out the girl with the longest hair would play the leading role. There was gossip on the playground that the only reason Faith got the role was due to her long Cinderella-like hair.

The play was a success with the closing scene taking place at the ball. We all sang a song about waltzing: "Swaying, swaying to and fro, round and round the room we go." And we swayed to what seemed like twenty-two verses of it. On and on it went…till the curtain was drawn. The best part for me was I got to wear an old cocktail dress Mom had borrowed from someone, which came to the floor on me, and didn't I think I was just the grandest lady at the ball!

For Mother's Day that year, we put on another show; we sang songs about spring and also motherly type songs, one being the old "M is for the million things she gave me…" When we learned it, the girls thought it was the most beautiful song we had ever heard. When we reached the end of the song and had sung, "Put them all together, they spell *Mottthhhhhher*, a word that means the world to me," we were practically in tears, especially if you really and truly loved your mother.

In the fourth grade, no more bus rides since the next level of elementary school was only a few blocks away. We got a teacher we weren't too fond of that year—Mrs. Richmond. All smooth sailing up till then… Of course, we soon came up with a nickname for her: Mrs. Witchmond. Or simply Mrs. Witch. Behind her back, of course.

One day after recess, we came back to class and were all seated in our assigned places. We were about to begin our lesson, and there came a faint knock on the door. Mrs. Witch promptly went and opened the door. There stood Donny Martin with a sheepish look on his face, hands behind his back. Mrs. Witch said, "What seems to be the problem, Donny?"

Donny, replied in a near whisper, "I tore my pants."

Then Mrs. Witch said, "Oh, let me see!"

Well, that was all it took, and thirty-some kids were howling with laughter. Heaven forbid Mrs. Witch would see Donny's underpants!

A big baseball game took place on the playground one day. A few different grades were participating, and everyone playing the game and those who weren't (me) seemed unusually revved up that day. As the game was in the last inning, a big girl named Janine was racing for home base. She was running a hundred miles an hour, buck teeth glinting in the sun. Just as she got to home, she tripped, toppling on to the catcher, embedding those great big teeth into the unassuming catcher's forehead!

There was blood and gore, and one of the teachers had to come and pry Janine's teeth out of the victim's head. Not since Mrs. McKinnon's close brush with death in the first grade had we all experienced what we thought would be the fatality of the catcher. The catcher finished his school career with a nasty scar, and Janine needed some dental work, but the two survived.

The best teacher we ever had for all those long and arduous school years, we all agreed, was the teacher we got in fifth grade. Thank God after that frightful year we had with Mrs. Witch. His name was Mr. Petersen, and he was fair, soft-spoken, and smiled easily...unlike that previous teacher. What a welcome relief. He reminded me of Mr. Rogers (of the neighborhood from TV). He actually wore a sweater with the leather patches on the elbows. We had lucked out big time having Mr. Petersen.

Remember Danny the Manny (the kid with the gross and awesome eyeballs)? Danny and Tom Benson had an altercation in fifth grade. Tom came into the classroom one day, steam coming out of his ears. Mr. Petersen, in his calm quiet voice, asked Tom whatever the matter was. Tom boisterously replied, "You'd be mad too if someone was watching you take a shit!"

All the kids in the classroom held their collective breaths. Swearing right in front of the teacher! The two boys had been in the bathroom, and "the Manny" had climbed on top of the toilet in one stall, peering down into the next stall as Tom did his business. Boys are disgusting.

Mr. Petersen, in his casual way, took the boys into the hall and evidently spoke to them in his reasonable manner. The boys were friends again by the end of the day. Man, Mr. Petersen was good.

Ally and I spent every waking hour together down at the swimming hole in the river at the end of our road in the summer months. In the wintertime, we went ice-skating on that same frozen river just beyond the swimming hole. Ally and I would spend all day shoveling the snow away so we'd have a nice big space to skate. After dinner, we'd grab our skates and head to our own personal rink. Well, not so personal as most of the time, we were joined by a group of the neighborhood kids. It didn't matter how cold it was. We were out there, skating and gliding by the light of the moon, our silhouettes moving to the sound of our blades scraping beneath us. It was a winter wonderland. All part of the fairy tale.

We stayed overnight at each other's houses and rode our bikes through hill and dale all over town, my best friend and I. Each morning, it was my mom's job to get us moving off to school. Ally always came to get me for school so we could walk together and yak, yak, yak all the way. We've never been at a loss for words and still have a hard time now hanging up the phone.

One night, I was staying overnight with Ally, and we were in her room, talking away (no kidding). Ally said, "I'd like some ice cream, would you?"

You bet! She then said for me to go to the big chest freezer in the garage and get the ice cream, and she'd get the bowls and the spoons.

I headed out to the garage in my nightie. I got the large chest freezer door open and had to lean way in to reach the ice cream. What a sight, my little butt poking out of the freezer. All of a sudden, I saw car lights shining behind me, and then heard a car door shut. Her dad had come home from his night shift at work. "Hey! What are you doing?"

Yikes! I tore outta there and ran all the way down the length of the house to Ally's bedroom! He had frightened the daylights out of me, and how well Ally and I knew what he was like. No messing around when he was about. We dared not to go back out of her room and we never got our ice cream.

Ally had a few things I was totally jealous of: pet monkeys, a pet skunk, a snowmobile, and she played the organ quite beautifully.

She was giving the monkeys a bath in the bathroom sink when I showed up to visit one day. She had two small spider monkeys. As she retrieved one from the sink, that mean little creature grabbed her finger in both of its little hands, clamped its teeth in, and bit her as hard as it could! Poor Ally was stunned and cried her heart out in extreme pain. Okay, I was less jealous of the pet monkeys after that episode.

The organ was bought specially for her because her dad loved organ music and wanted to be entertained daily with the selections he would request. She took lessons and would play the song about the Green Berets. I myself had always wanted to play the piano and never have. So for her to be able to sit at the organ and play various pieces—and so well at that—made me a bit green.

Then didn't Ally just win the coloring contest at our Small Town grocery store? Ooh, that was the most jealous I ever was. And the prize was a transistor radio! By all rights, my "expert" coloring job should have won. As jealous as I was at times in my heart of hearts, she was and always will be my dear friend.

Ally's mom would always call herself my second mom. Okay, fine by me because I treasured her for the rest of my life.

Little Nina was a small sprightly woman with dark hair and dark shining eyes. But do not refer to her as short. She hated when people pointed out her shortness. She had a quick wit and a quirky sense of humor, and she made the best damn chocolate cookies ever. She'd make millions of them at a time, and her kids and I ate about a million at a time. Everyone's mom made the regular recipe on the back of the chocolate chip package, but Mama Nina's beat the heck out of all the other cookies. I wondered what she did to make hers so good. I finally came to the conclusion that she must've kissed each one of them as they came out of the oven. Really, I think it was the real butter she used. I was privileged sometime along the line to be given her special recipe and use it even now. When somebody brings their chocolate chip cookies to a family party or gathering and some-one at the event compliments the cookie baker on their cookies, I think to myself, *No, mine are waaay better.*

Nina had been busy painting the kitchen one day and had become loopy from the fumes. I had never seen her so silly. First she sang, "My baby wears a rubber girdle (instead of 'does the han-ky-panky')," then she picked up some small, brightly colored toys Ally's little brother had left scattered on the floor, and as Nina picked up each one, she proclaimed, "This one is a strawberry! This one is a blueberry!" and named every berry known to man. What a nut!

But poor Nina had to put up with Ally's dad, so it wasn't all fun and games by any means. Her dad was callous and bitched a lot all the time. He was a smallish man with a temper, and the family felt his wrath whenever the mood struck him. Ally told me once that he came through the house one evening, all dressed up, aftershave, hair slicked back. "Dad, where are you going?" she had asked.

He replied with a smirk on his face, "Out to see my girlfriend."

And sure enough, that's just what he had been doing. Ally's mom and dad divorced. It was hard on the whole family, and Ally's mom had to work. Ally was in charge of the little ones and was stuck at home much of the time as babysitter-in-chief.

Nina, through the years after the divorce, got married several times. Just couldn't seem to find the right guy, none of them deserving of what she had to give. One of the husbands almost killed her by nearly choking her to death. My dear second mom didn't deserve any of it. Toward the end of her life many years later, she did find the right one, and they had quite a few happy years together. I'm so glad.

There was an extra person who lived at Ally's house—her Uncle Karl. He was a good-natured man, actually her dad's uncle. Ally's mom had taken him in, feeling sorry that he had such a hard life. He was deaf and mute, but that had been just part of the problem. As a child, he had worked on his family's farm. Since he was a strapping young man, he was used more or less as a mule, and from what Ally had told me, he was treated like an animal too. When he was still quite young, his parents decided to send him to deaf school so he could learn to communicate using sign language. That was a good thing. However, he was only a kid, couldn't speak or hear, and they gave him a small suitcase and put him on a train for places unknown. I don't know what happened in between until he ended up with Ally's family, besides her mother's goodwill, but I'm so glad he did end up there with them.

Ally loved him dearly, and in time, I did too. Ally had taught me the alphabet in sign language. All her siblings, mom, and dad knew the alphabet and whole words too so they could communicate with Karl. When I'd come to visit Ally nearly every day, I'd walk into the kitchen, and Uncle Karl's face lit up. I felt he was so genuinely happy to see me. I don't think I had ever felt so special in someone's eyes as I did with Karl. Immediately, Karl would do the *H* and the *I* with his finger signs, and I did it back. He beamed. Then he would spread his arms and make a guttural noise ("Come here"), wanting a hug. And when you were hugged by Uncle Karl, you knew it. He would give you the biggest tightest hug, and he really meant it.

Uncle Karl usually sat at the dining room window and watched the birds and squirrels. He watched TV and knew every single thing going on in all the soap operas. We marveled at his understanding of the story lines as he signed, made faces, and made some guttural noises to dramatize the plots.

One Valentine's Day, Ally came to my house with a card explaining that it was from Karl. On the envelope in primitive scrawled writing, he had written my name the best he could. I opened the card, and on the front of it was a pink heart with a small rhinestone at the top. The greeting was, "Happy Valentine's Day, Grandma. With Love."

I looked at Ally quizzically and asked, "Why does it say Grandma?"

She said, "Oh, he didn't pay any attention to that. He just thought it was pretty."

And it was. When I opened it and looked inside, in the same scrawling hand, it was signed "Love, HI." It is still one of my prized possessions, and when I happen across it in my memorabilia, it brings tears to my eyes.

He was a permanent fixture at Ally's, and we took great pleasure in conversing with him, Ally being better at it, knowing how to sign whole words and sentences. Ally now many years later works with deaf people, helping them to live their everyday lives in an easier and more efficient way. She also has done entire church services in sign language. Uncle Karl would be so proud.

A Poem from Ally
(A Treasure from Many Years Ago...
Just as It Was Presented to Me)

meet   have fun
  talk   run
    smile   walk
      joke   ride bikes
        argue   fall...
        fight   swim
          cool it   discuss
            get together   compare
            goof off   make decisions
           do things   tell jokes
           "bug it"   get along
                everlasting friendship
                yup...BEST FRIENDS

My Brother, My Friend

No, I haven't been avoiding talking about my brother, Vance. When you have a little brother, you go about your everyday life. We played and fought, got along, didn't get along—the usual sibling stuff.

Mom and Dad had made some new friends in Small Town. One couple had two kids. Their boy was nicknamed Skip who was the same age as me, and their little girl, Jill, was a year younger than Vance. The family came to visit ours one evening. All us kids were in Vance's bedroom, playing. Skip and I were having a great time doing whatever we were doing, totally leaving the little ones out.

First, Skip came running into the living room, holding his head, crying. I came out next, holding my head, crying. Then Vance came out, went directly to our dad, and declared, "Me be a good boy now, Daddy!" He had clunked each one of us with my majorette baton. Served us right.

Vance was known for his temper. Don't get the boy riled up. Because I knew this, I would pretty much rile as much as I could. I loved to make up stories as a kid and test them out on Vance (Auntie Shirley's influence perhaps?). At the end of our road, across the highway, was an old gas station not in operation anymore, but someone lived in the apartment above it. Vance and I were out on the road one day right in front of our house. The gas station/apartment was not quite a block away. I yelled out, "Hello!"

It created an echo bouncing off the apartment/gas station building. So of course, I told Vance that whoever lived in that apartment would shout from the window the same word you shouted to them. He was thrilled with that, and we stood out on the road for quite some time, bellowing every word and phrase we could think of.

When Vance was old enough to learn to play an instrument at school, he decided he'd like to play the trumpet. That meant he had to practice at home. It got on my last nerve. Those silly trilling exercises he practiced seemed to go on for hours in his room. There was one in particular that was so annoying. First, he'd play a few bouncy notes, then tap his foot for the beats in between. More notes, more foot tapping. And on and on and on. I'd quietly open his bedroom door and in my most smart-ass annoying voice mimic the tune he had just played. The usual loud response was, "Mommmmmmmm!" He was hoping she would come to his rescue, which she usually did, and then I'd get told off not to tease my brother when he was practicing. I just couldn't help it.

Another one of my evil tricks to rile Vance up was to frighten him each and every time he came down the basement stairs. I would already be down there, and I'd hear him open the door at the top of the stairs. I'd hide around the corner at the very bottom and would then wait for him to happily come down. The minute he hit that bottom stair, I'd jump out and not even loudly say, "Yah!"

Again with the, "Mommmmm!" And the kid never wised up. Each time he came down those basement stairs, I was waiting...

Now it sounds like I was just plain evil to my brother, but it was in retribution, paying him back for all his bugging of me. All of you who have a younger sibling know what I'm talking about. When he got mad at me, he would do this windmill thing with his arms. A regular punching machine he was. He'd start at one end of the main hallway in our house and get those arms a-whippin'! He'd come like a high-powered bulldozer, slicing the air with arms flying, head down, making a beeline in my direction. Vance, Vance, doing his punching dance!

I really loved Vance, and he loved me—just a bit of sibling rivalry. Once we went beyond our childhood years, we were really best of friends, and to this day still are. We have some fabulous conversations. He's one of my favorite people to talk to.

He's always been so good at helping me solve problems throughout my life. And for that, I will always be grateful. I've told him before but I'll say it again: "Thank you for being my brother, Vance. I love you."

Buddy and Brutus

We had our first dog, Buddy, a terrier-type dog, when we were kids. We had him for a few years till he came to his demise being run over by a car one day. A sad day it was.

About a year went by, and Dad said we could get another dog. Our neighbors had two Chihuahuas, and we loved playing with them when we visited. My brother and I asked Dad if we could have a little dog like that. Dad then asked the neighbors where they had found their dogs. They informed Dad that an elderly couple who lived way out in the woods had lots of Chihuahuas. The neighbors gave Dad the phone number of the old couple to see if they had any dogs available. Yes, they had a few dogs to choose from.

We all got in the car to go get our new dog. We found the right house out in the middle of nowhere and got out of the car. Dad knocked on the screen door; the inside door was open. No one came. Looking through the screen door, we saw an incredible sight. It was like the old movie with all the Dalmatians. There were at least 101 Chihuahuas! They were everywhere! On top of chairs, running around everywhere, on the couch, eating food, yapping simultaneously—it was like a circus of dogs in that house!

Eventually, an old man came through from the back of the house and showed us a few dogs out of the many we could choose from. We picked a little male and decided that his name would be Brutus. It was our little joke giving the tiny dog a name fitting of a much bigger dog. Brutus was so not a threat to anyone.

Brutus, we found, had a special talent. He could smile. And on command. Everyone who met him thought he was snarling, but he was just smiling. He was a friendly pipsqueak and never bit anyone.

Just smiled. After we had Brutus for a while, when I'd see other dogs, they seemed boring because they didn't smile.

Vance was on the front porch one day, banging a roll of caps really used with a cap gun; but instead, Vance was hitting the caps with an old hammer. Brutus grabbed a roll of caps from the porch and ran off. Soon Brutus was running down the road. *Bang! Bang! Bang!* He was chewing on the caps as he ran along, banging down the road. It was a funny sight to see.

I used to sit with Brutus on my bed and tell him all my woes. If I was having a bad day and had a few tears to shed, Brutus understood. I bet he would've had some good answers if he'd been able to talk. But even if he couldn't talk, he was a good listener.

It Was Only a Dream

I was walking next to the highway in Small Town. It was very windy that day. I found that if I put my arms straight out at my sides, the wind would take me, and I could levitate for a few minutes at a time. Oh, what a wonderful feeling. It was like flying. I was minding my own levitating business when just up ahead, I saw some sort of strange being coming toward me. As I got closer, I could see that it was a regular sized person with a giant head. It looked like a character from an old-time parade. In old-time parades, a cartoon character came walking along; the body was human-sized, and its head was inflated beyond reason. What was the purpose of that?

I then saw more and more of the giant heads coming my way. And I took off running like I had never run before. I came upon an old shack and tried the door. It was open! I went inside, locking the door. There was a small grimy window I had to wipe with my sleeve to see through. I didn't want it to be too clean because the heads might see me, and I would surely be killed! I peeked out the window, barely breathing, thinking they could hear me too. Finally, the coast was clear, and I ran like the wind back home.

*****

Back to my tale...

Sixth grade and the last year for going to that particular school till we went on to the "big" high school. Not big at all. Remember, it was Small Town. I had a marvelous teacher in the sixth grade—Mrs. Barber—and the vote was unanimous that whoever was lucky enough to be taught by her was relieved to have not had one of the other two sixth-grade teachers who left something to be desired. The one you did NOT want was named Mrs. Sargent. Everyone called her Drill Sergeant. She kept her troops in order daily, like any respectable drill sergeant would. Evil, she was.

The other teacher was an older woman, Mrs. Bertram, who had her own way of pronouncing certain words. Like "uglah" for ugly, and in math class, she would say, "One mill-ee-on, two mill-ee-on." Nice lady, but she had some odd ways.

But the best of the three by far was my teacher, Mrs. Barber, who looked like a shapely fashion doll. She had a short red hairdo, a nice and kind face, and a killer body, especially her perky boobs, which she used as a sort of desk. Someone would bring her a note to sign, and she'd put the note on her "boob shelf" and then sign it. The boys' eyes almost bugged out! And also with that shelf, she about took the eyes out of a few of the boys. Considering the height of most boys in the sixth grade, the shelf came about level with their view of the world. She "rocked their world" for sure and a few of the dad's that came on PTA night too, I'm sure.

Sixth grade was my year. Everything seemed to go my way, starting with the new kid in town, Dave Donaldson. What a hunk. And he was from a faraway exotic land called Iowa. He was one of the taller boys in our class. He had sandy blonde hair and a smile that could put the sun to shame. Wow. And he liked *me!* I was about as smitten as a sixth-grade girl could be. That smile.

He lived not far from my house, so he'd come over, and we'd sit in my fort Ally and I had built with old planks of wood, some spare nails, and plastic sheeting (for waterproofing) on the edge of the woods of my backyard. Dave and I would sit in the fort and talk and flirt. Not one kiss was had. All innocent stuff, but I was in love.

When Valentine's Day came around, I found out after the fact that Dave (probably his mom) had bought a heart-shaped box of candy for me, but Dave was evidently too embarrassed to do the whole lovey-dovey daunting presentation. I'm sure the other boys in school would've given him all sorts of grief over that…giving a girl a token of love on that special romantic day. I also heard later that day that the boys gathered together at recess and shared in my never-to-be chocolates. I hope they all, including Dave, got a belly ache.

The following spring, Dave flew the coop with his family for bigger horizons than Small Town, somewhere exotic again like Idaho, perhaps. My first real love was gone.

The biggest fluke of the sixth grade happened when we were all supposed to go on our annual bus trip to the big city of Monticello some hundred-plus miles away. This trip had been taking place for years, and all the previous sixth-graders had enjoyed an eye-opening trip. It was our chance to go on an adventure, and no way was that going to happen. It was due to the fact that our sixth-grade boys were absolute terrors. They were connivers, instigators and just wild in general.

The teachers got together and decided they'd rather have a root canal than to take those diabolical boys a hundred-some miles away in a bus, just to have the boys terrorize the big city. All the girls were so upset. Our reasoning was, why couldn't we, the angelic girls, go anyway and leave those horrible boys behind in Small Town? All the years previous and the years after us, all the sixth-graders got to go. The worst part was those boys were just getting started…

A Priest and the Lesbians

Priest:

One of Grandma Inga's brothers (the other one I'll get to later) was named Victor or simply Vic. We called him Uncle Vic or Father Vic. He was a priest. And everyone adored him. He was the calmest, gentlest, kindest man. He lived in another small town, not far away, in a stately white house. On the rare occasion when we visited him, the atmosphere there was so peaceful. The house was surrounded by large pine trees, and there seemed to be a holy whisper in the air.

Next door to his house was his tiny church, a woodsy looking church. The church could've been pictured on the front of a vintage Christmas card or a scene come to life from a snow globe, snow gracefully falling, invisible angels on high above.

Father Vic loved children, made apparent by the loving way he spoke to all the kids in our families—mine and my cousin's families. I always felt that if you ever had a troubling problem or some sort of crisis in your life, he'd be the man to confide in. And surely, he would pass on to you the grace of God, and all would be well.

My mom would say she thought it a pity that he couldn't marry and have some children of his own because he was so special. I agreed with her and would sometimes think how lonely he must be at times. I had to accept the fact that he was happy in his own way, choosing his solemn, solitary life to enlighten others and be of comfort to those in time of need. That's a pretty big and selfless thing to take on. God bless him, literally.

When I was a bit older, sadly, our holy uncle died. His funeral was held in a huge church I had never seen the likes of before. It was a very ornate chapel with lots of gold in it and vaulted ceilings that I felt almost reached heaven. The altar boys seemed to float down the aisles with their swinging ornamental containers of smoking incense. The whole ceremony commemorating his holy life was all very mystifying to me. And beautiful. It was a great tribute to a dedicated priest and a wonderful man, my uncle, Father Vic.

Lesbians:

Grandma Inga's sister was named Tina. Her name should've been Teeny—she was a mite of a woman, no taller than five feet, if that. We would visit Auntie Tina now and then in her also teeny dimly-lit apartment located above a store. She lived there with Auntie Mack. Auntie Mack was the total opposite of Auntie Tina. Mack was large, tall, and wore cowboy boots. Both aunties wore pants (called slacks back then), which you didn't see women wear much in those days, and they didn't have hairdos like other women did. Their hair was short and sort of slicked back with some sort of pomade. Big Auntie Mack, besides the cowboy boots (ugly), carried her wallet in her back pocket.

Auntie Tina and Auntie Mack were always so friendly and welcoming. Out came the milk and cookies. Great! My mom would chat with them for an hour or so, and we'd be on our way.

Not until I was in my thirties did I hear that they were gay. All of their mannerisms and the way they'd dressed suddenly all made sense to me. Wow. And that's just fine with me. And that is one of the most awesome things with kids. They don't judge. If you're nice to them, kids will see you for just that—yourself. It's so sad that as children grow, they become influenced by others and lose that sense of being open to whoever may come their way. Kids don't see color or race or sexual orientation.

They've both long since left this earth. May they rest in peace, my two lovely gay aunties.

Joyous Christmastime

On one particular Christmas Eve, Dad, Mom, Vance, and I got into the car after piling in all the presents, and started off for Utopia. The mood was jolly, Christmas music playing on the radio. We probably sang along. It was quite slippery for Dad driving along the highway. Whoa! Dad hit an icy patch, and the car spun around three times—*whoosh, whoosh, whoosh*—and suddenly came to a dead halt straight into a ditch in the middle of the highway. *Poof!* A big spray of snow flew up like a fountain all around us. Silence. Then Dad said, "Is everyone all right?"

We were all so stunned, we all began to laugh. Dad had to now figure out how to get out of the ditch. He trudged over to a nearby house and used their phone, and soon, a guy came in a truck and pulled us out. Off we went to Grandma Lil's to spend a few hours, and then we'd go spend the rest of the evening with Mom's side of the family.

Vance and I were mesmerized by Grandma Lil's tree. We thought it was the most amazing tree we had ever seen. It was a small tree made of silver foil hung with plain solid-colored balls here and there. The real attraction was the color wheel of red, green, blue, and yellow. The wheel was placed on the floor a small distance away, and as it spun and shone onto the metallic tree, it was a magical experience. We could hardly decide which color we liked best.

Since Grandma Lil was of the Christian Science religion, she didn't give presents, but it was okay. Vance and I understood that from the get-go. Years later, Mom told me that Grandma Lil would give Mom and Dad money for Santa presents. So really, she'd been giving us presents for years, and we hadn't even known. And Vance and I also knew we'd "hit the jackpot" at our other grandparents' celebration…

Christmas at Glam Gram's and Grandpa Sam's was a wild time indeed. They lived in a small duplex, and the house was packed to the rafters with Mom and Dad, Vance and I, Uncle Chum, Auntie Lovey, all of my ten cousins, Auntie Shirley and, of course, Glam Gram and Grandpa Sam and whoever else showed up. A mountain of presents extended halfway out into the living room. Grandpa would work his tail off all year to afford all those gifts and then work the whole next year to pay it all off. Then it was Christmastime again, and the poor man must've never had a penny to his name.

Midway through the festivities, we'd hear bells jingling outside the front door. And in came Santa in all his glory. He was larger than life and had a perfect "Ho, ho, ho!" He wore an immaculate red suit, had a silky white beard, and even his boots were polished to a sheen, completing the authentic look.

Every one of the kids got a small box of brightly colored wrapped caramels. With a few more "Ho ho hos," off he went to see the other neighborhood kids. When I reached the "beyond believing in Santa" age, I found out Santa's identity. His name was Frank, and he was a well-known resident of Utopia, married with no children, and had been playing Santa for years before I was even born. The parents in Utopia would call sometime before Christmas and request him to stop by on Christmas Eve. He used his own money for all those treats and gave his time to give so much joy to everyone, and all I can say is what a kind and generous man he was.

He didn't stop at just playing Santa. One year for Halloween, we went trick-or-treating with our cousins and ended up at Frank's door. He appeared at the door with a giant bowl of candy…in a wig, makeup, wearing a dress, fake boobs, and a pair of cat-eye glasses. One of my older boy cousins asked, "Where's Frank?"

The "woman" replied, "Oh, Frank had to go out of town. I'm his sister, Myrtle." The little kids bought it hook, line, and sinker, the older kids knew better but played along. What a delightful guy Frank was.

As Christmas Eve wound down, Grandpa, having had a few brandies, was asleep on the sofa. Wrapping paper waist-deep in the small living room, all the kids were getting sleepy but were more than pleased with all of their many treasured presents. The best ever gift I received from Grandma (Grandpa only furnished the money) was a matching set of a bra, half-slip, and undies. Who cared about the half-slip and undies? I had plenty of those. But I had never had a bra, probably being that I didn't really need one yet. The whole set was white shiny nylon, and the bra itself was no more than a flat piece of nylon with straps and a few hooks in the back. But it was a bra nevertheless, none of my friends had a real bra yet. I truly felt grown up as I had opened that important gift. Thank you, Grandma.

Joy

The summer before the seventh grade, I had been summoned by a little neighbor girl who lived a few doors down. "Come quick!" she exclaimed. She then explained that there was someone she wanted me to meet.

I followed the wee one right to her sandbox, and there sat a girl about my age who jumped up and excitedly said, "Hi! I'm Joy!"

Joy and I became friends. A lifelong friendship was born that day at the sandbox. Joy was always a good laugh. She just had a funny way about her in a good way.

Being the new girl in Small Town and the one with the most curvaceous body, most of the girls were extremely jealous of Joy. One little b-i-t-c-h had it in for poor Joy and relentlessly gave her all kinds of grief. The "B" would shout out obscene things at Joy from across the gymnasium! It made my blood boil because Joy had not done one darn thing to deserve the constant torment being relentlessly hurled at her. Joy had no choice but to avoid Miss Meanie by keeping out of view, hiding around a corner, or simply running in the opposite direction when needed. Some kids are evil. Yes, bullying was alive and well way back then.

A few years later, one day, Joy's older brother, Bud, drove by out in front of their house. Joy said he was eyeing me as he backed up, not paying attention. *Bam!* He backed right into a telephone pole! We laughed our heads off. Bud's car had a sizable dent in the rear end the same shape as the telephone pole. We still laugh about it to this day.

Joy's controlling mother just wouldn't leave poor Joy alone. I had never known anyone to have such a mother. Mother told Joy what to wear, what music she could or could not listen to, who she could be friends with, and heaven forbid if she was out one minute past her curfew; then surely, Joy must've been up to no good. I couldn't imagine the constant stress of having anyone lord over you, much less your own mother. It's a wonder Joy kept her wits about her and behaved like your average teenage girl when she was being watched and scolded for anything and everything she did, day in and day out.

Not until many years later, as an older adult, did Joy and her mother make peace. If memory serves me, I believe Joy finally spoke up to her mother and, in so many words, told her to lay off. When Joy's mother died, Joy was sad, but I thought to myself, *She's also got to be relieved having had a whole lifetime of scrutiny from her mom.* Especially when my mom had been my best friend, I would've left home long ago had I a mom like Joy had.

Joy and I have remained friends through the years. She makes me laugh and always tells me that I get her. Hmm… Maybe because I listen to her and always have, unlike all those years when she was growing up.

It Was Only a Recurring Dream

Ever since I laid eyes on Howdy Doody, I had an instant dreaded fear of that creepy, disgusting puppet. The big rotating eyes, the mechanical movement of its jaw when it spoke, and even those red freckles on it's ugly face scared the hell out of me. Actually, most ventriloquist dummies and clowns that aren't cute enough freak me out…to this day.

In my dream, first I would go through some very thick woods. All the tree branches tangled and gnarled together. So I would worm my way through the trees, bushes, branches, and foliage. As I was winding my way through, scary faces would pop out between the branches, like monster faces: a vampire face, a Frankenstein face, a Wolfman. Soon I came to a clearing, and there was a small cabin in the middle. The cabin had a front door and a side door, and I would always enter through the side door every time. Once I got inside, I'd immediately look for a place to hide.

There were very few places to hide. The items in the cabin included a small table, a refrigerator, a small camping cot. That's all. So I either hid under the cot or under the table since those were the only two places available. The minute I was hidden and barely breathing from sheer fright (I knew what/or who was coming), the door flew open, and in came a man-sized Howdy Doody with a mean snarly look on his face. He was looking for me! As I waited in hiding, he scanned the room, the rolling eyes rotating from side to side. He finally gave up, closing the front door behind him. And the very minute he left, I jumped up, went out that same front door, and ran my ass off. End of dream.

Wonder what would've happened had he found me. Maybe I would've actually died in my sleep from fright. I had that same exact dream for years, well into my teens.

Reading, Writing, 'Rithmatic, Boys, and Sex Ed.

On to the big time as I entered junior high, which was combined in the same building with the high school. We were the peewees that year, but we felt big. I just wanted to be a part of it all and to join everything: the band, the choir, the cheerleaders, and the majorettes…until I became disillusioned.

I started out by joining the band. I chose to play the drums. My dad was a drummer and earned extra money by working in several bars and supper clubs in the area every weekend. I always admired his drumming and thought it would be cool to follow in his footsteps. Hated it. Boring as could be.

Next, I got myself a baton, and my mom would teach me fancy twirls she had learned when she was a majorette in school. I tried out and made it, and Ally tried out and made it too. We performed at some basketball games and did a special arch with our batons that the homecoming candidates walked under. We thought that was the coolest. It was dumb looking back. We also twirled and performed an awesome routine at our coach's old college. It was really groovy, done to a menacing rock tune of the day.

The twirling lasted a couple years, and then I became the school mascot and danced around at sporting events. That lasted about a year, and I decided to try for cheerleading until it all went downhill, and I fell in with the "wrong crowd." Not wrong, exactly, just more fun.

It's what happens to not all teenagers but to the majority. It's more fun to mess around and act cool than to be part of the so-called in-crowd. In-crowd meaning those dedicated students who lived for school and to be the apple of every teacher's, principal's, coach's, and school administrator's eyes. I've never been a competitive person or had a burning desire to prove myself. Please people, yes, but not to be the greatest anything. As I've come to realize, maybe way back then, there's always someone who can do it WAY better than you. Someone smarter, prettier, faster. You're easy-breezy, just sailing through something, whatever it may be, and here comes Suzie-Q who can fly right by you with no effort.

Still, I thought I'd try out for cheerleading. The night before the cheerleading tryouts, someone said, "Party!" and I was in. Parents out of town = party. There were quite a few kids at the party. There was drinking, joking, dancing, and the usual merriment. I wasn't into drinking then (too young), but the best part was no supervision and hanging out and talking till the sun came up. Uh-oh, guess I won't be going to the tryouts.

I felt a bit guilty about the girl I was paired up with to do some of the stunts and her having to be paired up with someone else last-minute, but I was on a different wavelength now. When school resumed on Monday, I heard that my partner I had left high and dry had made the cheerleading team. Good. She truly wanted it and got it. She wasn't one of my best pals, so I didn't dwell on my misdemeanor.

Being in the choir at school was a whole different story. I can't read music, but I can carry a tune and follow along. Choir is what I stuck with the longest. Finally found my thing. Our choir director was a dark and handsome actor-looking type guy, Mr. Trudeau of French descent who proved it a few times a week by swearing at us in French when we'd hit a sour note. But he was an amazing instructor who could even get the dumb boys to sing the right notes. And Mr. Trudeau was in heaven when that happened. He would close his eyes, head tilted back, and look as if he had left this planet altogether in ecstasy. We always knew when we got it right.

He spent weeks teaching us how to sing a difficult piece in Latin. Little did we know he was grooming us to compete with some other big town choirs in parts unknown. When it got closer to competition time, he went into overdrive, rehearsing and rehearsing till, by God, we did a pretty good job of it. We went on to win a few of those competitions. Some we didn't win because the thing with that tremendous piece of music in Latin was halfway through, it had a break. The singing stopped; all was silent. Then we were to pick it up, in tune, and start singing again till the end of the song. We saw the trance-type look when we hit it on the money and a very sour look like Mr. Trudeau had just sucked on a lemon when we failed. Another cool thing about Mr. Trudeau was he introduced us to new music, old music, and everything in between. One of the best instructors I've ever had.

Well, the dreaded boys in my class were still at it, up to their antics as usual. On the last day of school, they once got the idea, collectively, to each bring a pea shooter, and each of them brought their own bag of peas. Oh, what fun they had with those pea shooters. But not quite enough fun. Soon they were letting whole bags of peas loose all over the second-story floor of the school. The floor was alive with all those peas, people slipping and sliding and falling all over the place.

The next year, last day again, they all brought squirt guns. A group effort again. Were they happy each having a squirt gun? Hell, no. They all got into the janitor's closets and filled buckets with water! Water, water, everywhere! It was like a major flood had taken place in the school that day.

But the real stunt of that school's history was the day they got the big idea to sprinkle a huge bag of parsley all over the boys' bathroom. A teacher had gone in to the bathroom and surmised that the green leafy stuff everywhere must be marijuana! The police were called to investigate. Didn't they all feel silly for making such a fuss over parsley?

Miss Hatton, our gym teacher, was with us from sixth grade on. From our first embarrassing showers all the way till we were old enough for Sex Ed., she was a "good egg," and we all liked her well enough. It was in those days that we all had to wear royal blue gym suits. Oh, for ugly. So happy for all the school-aged girls these days who don't have to wear those God-awful, totally ugly with the stretchy waist gym suits. I hated Gym, mostly because of my non-competitive nature. I liked jumping on the trampoline, and we had a few weeks learning folk dances, which I enjoyed, and any sort of floor exercises. That was about it. I'm not a sporty type whatsoever. A few girls, besides myself, weren't into sports either, and when Gym class took place, sometimes we had our time of the month…about four times a month. When I attended any sporting events such as football or basketball games through my junior high and high school years, it was usually in hopes of meeting a boy to flirt with.

When we weren't in the gym with Miss Hatton, we were in a classroom NOT learning all about the mysteries of sex. Miss Hatton would only say so much about the titillating topic at hand. Way not enough. We wanted more, more, more! Everyone in class would ask a million and one questions about all aspects of the birds and the bees, trying to get as much info as possible. Poor Miss Hatton had her hands full trying to explain without saying too much. All the parents in those days would've been up in arms if their children got too much of an explanation.

We got onto the discussion of VD one particular day. We all wanted to know just how exactly you contracted the deadly disease. We didn't even know how two people went about having actual sex. Film strip time. The lights were dimmed. We were all excited to finally know the truth. What we saw on the movie screen was mind-boggling. White silhouettes of men and women floated across the screen, and when the silhouettes passed by each other, suddenly, little white dots showed up on their crotch regions. What? So we didn't know anything before we watched the film strip, and guess what? We were still just as clueless when the lights came on. What a scam. And still, Miss Hatton was "Mum's the word."

Oh, Those Swaying Pines

I must reminisce about Sandy Lake, another kid's wonderland. Each summer for about eight years in a row, we packed up the car and headed out to heaven on earth. Approximately forty miles away was our fairy-tale getaway (again with the fairy tales). We packed the car so full that we barely had room to sit. Heaven forbid we'd forget an important piece of home for a whole week.

Vance and I would be squeezed in among all the household belongings in the backseat. We'd amuse ourselves by singing, making up games, and talking about all the fun we'd have once we got to Sandy Lake. About twenty minutes till our time of arrival, we would stop at a unique cafe that was fashioned from an old trolley car. That cafe and a gas station were the only two buildings in the town on the highway when you passed through. We knew what came next as we entered the familiar front door of the cute little cafe…ice cream cones! They had the best pink peppermint ice cream ever. It had tiny bits of bright pink peppermint candy in it and had to be scooped into a sugar cone. A plain cone wouldn't cut it.

Back in the car and after about fifteen minutes, Dad would announce, "Everyone, close the windows." It was the dustiest road on earth, and you'd be choking on the dust if you didn't do what Dad said. Vance and I loved the dusty road because we knew in a matter of minutes, we'd be at the lake.

There it was in all its glory. First you got a view of the lodge, which housed a bar complete with dance floor and a small grocery area. And beyond the lodge, the crystal clear gorgeous blue lake. Swaying Pines Resort—heaven on Earth. Each year, Mom and Dad rented one of the eight cabins. We tried them all, but our favorite was

#7. It had a sizeable front screened-in porch with a picnic table where we ate most of our meals, weather permitting. The porch looked out over the lake. Picture perfect. The cabins were big enough for us and had a rustic charm with two bedrooms, just curtains for doors. The cabin had running water, cold only. You had to heat water to wash yourself or the dishes, and it made it more fun somehow. There was a small bathroom with a toilet only, no sink, but it was a luxury not having to use an outhouse.

The lodge had some fun things in it—a jukebox, a bowling game, pinball machines, snacks and candy, and ice-cream treats of all sorts. There was a bar for the adults, a dance floor with a row of booths off to one side, and a pool table. The bathrooms in the lodge had small signs on each door as follows: Pointers (picture of an Irish Setter; men) and Setters (picture of a girly-looking poodle; women). We got such a charge out of that.

During the day at the lake, time stood still. We went swimming, fishing, played shuffleboard (the court being right behind the row of cabins), and generally ran around without a care in the world. There were always other kids to play with, and our relatives would come to visit for a day or two.

Sandy Lake is where I decided I love to eat fish. Dad would go out fishing with some of the men that were staying there also. They'd bring their catch in, clean the fish, and grill them with a bit of butter and garlic. Dee-lish.

All About Dad

My dad's family consisted of his three older sisters as far as I knew. It wasn't till I was about twelve or so that I learned of his eldest sister and his only brother who weren't with us anymore. With a mournful tone, Dad quietly told me that his sister, Joyce, had committed suicide. How terribly sad to lose a sibling in any way but especially that way. And poor Grandma Lil, her own child. How could Grandma even go on living with the memory of her firstborn giving up on life? Joyce had been mentally ill—smart as a whip, but for some reason just couldn't go on living. Mom told me behind closed doors that Joyce had a stiff drink and a handful of pills when she made the sorry decision to say goodbye to her life. Joyce had also left a note of which my dad never spoke, not even to Mom.

Dad's brother, Bert, Dad obviously had idolized. I had always assumed he was killed during his time in the armed services. How very sad for Dad to have two siblings gone before I was even born. I had seen pictures of Joyce and Bert and never heard an explanation of what had happened to them. The subject was always swept aside, dropped. In the pictures of Bert, he looked just like Dad— same twinkly eyes, same nose with the familiar friendly smile. He just looked like the nicest guy. Just like Dad.

Onto happier times:

Dad worshipped his three sisters, and since he was the baby, they fawned over him, no matter his age. The eldest, Sylvia, the middle sister, Laverne, and the youngest, Angela, were spread all over the country. We lived to the extreme north; two of Dad's sisters lived to the extreme south. We never got to see any of them very often but loved it/them when we did.

Auntie Sylvia was an intelligent bookish-type woman married to an intelligent bookish-type man, Uncle Ray. He worked for a branch of the government in a rather high position. He was also a lifelong member of The Audubon Society. Uncle Ray's important job took him all over the world, his kids (my four cousins, two of each) growing up in various European countries. And it was common knowledge that my cousins were exceedingly smart, just like their parents.

Next in line was Auntie Laverne, just the opposite of Sylvia. She was down-to-earth content to live her life simply being an attentive and caring mother to her three sons. She was loving and charming. Her husband, Uncle Larry, was a nice quiet man who could be seen at any given time just smiling and smiling all the time. Everyone seemed to like him the minute they met him.

Also, years into the future, Auntie Lav and Larry's middle son, my cousin Brad, would come to visit and stay for a few days now and again. We all got to know him and we all just love him. He's a funny, friendly guy who seemed to really click with Dad, especially since they shared the same warped sense of humor. Brad, you take the cake!

And then there was Angela, better known as Auntie Angel. She was a beauty. In her younger days, she must've been the talk of the town, another smart lady, and she had the kindest eyes, and I always felt loved in those eyes. She was married to Uncle Charles who was another smiler and a funny character. Auntie and Uncle had three kids (two boys and a girl) who we got to see more often than the others since they didn't live as far away. When I got much older and lived even closer, we made quite a few momentous trips to visit them.

It was so neat to see that as Dad and his sisters aged, they all began to look alike—almost identical. Especially around the eyes. They all had those same kind, sort of drooping, understanding eyes and the same crow's feet too. Dad and Auntie Angel, in particular, as they grew older, they could've passed for brother and sister twins.

I Hate Sunday

Ever since I can remember, I've hated Sunday. Any and every Sunday. Yes, it's the Lord's day, the day of rest, etc., but it's boring.

When I was a kid, I woke to the smell of roasting meat. Ick. It's supposed to smell good and maybe get your mouth watering in anticipation for the Sunday afternoon meal, but as the first conscious smell wafting down the hall and waking me up, no. Ick.

Especially Sunday in the winter months. Blah. Growing up in the north woods, everything is white. The sky is white, the snowy ground is white, birch trees are white. Blah. It can drain any energy you may have had to begin with as you look out the window out at all that "blahness."

What's on TV? Nothin'. More on the box these days, but as a kid, nothin'. Sports? Wild Kingdom? Sermons? Boring...so boring. What is there to do? Nothin'. Hang around the house and mope through sheer boredom. Even stores weren't open back then. Imagine that!

As an adult, Sundays being just as bad had an even worse factor. Right around 4:00 p.m., it dawns on you that tomorrow is the start of another monotonous workweek. How depressing. Now you're bored AND depressed.

I've never gotten over the Sunday blues. You may go for a picnic in the warmer time of year. You may go for a drive to distract yourself from the boredom. You can even eat a beautiful Sunday feast, but in the end, it's still Sunday and it's still boring. Sunday just has a different boring, blah, nothin', and somewhat depressing feeling to it.

Monday through Saturday would be just fine with me.

I digress...

Boys, Friends, Boys, Friends, More Boys (In That Order)...Did I Mention Boys?

I think I met him at the swimming hole. His name was Sheldon. Ally and I were always at the swimming hole in the summer since it was the place to be. It was a small park with benches built in a semicircle on top of a small hill that went down a slope to the actual place where we swam, a deep spot in the river that ran through Small Town.

Sheldon was a few years older than me, and I felt grown up being around him. He had a friendly way about him, and he drove a VW bug. Since I was still kind of young, Mom and Dad would only allow me to go with Sheldon before it got dark and for an hour per drive. We drove around and talked, listening to the radio. Ahh...The Carpenters and The Association...total swoon music. I could swoon right this instant just remembering how that music made me feel. At some time during our excursion around Small Town, he'd stop the car and kiss me once or twice if the mood was right. What do you expect with that lovely music on the radio?

I had a babysitting job that summer, and when I'd put the little girl I sat for down for a nap, I'd listen to the radio and I'd daydream about Sheldon and those kisses and hoped he'd pull up outside in the VW. He never did, but a girl could dream. Don't know what happened to Sheldon and me. I must've had bigger fish to fry. It was short-lived, and maybe he wanted more than a kiss here and there. In any case, I was not ready for any more than that. Maybe he scared me off. That's okay. No shortage of available guys around. I'd keep fishing.

My friend Joe-Joe lived in the next town over. I'll just call it Coolsville where all the cool kids lived. And their school was cool too. The school had what was called the modular system. It had something to do with how the hours of the day were divided...into mods. Oh, how mod! To me, it seemed like they could sort of do whatever they wanted at that mod school. They had some cool hippie-type teachers who presented cool new concepts that the Small Town school would never have dreamed of. All the cool hippie guys lived there too—the first guys to ever have long hair back then.

Back to Joe-Joe. We became fast friends. From across the street, you could always tell it was Joe-Joe. Taller than tall, stick thin, long khaki military coat, and the ever famous to-the-knee brown suede boots with fringes dangling down at the boot tops. Joe-Joe and I would meet up and talk for hours. He had the most fabulous album collection I had ever seen. He was all about the music. And we talked on the phone for hours, solving the problems of the world. We had two main things in common. He had been adopted from the same agency as me, and he and his family were also part-time residents of Sandy Lake.

Vannie

About that time at school, a new girl arrived. But wait, do I already know her? Yes, I do! It's Vannesa (otherwise known as Vannie)! Years before, I had been in dancing school with her. I told her we had previously crossed paths when we were small, dancing together. Then we went into a lengthy duet, singing the songs that went with the dances all those years ago. A lifetime friendship began that day.

We then started to pal around with Deanna. Deanna belonged to a large family who lived in an old farmhouse way out in the sticks, so it was an effort to get together with her, but we dreamed up all sorts of ways by bribing our dads and begging rides from anyone who was willing. Anyway, it was another friendship that would go beyond our high school years.

Vannie was so much fun, especially in our high school years. We did everything together and laughed all the way through it. She came up with pet names for everyone, including a few colorful teachers we had. And she had a collection of funny noises for incidents that came up. She was always high-strung and a bit jumpy, which just made her more funny.

To Coolsville we went, plenty of times in search of the cool guys. And we found them. Vannie found the coolest, a foreign exchange student named Franz from Denmark. This guy was not just from Denmark but from out of this world. He wore a big fluffy fur coat and smoked a pipe! And his accent was to die for. I admit to being a bit jealous that he had a thing for Vannie and not for me. We bombed around with him and his friends till Franz had to go back to Denmark. Pity.

Vannie and I then came across who we called the hippie hunks. We met them in the park one day where everyone met up in Coolsville. Where else would the meet-up park be? Bart and Bernie, one blonde, one dark-haired, were the quintessential hippies of the day, and they were both astonishingly good-looking. After about an hour at the park, they asked us to come to their place. They lived in an apartment right in Coolsville. We got there and went up some stairs into the apartment. Bernie said, "Come on, girls, you have to see this."

Vannie and I gave each other a "What are we in for?" look and followed anyway, of course. A door was opened, and the guys said to duck down and crawl in. What we crawled into was a room that had been entirely draped over on the inside with an orange parachute, one of the most far out things we had ever been invited to see. We sat in there and chatted with the hippie hunks inside the parachute for a while. When we left, we talked about the amazing time we had just had and just how pleasantly surprised we had been to be let into the secret hippie den.

In our junior year at school, Vannie actually lived with me and my family for about a year. Her mom and dad had divorced, and her mom remarried and was moving with her new husband to another faraway state. Vannie did not like her new stepdad and refused to go. I talked to my mom and explained the situation. She consulted Dad. Next, Mom called Vannie's mom, and they made arrangements for Vannie to stay with us. It was agreed that Vannie's mom and new husband would send a certain amount of money per month for Vannie's necessities, food, and board. Any teenage girl's dream come true to have one of your best pals move in with you! Yay! It made going to that prison known as school so much more bearable.

You would think that sharing a room would have led us to being archenemies, but we got along quite well. And we got up to mischief too. Nothing terrible, just normal teenage shenanigans...like crawling into a parachute with hippie hunks.

Deanna

Deanna, one of my other best friends throughout my school years, had a difficult upbringing but rolled with the punches and took whatever came her way, not letting her past get the best of her. She'd grown up in a falling down farmhouse way out in the country. She had older brothers and sisters, some so much older, they could've been her parents. She was from a large family, seven altogether. By the time she was high school age, the only kids left at home were Deanna and her two younger brothers.

Upon seeing her family home for the first time, I wondered how all those kids, before they left home, had fit in that house and where they all slept. The ground floor of the house was a regular size, but the upstairs had one bedroom. At the top of the stairs was a wide hallway that got narrower as you went along. The wide part was where her two brothers slept in a double bed shoved against the wall. Further down the hall was a door, and behind it was her mom and dad's bedroom. Another door on the left in the hall was a small closet. This is where Deanna kept her clothes. Finally, at the end of the short narrow hall was Deanna's bedroom, which really was just a small space overlooking the front of the house. No bedroom door, so she'd pull open the closet door to get some privacy.

Some of our best times together were up in that tiny space she called her own. We'd sit up there, talking and laughing, and her brothers who were mini comedians would come and entertain us. When it got dark, we'd light a candle and climb out the window of her room and sit on the peaked roof, which was over the front porch. Sometime late at night, Deanna and I would sneak downstairs to snitch a cigarette from her dad's pocket. There he was, sound asleep in his favorite chair. Deanna would tiptoe up behind him and, like a professional pickpocket, gently ease a cigarette out of his pack in his shirt pocket. Good going, Deanna, you little thief. Now we could sneak back upstairs and out on to the roof to share the stolen cig.

The reasons for the house she lived in being so rundown were: 1) Her dad being the sole breadwinner probably couldn't afford much else after providing for all those kids who had come and gone before; and 2) her dad was a drinker. There wasn't much money ever, at all. Period.

Deanna's mom was as a slight lady with a chiming voice like a fairy. She was sweet as pie and could cook up a meal out of nothing. No money to have much food in the house, but it was astonishing how she made delicious food out of nothing but her creative culinary skills. I ate many tasty dishes in wonder in that sorry little kitchen.

Immediately after graduation, Deanna got married to her high school sweetheart. Her new husband to be was a good guy who everyone liked. Before she got married, she made one solemn request to her dad, the only wedding present she wanted. She asked her dad to quit drinking. He agreed and actually did it. Deanna was so happy and proud of her dad. Quite a feat for her dad, and Deanna felt he really loved her for making such a sacrifice.

Deanna and her husband went on to have two kids, but I guess she got some of her dad's drinking genes because she became a drinker herself. Her husband couldn't deal with her ways, and they got divorced. After the divorce, she kept drinking. Maybe worse than ever. People would see her around town, looking worse for the wear. I've never seen Deanna again and haven't heard a word about her in years. I hope with all my heart that she's still alive and that somehow, she found her way to AA and she's now living a happy life somewhere nice.

Big Bad Chad

Deanna and I had met a group of guys from Coolsville. They were all friends and were a year or two older than us. We would ride around in someone's car and talk and smoke cigarettes. One of the guys asked me on one of our excursions around town, "Do you smoke?"

I replied, "Yeah, I should quit."

He got a sly smile on his face and chuckled a bit. *Weird*, I thought. Not till later that day did I realize he was talking about smoking weed. I was embarrassed that I was so uncool as to not know what he was referring to.

One of the guys in that group of friends was named Chad. He was gigantic, had a wide face, paw-like hands. I was dwarfed in his presence. He had a nice smile but also had a serious foreboding side about him. I had never met a guy before with such dark mannerisms. I was intrigued, but he would be way more than I bargained for. His parents were older, having had him when they were middle-aged, and Chad was totally in charge of at least one of them, ruling over his meek aged mother.

We drove to his house one day, got out of the car, and went inside. His mother stood in the kitchen. "Ma," he demanded, "give me some money."

I stood there in shock. Did he always threaten her? I think she was afraid of him. Had he hurt her before somehow? Physically? She immediately ran and got her purse and handed him a twenty. I think she even asked him if that was enough! He grabbed the money, and we headed back out to the car. He wanted beer. He pulled out of the driveway, and that day, I went on the most terrifying ride I've ever been on in my whole life. I live to tell the tale...

There was a long winding road through a long state park that connected several towns along the way. That was the route he took that fateful day. The whole roadway was nothing but winding hairpin curves atop high hills and treacherous gullies below. It was like an obstacle course of sinister twists and turns. And we sped through it at eighty to ninety miles an hour! I hung on like I've never hung on before. Miles and miles of road at a hellishly fast rate disappearing behind us as the car went faster and faster. It was beyond my worst nightmare.

Finally, we stopped at the end of the long passageway. I was never so happy to be alive. Thank you, Jesus, for saving me that day. I'm not an overly religious person, but Jesus or someone up there was definitely looking out for me that day. I should've demanded to be let out of the car that day, but when you're young and stupid, you don't want to act like a baby, even though you may be dead. Then we had to go back! But Chad managed to be a civilized motorist. Maybe he was content now that he had the damned beer he was after.

At the beginning of our weird relationship, Chad had given me a ring. Not a promise ring, just a ring, the first ring I ever had from a guy. I felt pretty special, I must say. A few months after the ring was bestowed on me, I lost it. I looked everywhere. Inside, outside. Gone. I was afraid to tell Chad I had lost it. When spring came around after the long snowy winter, the grass appeared again, and there in the front yard was my ring. Too late because between Chad being his serious, rather strange self, his lack of respect for his poor old mom, and being freaky in general, it scared me to be around him. I had to say goodbye. I stood in the front yard of my house, telling him it was over. And I couldn't believe what happened next. That great big lug of a guy started to cry. Serious, demanding, brooding Chad stood there and cried like a baby! Maybe he thought he would change my mind with such a pitiful display, but my mind was made up long before the tears fell.

Vinny, Derek, Dexter, and Joe-Joe Too

Vinny. Wow. He was the best guy I had seen in a while. Another smile that could outshine the best of smiles. Joe-Joe and he were friends. How convenient... Joe-Joe was one of those guys who would've given me the moon had I looked at him sideways, but alas, I didn't quite feel the same toward him. Everyone's had a Joe-Joe at some time in their life. He was a great friend but not boyfriend material in my eyes.

But Vinny, now you're talkin'. Vinny was about five-foot-eight or nine, wiry dark blond hair, and just, oh, that smile. He had beautiful teeth too. I always notice teeth because I've always hated my own. I didn't see Vinny much, partly because he lived in Coolsville, and he worked morning, noon, and night at his family's grocery store, which was located across the street from his family home. But when I did get to see him, I melted every time. But it was one-sided on my part, and one morning, I woke up and thought to myself, *I'm not going to swoon over Vinny anymore.* It was too much work. I scratched his name off all my notebooks and the collage I had made for my bedroom wall. I was done with Vinny.

Derek Donahue...well, well, well.

What a gorgeous specimen of a man. I'm saying speci-*man*. He was just seventeen and was a true hippie of the day, another one you could recognize a mile off. He was tallish and slim, wore the long army coat (popular with the hippies in that era), long flowing dark hair, and he had beautiful dark olive skin. To top it off, he had the deepest, brownest eyes you could get lost in, never to return. He hitchhiked everywhere, and there he'd be at the side of the road, looking like a tall Napoleon, one hand tucked just inside the front of his coat, the other hand, thumb out, hitching a ride. He was a fun friend, and we were together quite a bit. He also wore the most holey worn-out jeans he had abused on purpose himself, I'm sure, to pull off his signature look. His mother would give him a hard time for looking like a bum, and one time, she took his favorite scrappy pair of jeans and cut them right in half at the crotch. Next thing I knew, he was at my door, begging me to fix them. "Please, can you sew them back together? (giving me his best brown-eyed look)"

So I did and sewed a small flag on the back pocket and, as a specialty, lined one of the front pockets with blue crushed velvet. He was very pleased and strutted out of my house, hitching his way home to show his mom his favorite new old improved jeans.

Next came Dexter. Yes, he got a lot of grief for having that dorky name. We met in a most unusual way.

Our family had gone to Sandy Lake, off-season. The reason being for Mom and Dad to reserve our cabin for the upcoming summer. While Mom and Dad were at the lodge, I went to find Joe-Joe. After I located him, we started right in, having a fab day. Joe-Joe had a sailboat, and we took a spin around the lake. We listened to some records, had a chat solving all the world's problems again, and had a bowl of soup at his cabin. We ran into Vance sometime later, and we all hopped into Joe-Joe's dad's car to go back to the lodge to meet back up with Mom and Dad.

It had started to rain. Joe-Joe was trying to show off his driving "skills" and started whipping the steering wheel back and forth. Not a good idea on a wet sandy road. The car veered off toward the woods. Trees and bushes were coming way too fast at the windshield. The car came to an abrupt stop. I must've blacked out for a minute or two because I turned to Joe-Joe and said, "What happened?"

He took one look at me and said, "Oh my God!"

"What?" I said.

"Get out of the car," he replied. I looked at Vance and Joe-Joe, scanning them from head to toe. They both looked okay to me, undoubtedly shaken up.

We were now all standing out on the road when Joe-Joe said, "You're bleeding, and I can't tell where the blood is coming from-put your face in that puddle."

I did as I was told.

He then took off his jacket and said, "Here, wipe your face off with this."

I said, "No, I don't want to get it all bloody."

He then sternly said, "Take it, damn it!"

I wiped my face off, and he said he needed to get me somewhere fast. The car was wrecked. *Forget that.* Help arrived just then via a sporty red Mustang—Dexter. Joe-Joe knew Dexter and explained to him what had happened. I was quickly bundled into Dexter's car, leaving Joe-Joe and Vance to go tell Mom and Dad what had transpired.

Dexter drove straight to his cabin not far from where the car had crashed. He took me inside, and his mother immediately jumped out of her chair, seeing my messed-up face. What a wonderful sweet lady she was. She calmly sat me down and got a warm cloth and cleaned my face for me, all the while speaking calmly and assuring me that everything would be fine. I sincerely believe certain people are put there by the powers that be when you need help. She was like an angel that day.

When I had settled and my face was cleaned up, we got back into Dexter's car and headed back to the lodge. Mom and Dad were beside themselves with worry. But they saw that I was okay for the most part, except for my face, which looked like I had been in a fight with a large, mean cat. We drove to Coolsville where the nearest hospital was. Tiny pieces of glass were pried from my head, and my cut-up face was cleaned again. I was given some ointment to apply to the cuts and sent on my way. I had a black eye and a deep cut on my chin.

I lay around the house for a few days, taking it easy. Joe-Joe called and came to visit. The poor guy never would forgive himself for being a showoff and hurting his friend. He had stayed up all night the night of the accident, imagining what could have happened. I've never seen anyone so sorry in all their life.

One day, Mom came into my room and said, "Honey, you have a visitor."

In walked Dexter. *Wow.* At first, I thought sarcastically, *Don't I just look like a cupcake!* I didn't want him to see me all chopped up, not looking like my usual cute self. Any teenage girl would think that. But he was darling and hilarious and he had already seen me at my worst. From then on, he became my boyfriend. He was full of it and a lot of fun to be with. We went to dances in my town and his, went to the drive-in and had burgers and root beers, and listened to Santana (on 8-track) in his Mustang. It was good times.

On the night of a big dance at Dexter's school, we doubled with his friend, Rhino, and his girlfriend, Sue. The guys wanted to have a few beers before the big event. Way up high, overlooking his school, we followed his friend and date in Dexter's car to View Point Ridge, a famous make-out place in the area…until the cops showed up and your fun came to a screeching halt. Rhino had the beer in his trunk, and the guys kept jumping out, retrieving beers to drink in their respective cars.

First, the cop went to Rhino's car, asked what he was up to, and made Rhino pour his bottle of beer out. Next, the cop came to Dexter's car—same line of questioning. Right at that particular moment in time, Dexter didn't have a beer and had been throwing the empties in Rhino's trunk. The cop never thought to look in either car's trunk. Wow, what a miracle! The cop drove away.

Onto the dance. When we got up to the door where the dance was taking place, who should be standing at the entrance but…a cop! By now, both Rhino and Dexter were lit. Dexter walked a bit wobbly past the cop. The cop said, "Not so fast, buddy." He then asked Dexter, "Have you been drinking?"

Dexter said no.

The cop said, "I want to smell your breath."

And what happened next, I could not believe. Dexter got right in the cop's face, took a deep breath, and blew a cloud of beer breath right at the cop!

Next thing the cop said was, "You're outta here!"

Damn, I really wanted to go to that dance. I think for once, that night, I thought ahead and figured there would be a cop at the door of the dance, so I did not partake of the beer that was being consumed by those two dumbass guys.

Soon Dexter's school was having their winter dance. I needed a new dress. Mom was under the weather, so Dad said he'd take me downtown to North Haven, the biggest city nearest to where we were from Small Town, bigger in comparison to our town but nowhere near a big city like New York or Chicago.

This would be interesting having my dad take me shopping, not Mom, which was normally the case. Dad and I went to every store in North Haven. In those days, going into a store, first a salesclerk would pounce on you and, once in the fitting room, you'd be interrupted several times by the same or another salesclerk wanting to know if you needed help with the zipper or buttons. Now I ask you, when you're sixteen, do you need help? I wasn't an old lady or an invalid, for heaven's sake. Were all those salesladies pervs? Or what was that about? It embarrassed me and annoyed me.

I would come out of the fitting room and model for Dad, and he would say, "Not bad" or "No, that's not the one" or "That color is good on you." I could not have asked for a better shopping companion. Finally, when we were both getting tired of the whole shopping experience, especially with the fitting room pervs, I tried on a not-too-short forest green velvet dress. It was rather plain. I never went in for anything too fussy. I liked it. I came out of the dressing room to get Dad's opinion, and a big wonderful dad smile appeared on his face. "That's the one," he said with glee. We had a special dad-daughter moment that night, and I've thought about it many times since. When I recall that shopping trip, I say to myself, "That's my dad."

It Was Only a Dream

I found myself in an extensive upstairs warehouse attic, like a massive hayloft. The building was very spacious and open and had bulky wooden support beams. From one end to the other up in the loft were enormous overstuffed chairs, sofas, and beds. All of the furniture was so huge, it almost looked cartoonish. I started with the first giant sofa in its row. I jumped onto it, and then... *Boing, boing!* I jumped from one "boingy" item of furniture to the next. What fun! I jumped on every item in the whole place.

Freddy, Freddy...My Legs Turn to Jelly

For a summer, I had a part-time job right down the road from our house, around the corner, on the highway that ran through Small Town. A small family run business, The Coffee Cup Cafe, was an old-fashioned diner with a bitchy lady behind the counter who ran the joint. I guess I thought it would be nice to have my own money. I would babysit sometimes, but it wasn't my idea of a good time, and I got sick of staying up all night, waiting for the parents of the kids to finally come home.

The Coffee Cup had a few regulars, workmen mostly that came in for breakfast and lunch. Then the cafe closed for the day. When it came to lunchtime, the place was hoppin'. I ran around behind the lunch counter and ran back and forth to the row of booths. The men were typical workmen, telling stupid jokes and being picky, wanting condiments of all varieties, extra drinks, endless cups of coffee, and leaving tips that were nothing to write home about.

At that time, I had just gotten acquainted with a handsome older guy; just a few years older, but it's still heady stuff. His name was Freddy Johansen. Freddy strolled into the cafe one lunchtime, all six feet and three inches of his model-esque self. He was blonde, good-looking as hell, dressed like a million in a yellow checked shirt, high-waisted bellbottoms, and platform shoes and had the smoothest of smooth swaggers as he entered the busy lunchtime scene. His presence caught me by surprise, and my legs turned to jelly. The word *swoon* comes to mind.

I spoke to him briefly, knowing that the boss lady would embarrass me by shouting out a curt command of some sort right in front of Freddy. No way was I going to be humiliated in front of this new prospect. The more I tried to keep my cool, the more flustered I got. I screwed up a few orders and slopped part of a milkshake on the floor. My coolness had about run out, and it was all good-looking Freddy's fault.

Things progressed nicely with Freddy, and we were going steady soon after. A school friend and her boyfriend, myself, and Freddy went to a party one night. It was in someone's garage. Classy. I had a bit way too much to drink at the party and was having a fabulous time. When we decided to leave the party, it hit me. I wasn't feeling well at all. My friend's boyfriend had driven his muscle car to the party, and Freddy and I were sitting in the back seat, heading for my house first. "Motorhead" drove wildly on the back roads, and I didn't know how long I would last before all that alcohol would come spewing out. And then a terrifying thought occurred to me. The race car driver of the souped-up car was going to pull up in front of my house, come to a jolting stop, and the whole car would jerk forward. With no way to stop it, I'd be puking my guts out.

Just as I had imagined, the car came to a jolting stop and jerked forward. I flung the car door open and ran to the house. Vance was home. Thank God Mom and Dad weren't. I ran past Vance and puked a week's worth of everything I had in me, plus the booze. I was beyond sick. After that, I didn't hear from Freddy again. He must've thought, *What a stupid little girl, getting ridiculously loaded like that.* It made me sad because I really liked Freddy, but it was my own damn fault.

Freda and Veronique

Amid the "bliss" of living in Small Town, a new girl, Freda, showed up at school. I really liked her, and we became fast friends. She lived on the outskirts of town with her family that included a younger brother a grade below us, a sister, and a tiny brother. She also had an older brother and sister that had finished high school and didn't live at home anymore.

Soon Freda and I were doing the usual teenage stuff, and I was going to stay overnight at her house and she at mine. At her house, everything was mellow. Her mom even let Freda's friends smoke in the basement! Unheard of at that time. The basement was our hangout.

Freda's Mom was a chilled-out lady and always wore a necklace that was inscribed with "War is not healthy for humans and other living things." Her Mom baked everything from scratch, and she canned vegetables and fruit they grew on their property—Mother Nature herself.

My new friend had a different way about her (in a good way) and could be a laugh a minute. Freda loved to talk, and I can talk just as much. Doing just that, we had stayed up half the night in my room. At three or four in the morning, I was done and told Freda I was going to sleep. Freda said, "Do you mind if I just keep talking?"

"Be my guest."

Now and then, when I was at Freda's, her older brother, Roland, would come around and come down to the hangout to see what we were up to. He was older and funny with long dark hair and a handsome face. I had a total crush on him, but knew he probably thought I was just a dumb little girl, one of his sister's friends. He was way out of reach and too old for me, but I always wished he'd show up at the hangout when I was there.

Freda and I spent a lot of time together and went on double dates when we would go out with the guys from Coolsville.

At about the same time I was getting to know Freda, another new girl—I should say woman—came gliding into town. She was statuesque, sleek, elegant, and smoother than any girl my age or anyone at the Small Town school—a real beauty with a gorgeous mane of hair and looked like a fashion model from a magazine. She was not a girl. She was a woman. But she was my age. No one could believe their eyes. Where had this stunning girl/woman come from? She was absolutely polished and fabulous. With one look at her, all those dumb boys in my class went weak at the knees and fell all over themselves, waiting in line to get her attention. She towered over the miniature-sized fools but treated them with all the radiant grace that exuded out of every pore of her being.

To top it all off, her name was Veronique. Exquisite. Her style was southwest chic, and she wore her jeans to perfection on those long splendid legs topped with a formfitting shirt. Around her neck, she wore an unusual stone necklace, and then there was her glossy, shimmering hair—a vision from the floor up. Not to mention her professionally applied makeup. Every other girl in the town shrank into themselves when she passed by, feeling like nothing but country bumpkins.

Most people avoided her at first, thinking she would be too full of herself to bother with any of us Small Town hicks, or maybe they were just intimidated by her stature.

I tend to make the first move with someone new on the scene no matter who they are because I always think how awkward and new they must feel. It only takes one person to approach the new person, and at least then they know they're not completely alone. From my experience, the new person seems more than relieved once I've broken the ice. And poor Veronique, ending up in Godforsaken Small Town, thinking to herself, *Where the hell am I?*

Before long, Veronique and I started to do things together, sometimes as a threesome with Freda. She was really down to earth when I got to know her. She could've cared less about her immature classmates, the ridiculous boys that wet themselves in her shadow, but when she met the guys from Coolsville, she could take her pick. Some of those guys that were too cool for any of us other bumpkins made a beeline for those long legs and curvy hips that Veronique possessed so amazingly.

I think her class and style rubbed off on some of the girls, and some started to dress a bit more upscale in an attempt to keep up with the goddess that had come floating in on air one boring day in Small Town.

Deaf Jeff

Sometime during high school (so many boys, so little time), I became aware of an attractive guy who was a grade ahead of me—Jeff. Jeff was deaf. The smart-ass kids called him Deaf Jeff. Being the funny light-hearted guy he was, he shrugged it off. Either that or he threatened to beat them up (Jeff was a big guy). The smart-asses would run away, believing every threatening word Jeff said, and left him alone for a while.

We had a short-lived "romance," which was difficult at times because of his hearing loss. For instance, when we wanted to meet up for a dance or a date, I had to call his house and get his brother on the phone to make arrangements. This would take some time relaying back and forth. I would always hope that his brother or another family member would be home to answer the phone. I would speak to his brother, he would relay to Jeff, and he would come back to me. Speak, relay, come back. Speak, relay, come back. It took some work having a deaf boyfriend.

After a dance, Jeff and I would sit in his car and "talk." Jeff was very good at reading lips, and then I didn't have to use the alphabet sign language that Ally had taught me. When we kissed in the dark car and I wanted to say something to Jeff, I'd have to turn the dome light on. I'd mouth my thought to him, then shut off the light to get back to the business at hand.

Jeff wasn't totally and completely deaf. If you came up behind him and hollered his name, sometimes he heard and turned around. He could feel vibrations at a dance; the low bass would give him the beat, and he danced better than most.

After Jeff graduated, I heard that he married an older woman with kids, and they lived happily ever after.

Goodbye Glama, Goodbye, Mein Papa

Glam Gram was sick again. After having one lung removed (a result of her nonstop smoking), now the only lung left was on its last breath. Always, everyone in my immediate and extended family were forever optimistic. Never did anyone say, "This is it. The end is near." It was always, "She'll be fine" or "He'll be fine." I think I like it that way better than taking a fatalistic attitude, all doom and gloom. Sometimes the ailing person will pull through, and you've worried yourself into near hysteria for nothing. This time, Grandma Inga was not fine, and she died. I have two priceless memories of her that make me smile each time I think of her:

I was a child of maybe four at the time when we went to stay with Grandma Inga and Grandpa Sam at the cabin they had rented at Fish Lake. We may have stayed just for the weekend. One morning, asleep in bed, I heard my name softly spoken. Rubbing my eyes, I looked up, and there stood Grandma. She simply said, "Come on."

I thought something was wrong.

Again, she said, "Come on."

I got out of bed and followed her out the front door which looked out over the lake. The sun was just about to come up, and we sat on a wooden glider facing the lake. She had a cozy blanket with her and wrapped it snugly around both of us. I don't remember even speaking to one another. We just enjoyed the peaceful rising sun as it came up over the sparkling lake, just me and my grandma. I felt so loved and so special in that moment with her. She had chosen me to share the new morning with.

A few years after that memorable lake moment, Grandma and I had another fond moment together. It was on the Fourth of July, and we were at the carnival with the whole family (Auntie Lovey, Uncle Chum, all my cousins, Grandma Inga, Grandpa Sam, and Auntie Shirley). Grandma Inga, being the fun outgoing person she was, would go on every ride at the carnival. It's how I found out that I could not tolerate the Tilt-A-Whirl. I had such a screaming, crying fit out of sheer terror one time previously with Grandma that the operator of the ride stopped the death trap just to let me off. He then started it up again for the die-hards (like Grandma) that were enjoying it.

But this time, we didn't ride the Tilt-A-Whirl. Grandma and I decided to go for a calm ride on the Ferris Wheel. Up we went, and it was wonderful looking at everything below. "The fireworks are about to begin," a booming voice announced over a loudspeaker. The Ferris Wheel made one last full circle, then stopped. Grandma and I were on the very top seat! The lights went out in the whole place. The fireworks began, and there we sat at the very top, taking in the wondrous display from a bird's-eye view. How lucky can you get? When the fireworks were over, the lights came back on, and the Ferris Wheel was put into motion. We got off the ride and went to find the rest of the family.

When we found our group, they all spoke at once, "Where were you guys?"

With big smiles on our faces, we exclaimed, "We had the best seat in the house!"

A year to the date of Grandma's death, Grandpa Sam died. After a long day at the funeral home, we were on our way home, driving back to Small Town. It was late and dark outside by then. Dad had the radio playing, and the old old-fashioned song, "Oh, Mein Papa," came drifting to the backseat. I cried my heart out for my sweet grandpa.

Now with both my grandparents gone, Auntie Shirley was alone. She was perhaps nineteen or twenty at the time, old enough to live on her own but never had, and she didn't know where to turn. It was so very sad and lonely for her. She had missed some time from work and had a bout of narcolepsy for a time. She was truly beside herself.

School, Yuck

As I got a bit older and got the real gist of things, I started to hate school. If you weren't number one, you were nothing. Compete, compete, compete. And there was so much gossip at the school and all over Small Town. I would cry and beg Mom to let me stay home from school, and many times, she'd let me. I completely hated it and dreaded it.

Report card time came around, and I wasn't even there to get my report. One such time when I returned to school on Monday, I went to the principal's office. The secretary was sitting at her desk, and I asked for my report card. She said in a snippy voice, "You got all Bs. Just think, if you were here half the time, you could have all As."

I was not amused. For one, I thought all Bs were pretty darn good, and plus, what was she doing looking at my report card in the first place?

It Was Only a Dream

As I walked along the highway that ran through Small Town, a car pulled over on the side of the road next to me. Not just any car and not just any driver… The car was a slick, shiny, silver Maserati. I was stunned. When do you ever see a top of the range, primo, dream come true ride like this in Small Town? That's right—NEVER! I was in total awe with my mouth agape.

The passenger door seemed to open on its own, and I heard a deep man's voice boldly say, "Get in!"

I got in (like I always did when a strange car drove up and someone told me to get in…yeah, right), and as I sat in the plush purple seat, I noticed that the floor inside the gorgeous vehicle was made of purple metal flake. It reminded me of a sparkly purple drum set. I was completely mesmerized…until I turned my head and saw who was driving this fabulous car: James Taylor! REALLY…

We took off driving, we chatted casually, and smiled and smiled since we were having such a good time.

My Shining Light

From day one, my mom was my shining light. She was my most ardent fan and constant supporter in whatever I did. She wasn't beyond telling me off when I did something dumb, and when she did, she always said her words of wisdom in a calm and meaningful way. I could really talk to her, and she knew more of my hopes, fears, and dreams than my closest friends. After all, over anyone else, she was my best friend.

And she always had the right answer. Every single time. Whatever the dilemma I faced, whatever the woe, she had a perfectly sound solution. How did she know? She was an amazing soothsayer and the best secret keeper—my secrets and those belonging to others.

The phone rang one day, and it was one of the nosy neighbor ladies. This nosy busybody was calling to pump Mom for information about Ally's mom, Nina, who was recently divorced from Ally's dad and now had a new boyfriend. Mrs. Nosy began the phone call with, "Have you talked to Nina lately?"

Mom had just hung up with Nina (having had a lengthy conversation) not ten minutes previously. Mom then told the nosy one, "No, I haven't talked to Nina for a long time." Served the batty old neighbor right!

I was very close to my mom who always loved me unconditionally and was right by my side every step of the way. The very best mom in the world. I hoped I'd have a daughter someday that I could share the same type of relationship with like me and my mom.

Lasers and Jesus, Oh Bless My Soul

The big city of Monticello that we never went to in the sixth grade, we went to for Mom to have laser treatments on her eyes resulting from diabetes. The way Mom described it was like looking a foot away into a bright headlight of a car. They burned off the bad stuff behind her eyes with the lasers. She couldn't see well for days afterward. She said on one occasion that she had the shape of a pine tree in her sight that was always there at whatever she was looking at. We went to the university hospital for her to have the treatments. It was a long day for Vance and I, but we managed to find things to do.

We happened upon a chapel one day. We peeked through the door, and it was empty, so we went in. The room itself was an octagon shape made of brick. At each point of the octagon was a thin tall window. Within each window were horizontal strips of different colored glass. Beautiful. The colors started at the bottom with earth colors, then graduated into different hues of yellow, orange, and red and finally every shade of blue for the sky. The strips of colored glass went from floor to ceiling. Vance and I would crouch down in a squatting position and slowly come up to a standing position, the colors changing as we rose. You had every color of the rainbow and every variation of it. That would keep us busy for a good hour. Sometimes we visited the chapel several times in one visit. It was a magical place, and I think it gave us some comfort and quiet time.

Sometimes when we went to the city, we stayed with our Auntie Dolly and Uncle Floyd. They had three children, the oldest boy named after his dad, Floyd. Then Robby, who was a year or two older than me, and the youngest was a little blonde girl, Melly (Melissa).

It was always fun and games staying there. Uncle Floyd was Grandma Inga's brother. I guess that made him my great-uncle. Uncle Floyd was a wheeler dealer and very enterprising. One of his businesses was selling Christmas trees. We marveled at stories he'd tell us of flocking trees, pink or even black at the customer's request. He was a nice man and a lot of fun.

Auntie Dolly was a doll of a woman. She had long, flowing, light-red hair and freckly skin. But that's not what made her a doll. She was soft and radiant and lovely. The kids were funny, and Robby was full of the dickens. Melly, being the youngest and a girl, had a bedroom with a princess suite of furniture (white with gold trim) and tons of dolls with miniature baby carriages for all. But her favorite thing to do was to put their family dog in the carriage and stroll around the house. The dog's name was Cutie Pie, and that miniature white dog with the big fantail just loved her trip from room to room.

Auntie Dolly and Uncle Floyd were very religious. Our family went to church, and Vance and I attended Sunday school, but Auntie and Uncle were way more religious than that. There were pictures of Jesus all over the house, and old Gospel music played on the hi-fi day and night. In the middle of the night, you got up to go pee, and lilting out of the living room, you could hear, "Oh, bless my soul," and then an octave lower again, "Oh, bless my soul," and on it went. That's just what they did at Auntie and Uncle's house.

Vance and I went with Uncle Floyd once to their church. Well, that was an interesting experience… They did things differently in the big city. The church was a refurbished old movie theater, and it was huge. The congregation sat in all the movie seats, and up on the stage were four or five easy chairs. Vance and I were bewildered. Church was nothing like this in Small Town.

A man rose out of his easy chair and began to preach. Someone behind us hollered out, "Amen!"

Vance and I jumped and gave each other the "What the heck is going on here?" look. Then a different man rose from his chair on the stage and preached for a few minutes.

Uncle Floyd got out of his seat and loudly exclaimed, "Praise the Lord!"

Once again, the look was exchanged between Vance and I. As odd and surprising as it was to both of us, it was an enlightening experience. I'm glad we went to church that day with our uncle because sooner or later, you have to learn that people everywhere have their own beliefs, and that's okay.

My Other Shining Light (The Dad Version)

Dad was all about exposing Vance and I to as many new experiences, happenings, and cultural events that he could possibly afford. Even if it was a free experience, he'd find a way to get us there, no matter what.

Our family was out of town the day of the first moon landing. I can't recall exactly where we were or what we were doing there, but it was a few hours' drive from home. Approaching a larger town on the way back, Dad pulled the car over in front of a hotel, got out, and said, "Wait here."

Mom, Vance, and I gazed at each other, puzzled looks on our faces, thinking, *What's he up to now?*

In minutes, Dad hopped into the car and excitedly said, "Come on, let's go!"

When Dad said, "Go," you went. We followed Dad into the hotel, through the lobby, into an elevator, and up a few floors where he led us to a room and opened the door with a key. Surely, we weren't staying here, and all of our stuff was out in the car. Dad then sprinted across the room and switched on the TV. And then looking at me and Vance, he said, "I really wanted you two to see this. It's a big moment in history." I must say he was probably dying to see it himself, kind of like when just Vance and I went to the grocery store with Dad alone, we got to throw all kinds of goodies in the shopping cart. Why? Because Dad liked "gooders" too!

After we had viewed that astounding moment in time, Dad told us to go directly out to the car and wait for him. He then explained that he had told the clerk that he really wanted his kids to see the landing and asked if we could use a room for a short time long enough to witness it. The clerk, when he had given the key to Dad, said that when we left, "Don't make a production, just leave the key on the desk (be discreet)."

On another occasion, Dad had bought tickets for all of us to go see an old jazz band at the auditorium in North Haven. I was perhaps fourteen or so and I did NOT want to go to something as boring and dumb as that. Vance was not in the mood either. Dad just about begged us to go, saying, "I really think you kids will like it. I really do. Please trust me on this."

After much protest and with a lot of further ado, we begrudgingly got into the car, hating every minute of the dumb car ride there.

At the auditorium, we found our stupid seats, and the lights went low. Then we had the surprise of our lives… The lights came up, and a sizable group of elderly black male musicians began to play with all their hearts and souls. There were lots of horns, especially, and I had never before seen anyone absolutely wail on a horn the way they did. At one point, a tiny horn player stood on his chair and almost blew the roof off the place—amazing!

For the finale, the whole ensemble came marching down the aisles, playing a boisterous "When the Saints Go Marching In." From then on, when Dad made plans for us, we happily got ready to go.

Through the years, we also went to a few professional baseball games (to experience it live), various museums, concerts, nature parks, and amusement parks, Dad always being in charge of these outings. I have no idea how he managed to do all this. He wasn't a rich man. Not poor either, but he figured out a way to give us experiences that all these years later, I hold in my heart with fondness. Thank you so much, Dad.

Being the swell guy Dad was (*swell* being one of the words he used his whole life as in, "That'll be swell" and "Look at that! That's swell!"), he had one weird and annoying habit that was his own invention. I call it "The Voice."

He only used it when he was extremely irritated or extremely mad about something. And maybe the reason he devised this unique method in the first place was so he didn't have to holler. I only ever heard him actually holler twice in all my years with him. And he really didn't have to holler ever…because he had the secret weapon: The Voice.

The Voice was quiet, menacing, with just a touch of sarcasm thrown in for the full effect. Dad would also stare a hole through you simultaneously while using The Voice. And when The Voice was softly spoken, it was way worse than hollering, a spanking, or a slap. And it always made me feel worthless, ridiculous, or just plain ashamed of myself. Totally. Dad used The Voice on both Vance and I and just about anyone else he was after at the time. Never used it on Mom, though.

Not until years later when I decided that I could never ever hear it ever again did I call him on it, and he pretended to not know what I was talking about! "I apologize if that's what I'd done," he told me. I then talked to an assortment of people, including some relatives, and asked if they knew The Voice. Auntie Shirley and a few others said they definitely knew The Voice. The funny thing is after I had confronted Dad, he never used The Voice on me again. Yeah, he knew damn well what he was doing.

It Was Only a Dream

Dad, Vance, and I were in the family car traveling on a freeway. It was nighttime. Gazing out the window, on the side of the road, I saw a massive bright-red statue of an angel. It was also lit up with red lights and had a fountain around it at its base. It was gaudy and beautiful.

We all gasped at the same time when we saw the main attraction (Dad must've wanted us to have another experience). It was a shopping mall: Shopping Mall of the Future! Each store was on its own spinning disc, each disc resembling a gigantic record. The discs were in sets of five on different levels. A rainbow of neon lighting spelled out the name of each store. There were four sets of five discs in total. It was a fantastic sight to take in. It was truly out of this world, like something from your favorite space-age family featured in the familiar cartoon of the sixties (good call, Dad).

The Times, They Are a-Changin'

The years in which I grew up included the '50s, '60s, and '70s. I came into the world at a very good time. At times, I've wished I would've been a teenager in the '50s and not just a kid. The fifties were a simple time, and the world was a fairly safe place. You hung out at the malt shop in your poodle skirt, listening to doo-wop. Not to mention the fabulous cars on the streets with their sleek silhouettes and pointed fins. How swell was that? There were claddy suits, penny candy, and if you were lucky, a new Schwinn bike. Your mom stayed home and made pot roast on Sunday. You weren't allowed to interrupt a conversation when adults were speaking, and you couldn't talk back. Yakkity-yak.

Things began to change in the '60s when fashion evolved, and everything else seemed to modernize too. It was the time of miniskirts and pop art. All was groovy, except for the part where young men were drafted. Some burnt up their draft cards in protest, but most of them went, and too many never came home. The whole war and everything about it was atrocious.

But if you were at home on safe ground, everything was really groovy, and because of the war that was happening millions of miles away in some jungle, the hippies were born. And they were really a peace-loving bunch. The ones I knew were, at least. I guess I considered myself a hippie too. I was all about peace, love, and "People, let's stop the war." But I wasn't old enough to be politically involved. I just liked the idea of the movement, wearing my love beads and going barefoot.

All the young guys in the small towns all throughout the area where I lived were growing their hair much to the chagrin of parents and the older generation in general. Actually, my boyfriend, Lance, and his brothers started the long hair trend in Coolsville, and it then extended from town to town. All the Small Town people were mortified. I once saw an older man bump into a younger man on purpose for an excuse to rudely remark, "Excuse me, ma'am."

Needless to say, the young man lurched at the old man but then backed off when a few older men came to their rude friend's rescue.

Woodstock was all the buzz, and I would've given my best Nehru shirt to go, but I was fourteen at the time. And since my mom and dad weren't hippies, it wasn't happening. All the older hippies were going, and if they didn't have the bread to travel to the three days of peace and music, they went to the movie when that came to a theater near you.

It was showing in Coolsville, and I wanted to see what it was all about. I asked Mom and Dad if I could go with a group of my friends. Without the two of them even considering it, I got a flat no. Hell no. They may as well have said, "Hell no, you won't go!"

I was furious. Did they think I didn't know what naked people looked like? Did they think I had never heard the word *fuck* before? I seem to recall that being one of their reasons for not letting me go because that F-word was going to be said…in technicolor. I was so sure I was plenty old enough to go to the movie about the greatest concert that has ever taken place.

There was pot-smoking, strobe lights strobing, and some psychedelic drug usage going on, but all of it was partaken in the peaceful brotherhood of man. I honestly never saw anyone fight or have words during this era. Were they all so mellowed out on their high of choice that all harsh words had simply been erased from their vocabularies? I'm not condoning the usage of drugs of any sort, but maybe a few hotheads, (not potheads) of today could try a few puffs. At any rate, those days were mellow, mystical, and far out, man. And I wouldn't have changed a thing.

Jesus People

Besides the hippies, another new movement took place right around my sixteenth year. I don't even know if the particular movement had a specific name, but suddenly, there were people called Jesus people or Jesus freaks everywhere.

I had my own theory what it was all about. There's always those kids you went to high school with or regular grown-up people in every walk of life that are misfits. Sad but true. As for the kids I recall at the time, they were deemed hopeless in some way. Maybe they were extremely shy. Maybe they were labeled ugly because they had red hair and freckles or maybe they were tall and gangly. Whatever the reason, they weren't "in with the in-crowd." They were usually bullied mercilessly, teased, or taunted in one way or another, which in my view is always so terribly unfortunate. It's hard enough growing up if you're considered so-called "normal." Whatever the definition of that is exactly. Does anyone know?

So when this religious movement of sorts started to emerge, all those poor misfits were finally accepted. If you were a child of God and really meant it with your whole being, then you were committed to be accepting of everyone, regardless of their looks, background, or their personal shortcomings. Perfect. Now all those downtrodden souls became Jesus people and had a place to belong and were wholly accepted by the other Jesus people. In a way, it was a beautiful thing. When they were ridiculed by the non-Jesus people, they didn't have to go home and cry themselves to sleep. No, they could just go to a Jesus meeting and be taken in with open arms and feel the love from their "own kind." At last.

Enter Harold and Steven. Steven was who I refer to with the red hair and freckles, and he also had a cleft pallet, poor guy. He wasn't the brightest crayon in the box either, but nevertheless, he was a nice decent human being. He had been there in the background since kindergarten. And then you had Harold. Harold was a giant, one of those guys that was always the tallest in the class, towering over all the other shrimpy guys outweighing everyone. But as nice as he was always, he was kind of dorky too. They were prime candidates to become Jesus people, and so they were.

One night, as Vannie and I sat around, bored, the phone rang. It was Harold. We would see Harold and Steven in school, and being one who was never mean to the misfits, I would always say hello to him and give him the time of day, just for the fact that he was always nice to me. Just because everyone else was a shit didn't mean that I had to be one of them.

In those days, you could look up anyone's name in the phone book and get their number, which is just what Harold must've done because he had never called me before. He said, "Would you girls like to come with Steven and I to a Jesus meeting tonight?"

I told him to hold on. I then whispered to Vannie that we were being invited to go to a Jesus meeting. What did she think? We decided it might be interesting to see just what went on at these meetings. I told Harold we'd go. He said they'd be over in a few minutes to pick us up. The meeting was being held in Coolsville.

Harold and Steven drove up outside in Harold's old car. And I do mean old. It was one of those big old cars from the '40s with the big rounded bumpers, and the inside seats were like comfy overstuffed sofas. Vannie and I got into the back, and away we went to have our interesting religious adventure.

As we came to an incline about a quarter of the way there, the car just died. Harold got out and lifted the hood. He tinkered around for a minute and got back into the car. The car made a pitiful "I'm not going anywhere" noise. Harold moaned and got back out, hood lifted, more tinkering, and tried to start the car again. Same pitiful sound. More moaning, and maybe the third try would be lucky. No. No go.

Suddenly, Harold exclaimed, "I know what to do! I know what to do!" He then shut his eyes and put his hands palm to palm in a praying position and quietly said most sincerely, "Jesus, help me start my car." *Vroom!* The car came to life!

Vannie and I almost peed our pants trying to stifle our laughter.

We reached our destination and went up the stairs in an old apartment building. Inside a small apartment, quite a few people were seated on the floor in the tiny living room. We noticed a podium at the front of the room. A young man then entered the room and took his place behind the podium. He began by saying, "Before you all came, I had a problem with the plumbing, the bathtub backed up, and there was all sorts of stuff in there—coffee grounds, noodles, you name it. I got out the plunger and tried that. It didn't work. I had some liquid drain cleaner, and that didn't work. I ran some hot water down the drain, but nothing worked. So I realized how silly I had been, and the answer came to me, and I prayed to Jesus to help me unclog my drain, and then I left the room. Moments later, I heard a noise, and lo and behold, blub, blub, blub! Everything went down the drain!"

Well, that was it. Vannie and I looked at each other, and I said under my breath, "Jesus is a mechanic and a plumber too!" God and Jesus really do work in mysterious ways... No doubt in my mind.

A Wild Bunch of Finns

Small Town was very far north, so I guess it was a familiar environment for Scandinavians to settle when they came from their respective countries. We had Swedes, Norwegians, and Finns. Mostly Finns. I might as well have lived in Finland; that's how many Finns there were. All the kids I went to school with and many of my friends were Finnish. They're a good group of people on average; likable.

When they spoke in their language or even in English, it always sounded proud, choppy, and precise. Any bread, rolls, donuts, pretty much anything made with flour is called biscuit. Just biscuit. Funny. They eat strange fish dishes with even stranger names, most ending with an a as in *mojakka*. (moy-a-ka).

There are quite a few distinct last names for the Finnish. To name a few tongue twisters, there's the "ilas," "olas," and "alas." The "inens" and the "yas" or "jas." Ready? Heikkila, Hattila, Rahkola, Kantola, Ketola, Antila, Nickila, Jokela. Kinnunen, Jarvinen, Leponen, Pykkonen, Juntunen, Repponen, Lyytinen. Oja, Turja, Leppioja, Haapoja, Haataja, Ruokaja, Maanoja. Sounds incredible when you rifle them all off real fast.

The Finns, they are party animals. Vannie came from a long line of Finlanders, and she had some wild and crazy uncles. Uncle Toivo, Uncle Aino, and Uncle Urho—her mom's brothers. My favorite was Uncle Urho. He lived in a house next to the highway with her Grandpa Viijo. Uncle Urho was a brilliant architect, and you could see all the houses he had designed all over Small Town. They had unusual angles, very modern and Scandinavian-looking. The house Urho and Grandpa shared, Vannie shared too for a time.

Urho had decorated the house in his avant-garde way. Going upstairs, there was a door hung on a wall that led to nowhere. Maps of the moon were randomly scattered all over Urho's bedroom ceiling. But the small sitting room on the first floor was my favorite. He had painted the walls white and then drybrush-painted birch trees around the perimeter with black paint, giving the trees a muted effect. Grass green carpeting covered the floor, and for lighting, a single thick black cord swung across the ceiling with a bare lightbulb that hung down in the middle of the room. I had never seen such a room and I was well impressed. Simple and odd and unusual. Just like Urho.

There were other quirky bits of furniture and objects d'art sprinkled throughout, but something caught my eye in particular. It was a small, rustic, handwritten sign that hung above the kitchen sink which read: EPAJARJESTELMAYTYMATTOMYYDELLAANSA-KOHAN. I was intrigued, needless to say, and I asked Urho what it meant. He said it meant all three: disorganized, proud of it, and not sure of. Whether that was true or not, I'll never know, but I thought it one of the most peculiar and wonderful of houses I had ever seen. Recently, I made a small sign with the same long word that hangs in our house in memory of Uncle Urho.

Another interesting property belonging to Urho was out in the country—an old falling down barn. Strictly used as a party place where quite a few parties were enjoyed, it was called something like the Juunta, which I think meant something like "the Joint." The rough wood the barn was made of had spaces between the slats, so the wind freely blew through it. It was a large structure and really was the perfect place to party. Urho had built a catwalk across the top by the ceiling that led to a long balcony running the length of the place for the party goers to have a vantage point of the festivities going on below. There was a round table on the floor level with benches made of sawed logs, seat-height, for guests to sit on and enjoy their beverages.

A long bar for mixing the beverages ran along the back wall, a small kitchen in an adjoining shed. In a tiny separate shed was a bed for Urho, just in case he had a few-ten-too many cocktails and decided to just stay put. That miniscule shed held the bed and nothing more. Urho made the ceiling of glass so he could lie on the bed and get the whole sky's view of the stars.

The partying brothers who were Urho's siblings and Vannie's uncles were popular around town, and everyone knew of their partying and other crazy antics. One of the brothers, Aino, worked at a banking office in Coolsville. After closing hours at the office, having had a few (probably quite a few), he came up with a great idea. He had a recording of a popular song at the time, something mentioning sex in the lyrics, and pressed play. He then started to strip. Some ladies who had stayed to get caught up on their work got in on the "show" and were thoroughly shocked, disgusted, and appalled. Uncle kept going and stripped down to a G-string (and he was not a bodybuilder by any means)!

The ladies fled the office, some in tears. That was just one episode of many performed by one of the famous brothers.

Vannie told me of another stunt. This time, Uncle Urho was seated at the bar in his favorite seat at his favorite watering hole. One evening, a stranger came in and sat in the seat next to Urho. Urho turned to the stranger and bluntly said, "Who the fuck are you?"

What can be said? To know him is to love him...

I loved Urho almost as much as Vannie because he was just so quirky, talented, and had his own way of viewing the world. He was one in a million, and with everyone in Small Town being pretty run-of-the-mill, he was a million times more unique than all of them put together.

My favorite Uncle Urho story relayed to me again by Vannie was about a time when he and Vannie's cousin Janice were staying at a cabin together. They slept in sleeping bags on the floor of the cabin, and when they awoke one morning, first Urho wiggled around a bit in the sleeping bag, and when he finally emerged, he stated that he was now a beautiful butterfly leaving his cocoon. He then stood, arms extended and, flapping his arms, pranced around the room as his beautiful butterfly self.

I think there should be more Uncle Urhos in this world.

Good for You, Grandma Lil!

Grandma Lil seemed content living in her comfy apartment after she had adjusted to living on her own. She had belonged to a club for years for older men and women—a nice way for her to socialize. She was socializing, all right. Soon she was seeing Henrik on a regular basis. She had known Henrik and his wife for years from the club, and now that she was a widow, and Henrik a widower, well, they might as well keep each other company.

Everyone was delighted that Grandma Lil had a "boyfriend." Henrik took Grandma out for dinner or they would go for a drive. It was comical to see them together; little and large. Grandma was not even five feet tall, and Henrik was well over six feet tall. He would put one arm out straight to his side, and little Grandma would fit under his armpit. They would do this as their standard trick, the big Norwegian that he was. He was a real character if there ever was one. He'd embarrass my mom at our house, looking on the top of the fridge, level to his view, and proclaim, "It's dusty up here!"

A few months went by, each of them enjoying the other's company, and then they made the big announcement. They were getting married, both of them being age seventy-three. Wonderful! Grandma moved to Henrik's house in a nearby town. We had a new grandpa. And he could not have been a better grandpa than he was to Vance and I.

Many times, he took us for dinner at Sterling's Super Club. Grandpa Henrik couldn't hear very well, and he'd make comments about the other diners. If he saw a woman at another table wearing a lot of face makeup, he'd too loudly declare, "Look at all that calamine lotion!" followed by Vance, me, or Grandma's, "Shhh!" Or he'd notice a different woman with too much rouge and say too loudly, "Oh, look at all that barn paint!"

"Shhh!"

If he saw a couple kissing, "Oh, ain't that cute!"

Since he was a giant of a man, no one ever called him on it, but I'm sure if he would have been shorter in stature, there would've been trouble.

On one occasion, Grandpa, Grandma, and I were headed for the supper club. I said from the backseat of the car, "Hey, Grandpa, got any good jokes?"

He told me one of the dirtiest jokes I think I've ever heard. And I've heard a few... It was pretty funny, and I chuckled, but Grandma was not amused. "Shame on you, Henrik, for telling a child such a terrible thing!" Grandma was silent for the rest of the ride.

Grandpa Henrik was a very generous man and always gave me and Vance five dollars each time we saw him after taking us for dinner or buying us a special something we wanted. At any restaurant or his favorite supper club, looking at the menu, he would always say, "Have whatever you want." He had retired from the railroad, having quite a nice pension for Grandma and him to live on. Sometimes he took us to the Have A Snort Inn, a small, dark, bar-cum-restaurant on the outskirts of town. They served pizza there, and as we sat down and looked at the menu, he would promptly say, "I suppose you kids want a pizza pie."

Vance and I would giggle at that since he was the only person in the world who would ever call a pizza a pizza pie.

A woodshop in his garage, Grandpa had all the tools you could imagine, and one was a jigsaw. He would take Vance and I out there on occasion and guide us using the jigsaw to cut different shapes. He made windmills for his yard and carved beautiful figures of animals to give to people. But the most astounding, most stunning thing he crafted was a violin. It was a perfectly made instrument. He worked on it for months, curving and bending and gluing the thin pieces of wood to get the beautifully rounded shape for his creation. He stained it a rich red cherry color, and when it was finally finished, he then walked around the house, playing it. It was usually "Turkey in the Straw" or "Oh Solo Mio," which he also sang to. What a guy.

It Was Only a Dream

I was standing in the living room at Grandma Lil and Grandpa Henrik's house. The TV was off, the screen was dark. Next thing I knew, I was inside the TV! Obviously, I had shrunk somehow to fit inside. It felt very claustrophobic inside there. I felt as if I was trying to swim in some thick, murky water. It was cloudy and slimy and gray all around me. I wasn't afraid. I just couldn't see much in the midst of the dim murkiness.

The Day I Met My Lancelot

The carnival came to Coolsville, and Derek called. "Hey, wanna go to the carnival? I'll come get you."

We got to the carnival early evening and walked around, taking in all the games, rides, the usual.

A long-haired, unusual looking, guy was approaching. Derek and the guy greeted each other and had a short conversation. This guy was new in town, and word had it that he had come with his family from New York. How exciting. No one new ever came from somewhere so amazing as that.

Lance. Like the knight, Lancelot. I decided right then and there that everything about him was for me. He had just a bit of an east coast accent. Not the same old northern accent I was so used to hearing. His first words to me were, "Do you want a dish?" He extended his hand and held a dish out to me he had won at one of the digger games. An ugly turquoise melamine dish. I was in love.

Don't know what happened after that. Lance must've called Derek after that first meeting and asked Derek to fill him in about the chick he met at the carnival. It went from there, and for the rest of my high school years, Lance and I were inseparable. It really was love.

Lance had an older sister, three older brothers, a way younger brother (an "oops" baby), and the most likable mom and the oddest dad. His mother could've been my mother; that's how much I thought of her. The older brothers lived in Monticello. Two brothers were musicians, and one was an artist. When I was around any of them, I felt like a child. They all seemed so worldly and hip. His sister, who lived in the family home, kept to herself, never speaking or showing her face, watching funny things on TV in her bedroom. The only way you knew she was home was when you heard the cackling coming from behind her closed bedroom door.

When I spent time at Lance's house, if we weren't getting up to all sorts in his room, I was sitting at the dining room table, talking to his mom, Vi. Since she had already raised Lance's older brothers, nothing much fazed her, turning her into such a mellow lady...until it came to keeping her house spotlessly clean. Honestly, at any given time, you could eat off the floor in that house. Lance would open the fridge for something, and she'd be right behind him, kitchen towel in hand. "Lance! You've put fingerprints on the refrigerator door!" She made his bed every day and had to perfectly line up the plaid design from where it covered the pillows extending out to the foot of the bed. His little brother, Buddy, would be playing with just a few toys on the living room carpet, and she'd exclaim, "This house is a mess!" And besides being the cleaning queen of the universe, she could cook like nobody's business. She even made homemade noodles for pasta dishes. Wow.

Her cleaning regimen rubbed off on me, and from that day forward, I was a younger version of the cleaning queen. I had been so impressed. I had never met such a maniac cleaner in my life. Not that the house I grew up in wasn't clean. It was, but not to that degree of perfection.

I loved Vi's distinct New York accent, the ethnic look of her, and her witty sense of humor. And I knew she liked me too for whatever reason. She told me a humorous story one day over coffee. One of Lance's brother's girlfriends, Bebe, had come to visit earlier that day. Vi and Bebe were having coffee, and Bebe asked Vi for an ashtray so she could smoke. Bebe reached into her purse, tilted her cigarette pack upside down for a cig, and instead, a joint fell out, right into her cup of coffee!

Vi thought it so amusing and said to Bebe, "That's okay, we'll put it on the window sill and let it dry. You don't want to waste it."

See what I mean? Anyone's mother I knew of would've been horrified that you had "evil weed" in your purse! Small potatoes to Vi who had been through it all with those older sons.

Lance had the most awesome stereo in his room. Besides sounding good, it had speakers that lit up to the beat of the music—Bright pink, blue, yellow, and green—lighting up the darkness as we sat, mesmerized.

We'd bomb around in Lance's little car, and as a joke, but not really funny to the recipients, he'd spot a group of kids walking along the sidewalk and suddenly jerk the wheel right toward the group of pedestrians. The group of kids would scream and leap out of the way, but Lance had by then jerked the wheel away from them. He then laughed maniacally as we drove off.

Lance was a really good boyfriend, kind and considerate, and he got me a few beautiful presents through our time together. We had been to the carnival a few times since the day we met, and for some reason, on one occasion, I was angry with him. We passed by the digger game in which you picked your own prize out of the pile of junk behind the glass but only if you had the skill to do so. You know as well as I do, just when you seemed to get hold of the thing you wanted most, it fell through the claws of the digger. Lance had been trying to do everything in his power to win me over so I would quit pouting and we could go back to having a good time at the carnival. As a last-ditch effort, he looked at the digger, looked at me, and asked, "What do you want?"

I spied a small beauty through the glass of the game. It was a tiny Chinese lantern: a gold elongated dragon curved gracefully from tail to mouth, the mouth holding the delicate lantern part. The tail of the dragon rested on a black stand, which had a switch so the tiny lantern could light up. I clearly stated, "I want that."

Lance fed a quarter into the game, grabbed the handle, led the claws just above the lantern, released the pulley, and clamped onto the prize. With one more maneuver, he swung the claws over and dropped the lovely trinket into the safe zone. The guy attending the game took it out and handed it to Lance. Lance handed it to me. Lance had been bound and determined to make me happy again. Who could be mad after that?

Lance and I attended my junior prom. I had never been a girl for fluffy, puffy, frilly "look like a wedding cake" attire. My mom knew this and hired a lady in the neighborhood to make me a dress. I wanted it to be made of denim. It was the hippie days, after all. I wanted to stand out in my own way, and stand out I did. The dress was light blue denim, floor length in a halter style, halters being a popular look back then. But the icing on my cake was the baby-blue satin pointed collar and the long baby-blue satin, past the knee necktie. Can I get a "Far out"? The night of the prom, Lance showed up in a far-out ensemble too, especially for a guy—navy blue dress pants, light-blue silky shirt with a pattern of muted yellow roses, and a navy-blue tie. No tux for my hippie guy.

We happily went on our way, and I'd promised Grandma Lil we'd stop at her house to model our look for her and Grandpa to see. Grandpa let us in when we arrived, and there stood Grandma in tears.

"Grandma, what's wrong?" I asked her.

She softly spoke through her tears, "Something terrible has happened." And then it all came out. "Your cousin, Marion, has been murdered."

Well, the prom mood wasn't so "prommy" anymore. Grandma didn't have details of what exactly had happened. My cousin (one I hadn't really known) lived on the east coast somewhere. Because of the distance or maybe because no one knew yet, Grandma had no full story of what or how the horrific tragedy had taken place. Seeing her so upset, I felt so sorry for my sorrowful grandma. I hugged Grandma and told her I loved her, but nothing could be done. Thank God Grandpa was there to comfort her. On we went to the prom, our moods a lot lower than when we had started out.

The prom was the prom. So many big hairdos (I did my own normal version) and so many poofy dresses I had a hard time recognizing some of the girls in my class. There was food and dancing. Ho-hum. Bet it would've been fabulous had it been Coolsville's prom. The real highlight of the evening took place on the highway on the route home. A line of prom-goers' cars were heading south to their respective homes when a car up ahead pulled over to the side of the road. The driver stuck his arm out and motioned for everyone to pull over. What was happening?

We got out of the car, and someone in the small crowd pointed to the sky and said one word: "Look!"

There above us was the most dazzling spectacle of the northern lights I've ever seen to this day. All the prom-goers got on their car hoods, lay back, and watched the show. Pastel colors of blue, pink, and white lights were dancing and leaving beautiful trails in the dark night sky—by far the best part of the entire evening.

Cousin Jake

Vannie and I used to hang out with my cousin, Jake. Vannie had come with to a family picnic, which was a regular occurrence with the family on Mom's side. Glam Gram, Grandpa Sam, Auntie Shirley, Auntie Lovey, Uncle Chum, all the cousins and our family, and whoever else wanted to tag along was there. Another of my grandma's sisters, Anna (whom we rarely saw), her husband, and their son, Jake, a few years older than me, had come to the gathering. We didn't see these relatives very often, so Jake was someone new to talk to.

Vannie and I hit it off with cousin Jake who really wasn't a blood cousin to me. Actually, none of my relatives were blood-related if you want to go on the adoption angle of it. I always thought of them as my immediate family because they were, but now and then, it struck me that in all actuality, I could fall for one of the boys as we got older, and it would be weird, but I could marry one of them because we weren't of the same blood. Stranger things have happened, I guess.

Practically overnight, me, Vannie and cousin Jake were best of pals. Jake had a car and would come pick us up, Vannie and I. If I wasn't available, he'd come get Vannie and vice versa. Jake would take us places we wanted to go, and most times, we just drove around for something to do. We always had such a good time with Jake. The thing we girls loved to do most was go to the big house where Jake lived with a bunch of guys in North Haven. All these guys were out of high school by a year or two, a bunch of long-haired characters we loved to visit. Each one of those guys had a unique personality. One had the deepest voice. We thought we heard talking on the radio in the kitchen. It was a guy named Dave. He was the radio! Another guy, Mike, knew I loved dill pickles (we had that in common), and as soon as Vannie and I arrived, his first words to me were, "Want a pickle?"

They were all fabulous storytellers, but the master of storytelling was Jake. His arms would be gesturing in every direction, like a compass gone wild. His voice would go high in places and low in others at just the right time. And he was so funny. It was like being at a comedy club. He'd tell his stories as we sat on the big front porch of their house, which was perched on a hill overlooking the freeway below. From way up there, the cars on the freeway looked like toys. Jake told this story about walking up the hill:

"I was on my way home one day, just 'truckin' up the hill. It was a beautiful day, and I was just truckin'." At this point, his arms were in motion as if walking briskly. He carried on, "I looked to my left and I noticed some people sitting on their porch across the street. So I waved to them (hand-waving gesture). They waved back (hand gesture again, now with his other hand mimicking the neighbors). *Bam!* A big bush right in my face (hand in front of his face, imitating the bush)! I got up and brushed myself off. What an idiot, I was so embarrassed."

A few of the guys from the house played in a band, so if it wasn't in a bar (couldn't get in), we'd go see them play. Vannie and I were still in high school. We had a good thing going with all those guys fawning over us. They probably got a kick out of us too. And they were perfect gentlemen and never ever acted like pervs or were the least bit rude around us. It was a blast.

One day, in the boredom of Small Town, Vannie and I were trying to think of something exciting to do. Yeah, right, in Small Town. "Ah-ha! We'll go see Jake and the guys!" But how? No transport and twenty-five miles away. We hatched a plan: Hitchhike. A bit dangerous, not as much in those days, however. Would that stop us? Hell no.

Out to the highway. Not much traffic that day, and no one was going quite that far. We walked a lot of those miles that day, bound and determined. At last, we stood at the door of the party palace. We knocked, and Dave came to the door. He got right to the point and said, "You girls can't stay here, the WTFs are after us!"

"Oh, no! What happened (plus, we had just made the long, grueling journey from twenty-five miles away)?"

Dave then explained that one of the guys from their house had parked in one of the WTF guy's parking spot. And there'd be hell to pay.

The WTF doesn't stand for what you think of today (WTF didn't even exist back then). It was a motorcycle gang, the letters standing for Wheels to Freedom. Some people made up other meanings for the letters. No one really seemed to know what the letters really meant. Some said the W stood for Womanizing or Wine, the T for Terrorizing, and the F for the obvious. Whatever they thought the letters meant, one thing was for sure: the gang was badass, and you were not to cross them. Our guys were ready and equipped with butter knives, other miscellaneous kitchen utensils, and a few baseball bats. All prepared to go into combat, if need be. Our guys were mellow hippies, not warriors, obvious by their choice of weaponry.

So we were driven a few blocks away to another friend's house. Well, that was boring after all our efforts just to have some fun that day. A few hours later, when the coast was clear, Dave came and picked us up and brought us home (we never did see Jake that day). Of course, I had told my mom and Dad we were just going for a walk. Better get home before they got suspicious.

Soon the fun came to an end when Jake decided to join the army. I didn't see him after that for many years but missed all his crazy stories and all those great friends—the hippies on the hill.

Things Can Change Overnight

All had been fun and laughs with Lance and Jake and my handful of friends till Dad made a family announcement halfway through my senior year in high school. We were moving. The factories in Utopia weren't making enough money, the industrial era was coming to an end, and the factories were closing down. Dad would have to transfer, us in tow, to another state some four hundred miles away.

I was torn. I had to say goodbye to Lance. I was about to finish high school and had to leave with my family. I knew darn well that a long-distance relationship wouldn't last. Not at our ages. But on the other hand, part of me was elated that I could at last leave pitiful and small Small Town far, far away in the dust! Yes! No more gossipy neighbors, no more never-ending chants of "We're number one!" ringing in my ears. A new school, a new life, a new start—yippee!

After Dad's sheepishly announced announcement (he thought Vance and I would be devastated), I was the first to speak up (big grin on my face). "When are we leaving?" Sure, I had Lance and my best girlfriends, but as far as that damn school and most of the people in it were concerned…one word came to mind: Goodbye. Forever.

Okay, two words.

It's Just Grand in Grandville

What a difference to move to a totally new location. About four hundred plus miles south of Small Town, it was a welcome change. This new place was bigger, crazier, and way better than the hick town from whence I came. Being that we had moved further south, the people spoke differently. Not necessarily for the better, but different nevertheless. And the climate, unlike where we'd come from, was like the tropics in the summer, no jacket required when the sun went down.

Grandville, our new hometown, as I said, because it was quite a bit farther south on the map, it meant that the inhabitants had somewhat of a Southern accent. Some had a heavy accent. It was either because of the closer proximity to the real Southern states or some of the area residents were actually from the South originally. Some folks said "Ha" and "Ba" (hi and bye). Sometimes I asked for a repeat if the words were drawn out. In the north, we would tend to speak more quickly and choppy, sounding a bit French Canadian. The Finnish had an accent all their own but still chopped words out. The minute I opened my mouth in Grandville, I would hear the same words every time, "Whereya from?" I got teased a bit in a friendly way; they had never heard the likes of my accent.

As I got to know my new territory and the colloquialisms, there were two phrases I never got used to, and each time I heard them, I shivered from their atrocity. 1) "Where's it at?" 2) "Ain't it?"

What in the hell is that? I don't profess to speaking the king's English, but I try to speak a bit more concisely. Could no one simply ask, "Where is it?" You need not add the "at."

"Where's the store at?"

Excuse me, do you mean, "Where is the store?"

"Where's your brother at?"

Did you mean, "Where's your brother?"

It was so sour to my ears. And "ain't" ain't the best choice of words, but then to use it out of context is another one that made me cringe. If a person were to say, "This is good ice cream, ain't it?" I could live with that, but to use it as such: First person says, "I don't like the look of that."

Second person replies, "Ain't it?"

WHAT? Instead of replying back by stating, "I agree," they say, "Ain't it?" I made a vow to myself not to fall into the trap of adopting these misused words in my vocabulary, not even to blend into my new surroundings. Vance, however, being younger and really wanting to fit in, fell into the lingo trap and has never escaped. Poor Vance.

Of course, I was the new girl at school, my new school being three times the size of the school I had left behind with pleasure. The first girl I met and liked a lot was named Haley. She was short and blonde like me with a wild laugh and boobs I wished I had. We became best of friends in the fun town of Grandville. She was a year younger than me, but that was fine. I had a friend. She could show me around and introduce me to her friends. Great!

In a class I had at the end of the school day was a burly blonde guy named Dean who sat in the desk next to mine. He asked me (he was checking out my coolness or lack of), "Whereya from?"

I said, "Up north." Like he would have any clue where Small Town was.

Next question was, "Do they party up there?"

What was he up to? He had a beautiful smile (those smiles get me every time). Not my type, but he would become a good friend, always there for me. I told Haley about Dean, and she knew him, confirmed he was a nice guy, and knew his two best buddies whom I met next. The two pals of Dean's were Tucker and Shane. Shane was a tall string bean of a guy and very friendly, a bit shy. And Tucker, well, he was just the most impressive hippie I'd ever laid eyes on. *Ding! Ding!* That silky long hair and bright face bowled me over from the start.

Haley and I would always be together. She'd stay overnight at my house, and I'd stay at hers. She lived in a large house on the outskirts of town with her large family. Her sister, Lucy, who was in Vance's grade, had her room across the hall from Haley's. We always went and knocked on Lucy's door and told her we were coming to visit like we were neighbors. Lucy most times had a friend staying too, and what a great time we all had talking the night away. Then Haley and I would return to her room and write poems, forlorn verses of lost loves and such.

Way bigger and wilder than Small Town, in Grandville, there were plenty of strong drugs around, and I'm not talking about pot. I'm talking the heavy-duty stuff. You always heard of some teenage kid OD'ing, falling out of a window, thinking they could fly or spending time in the hospital or being locked away in the town jail. The people who were taking all the drugs weren't criminals, just stupid and a bit crazy. It's one thing to experiment, but if you don't exactly know what you're about to ingest, do not eat a handful of pills. I hate to say it, but if you're that stupid, you've got it coming.

Some of the real hard cores would shoot up peanut butter if they thought they'd get off. Don't be ridiculous. If someone offers you a pill, for instance, break it in half and see what happens. Do not take five at a time. Both Vance and I lost some good dumb friends this way. The more this happened and certain kids and young adults were lost to drugs, it just made you realize all the more not to be messing around with deadly potions, pills and, God forbid, needles.

Jim the Junkie

One of our favorite places Haley and I liked to hang out was the infamous soda shop in town. We didn't go there to drink soda. We went to hang out. The place was buzzing most nights of the week. And it's where I met Jim, a figure out of a movie; a hippie-goth movie. Jim was a lanky sort, and wore a long wizard's coat. I think it was velvet. He had long hair like every other guy in that time frame, but he dyed it a dark red, said that he was disguising his identity from the cops. He wasn't a criminal. That was just his way of being his own legend.

Jim and I went on some dates; nothing spectacular, just enjoyed spending time together. I knew he sold pot sometimes to friends about town, and out in front of the soda shop one night, he said to me, "Let's go."

I said, "Where?"

"My house."

"Why?"

He replied, "I'm gonna do a deal (weed)."

I went along, and once there, we headed to his basement bedroom that he shared with his older brother. Sitting on the edge of his bed, we soon heard a quiet knock on the door. Two guys and a girl I'd never seen before came into the room (Jim's mother wasn't home, and even if she had been, she seemed oblivious to what went on around there; Jim's dad had died a few years prior). The visitors had taken their places on Jim's bed and also took seats on his brother's bed. Then the "equipment" came out. Jim already had some of his own equipment, and the people who came had some too (what I mean by equipment is all the assorted paraphernalia it takes to shoot up).

One of the strangers tied off another one of the participant's arms, and then I saw a frightening sight. The syringe was being plunged into the girl's arm. I didn't know if I should run for the door, have a meltdown, or go hide in the bathroom. I kept my cool. When the last one had shot up, one of them said to me, "Do you want some?"

Hell no, I do not want some! I thought silently, but I remained cool, and like a schoolgirl, said politely, "No thanks, that's okay." Schoolgirl or not, I wanted to be about as far away from that basement drug den as possible.

After a few minutes, Jim's company left. Good. Jim then laid back on the bed, looking like he was on cloud nine. (no, closer to cloud twenty-nine). I remember thinking at the time, *It must be good stuff because Jim is in la-la land.* I asked him, "Why did you do it?"

He drawled, "I have a monkey on my back."

He was hooked on heroin! That closed the chapter on Jim. I just couldn't be around him, his friends, and the junk.

The Sun God and the Englishman

Now I don't know which one came next, Frank or Miles, or maybe they came along simultaneously, however it took place. I honestly fell for both of them at once. At the time, there was a song called something like "Trio" about a girl trying to choose between two guys. I listened to that song quite a few times; so appropriate in my dilemma.

Let me describe each of the two candidates, and you'll see what a quandary I was in. Frank was Italian—tall, dark, and handsome, to use the old cliché. I wrote a poem about him once (probably in Haley's bedroom) entitled "The Sun God." He had beautiful brown skin, brown melty eyes, black wavy hair, and an amazing white-toothed smile like in a toothpaste commercial. Gorgeous. Besides the physical attraction, he was really an agreeable person.

Miles was shorter, very wiry curly hair, a fit wiry physique, and a quirky sense of humor, and he was just so adorable! His mother was British, which made him half-British, and Miles could put on the accent when he was in the mood, making me laugh and like him even more. Besides being so darling, Miles would've given me the moon just for the asking.

Frank was so tempting. Miles was so alluring. Now what was I to do? I wanted both of them in different ways, and they wanted me back.

For a time, I went out with both of them; no rules anywhere saying you can't have two boyfriends. But it gets confusing and hard to deal with two sets of feelings.

As high school was about to an end forever, just as I had started to enjoy it, Frank, my sun god, decided he'd go away to college after graduation to the southern part of the state. He wanted me to come with him. Hmm… Should I?

At the same time, Miles had similar ideas. He wanted us to get an apartment together when school ended. Should I take one of the offers? Or should I do something completely different?

Saved by Three Musketeers

In the meantime, just for fun, I went out with the Dean, Tucker, and Shane trio. All three of them were great friends of mine. I still had a big crush on Tucker, but he never seemed interested in me. He seemed to be attracted to very petite girls (I was quite petite myself, but I'm talking teeny-petite; childlike was Tucker's type), and also, they were the girls who wore the most makeup and the thickest eyeliner. Whorey looking girls, you might say. I was out of the running… That's okay because I had the best and most fun time with all three of those guys.

After dinner, on most nights of the week, one of the three would call on the phone and say, "Get ready, we're coming to get you."

I would no sooner hang up the phone, and there they would be, out in the driveway, waiting for me to go on a joyride. And joyride we did, all over through the endless cornfields, out to no-man's land, and back again. A few beverages were consumed, and we laughed our heads off at just about everything each one had to contribute on our nightly excursions. It was a blast. Why they chose me as their mascot, I couldn't say, but I was glad they did.

We ended up in a forestry one night, and Tucker, the driver that evening, stopped the car in the middle of nowhere among the towering trees all around us. A few beers were downed, and we were all talking and laughing at once, the usual ritual. After a time, Tucker started the car to leave, and the car was going nowhere; tires spinning, we were stuck in a pile of mud. Dean and Shane got out of the car to push us out. I stayed in the car, Tucker behind the wheel, giving it gas.

At last, the car lurched forward. We were unstuck. A cheer went up, and Dean hopped in front with Tucker, and Shane got in next to me in the back. Then I noticed something funny; actually, hilarious. Dean and Shane were completely covered with mud from head to toe. Tucker hadn't yet noticed in the dark. I loudly spoke over all of them and announced, "Tucker, turn on the light and look to your right." They were all talking and laughing. I said it again, "Tucker, turn on the light and look to your right."

This time, he heard me and did as I said. The light came on, he looked to his right at Dean in the front and then in the back at Shane, and the whole car was in an uproar. It was so funny to see the guys caked in mud. Both guys who had gotten out to push looked like they had partied in a pigsty! What a funny good night that was!

The Day the Earth Stood Still and Then Ended

Mom had gone into the hospital, having diabetic complications. The doctors were doing tests, and all seemed normal. She had many episodes the whole time she raised my brother and I. At times, her sugar went too low, and she acted like she was drunk. We tried not to laugh. It wasn't funny, but she said the funniest things when she was in that state. Dad would feed her a bowl of cereal with milk and tons of sugar. Once, he was feeding her the cereal, and she kept complaining, "This is yucky, this is yucky."

Dad was ever so patient and gentle and told her just to keep eating it. She still said it was yucky, and we all chuckled a bit, and then Dad decided to try it himself. He was so terribly sorry when he discovered the milk in the cereal was sour. Mom had been right. It really was yucky.

Many times, I had seen her throwing up, not being able to stop. Never mind all the times I saw her pinching her thigh and inserting that dreadful long needle. When you see that at a young age, that horrible image stays with you for years, maybe forever.

But through all her trials and tribulations with her horrendous disease, this time was way worse. She lost consciousness in the hospital. When Vance and I went to see her, we stood on either side of the bed and told her that we loved her. She squeezed our hands but did not open her eyes.

I walked around in school like a zombie. I just knew we were going to lose her. And we did. And my world as I had known it came crashing down around me.

I had never felt so utterly lost now that my best friend was gone. Who would I talk to? Who would give me better advice than my mom? Who would console me? My best friend was gone. My best friend. Gone. I had a better mom than any of my friends, maybe anyone else in the universe.

My best friend. My mom. Gone.

Mom was buried and gone forever; my life changed and was unfulfilled from that day forward, and I still had the task of getting through three more months of school till graduation. The light had gone out of my life, and it was so hard to get through studying, tests, and the sorry looks I got at school. As completely shattered as I felt, I was also mad at Mom, the one who had gently made me and encouraged me to keep going to school, especially that horrid school in Small Town. And where was she to see me graduate, at last? Thanks, Mom, for dying on me now, the person I wanted most at that ceremony. I had made it. *And where are you?* It's a confusing feeling to be sad and mad at the same time.

Dad made it nice for me on my graduation day, and there was a small party at our empty-feeling house with a cake and presents. We all got through it, our favorite person missing.

After getting through graduation and deciding not to go with Frank or with Miles, my real plan had always been to spread my wings and fly away to true independence.

I stayed at home for a month or two and, feeling guilty, told Dad it was time for me to test the waters of the next phase of my young adult life. That meant leaving Dad and Vance to fend for themselves, but Dad was a grown man and he was Dad, so he would have to carry on without me.

Flying Far, Far Away from the Nest

With Dad as chauffeur, the car was packed, and we headed north but not nearly as far as Small Town. My friend, Melissa (I haven't mentioned till now; some hard feelings from years later in my life. I won't even go there…), was waiting for me to move in with her in a basement apartment she had rented for us. The apartment was in a college town, and Melissa worked in a big popular bar that had live entertainment each weekend. She said I could get a job there with her, and what a fab time we'd have!

After hugging Dad goodbye and sadly waving as he drove out of sight, now my independence began.

It was beyond exciting adding my stuff to Melissa's and making our apartment comfortable and what we thought was cool-looking at the time.

Also, I got the job at The Showcase Bar and was meeting tons of new people and the bands that came to perform. Before long, I met Brad. He looked as though he could have had some Native American ancestry in his past. He had beautiful shiny dark hair, flawless brown skin, and a chiseled face. We spent a lot of time together—he at the apartment with me, and I going to his family home with him. His parents were so warm and welcoming. Nice, nice people.

Brad had called me Von (La Vonne) almost since the day we met. Before I met Brad's parents, when Brad's dad asked where he had been (sometimes for days on end with me), Brad would say he had been with Von. Brad's dad thought I was a guy because of the name Von and started making hints to Brad, thinking Brad was gay. Brad assured his dad that no, he was not gay, and that I was truly a female. We had a good chuckle over that. His dad would've been fine either way but secretly was relieved that his son was straight.

I had received a few letters from Jim (heroin Jim) back in Grandville, nice newsy letters, and I was happy to hear from him. Even though he was someone I had left behind because of his drug habit, basically, he was still a good guy. Then the letters just seemed to stop, and I thought the worst. I had no way of finding out what was going on with him. Hopefully nothing, and he would write when the mood struck him.

The job at the Showcase was going okay and could be really fun some nights, but between Melissa and I both working there, it barely paid the bills and whatever utilities we had to pay. We lounged during the day and worked at night. There was hardly any money. We had no food. It was nice to be skinny, but we were also hungry. One day, I opened the fridge, and we had apples and Jell-O. Great if you were a mouse. Another time I was starving, I opened the cupboard and found a box of that famous stuff you mix with ground beef to make an instant meal. *Wonder if you can make this without the hamburger?* I thought to myself. I prepared it, less the meat. And I got my answer with the first bite. Straight into the garbage can it went. Yes, you can make it with no meat, but it is god-awful.

For the lack of food and getting run down from the late nights, I came down with two infections, a yeast and a bladder, maybe caused by something else in the first place, but the lack of sleep and no food didn't help. No money to go to the doctor. Now what? Things got worse and worse, and I knew I needed antibiotics. When there was no way not to go, I went to the doctor. I don't know where I scrounged the money from, but when you feel that bad, you'll find a way. I soon improved and felt like myself again. Funny when you feel so bad and then you feel better, you think, *Do I always feel this good?*

I had another letter from Jim! As I began to read, I was over-joyed that Jim had been to rehab during the time lapse when I had received no letters from him. He wrote that he was a bit shaky, but he had kicked the heroin and was doing okay. What a relief. I was genuinely happy for him. He was still alive. I walked around at work that night with a smile on my face and with the knowledge that Jim was going to be okay.

Melissa had some friends, a girl and a guy that were a couple she had met at the bar. I didn't know them myself but knew of them through the stories she had told me. Mary Ann and Mort. Melissa said something had gone wrong where they had been living and now didn't have anywhere to stay. She then informed me that she offered for them to come stay with us. Fine and dandy, but as it was, we had one bedroom and one bed that Melissa and I had to share. No, it wasn't like that; both of us were straight as could be. We were on our own, and it was what we could barely afford, so necessity it was. I guessed the visitors would sleep on the couch and living room floor.

Shortly after Melissa told me of our guests coming to stay, Mary Ann and Mort came through the door with bag and baggage. They moved right in. Melissa then offered them the bedroom and the bed! Oh, how accommodating of her! And in they pranced and proceeded to get all set up in our only bedroom. Now I tell you, if you beg and shed crocodile tears to crash at someone's place, well, beggars can't be choosers, and you should be grateful to sleep practically anywhere. I wouldn't dream of kicking someone out of their own bed! But not Mary Ann and Mort.

One night, during there "hotel" stay, the two of them decided to take a bath TOGETHER. Whatever turns you on, but at someone else's place? After their communal bath was over, I went in to use the bathroom, and what to my horror did I see? A "beautiful" black ring all around the inside of the tub. Pigs. Not a word of apology from either one of the swine or an offer to clean up the disgusting tub. They stayed three or four days too many. Way too many. They didn't pick up after themselves, offer to help with anything, and totally camped out.

Melissa didn't say a word, and I knew better than to comment or Melissa would've had a hissy fit and say to me, "But they're my friends!" Who cares? They're PIGS!

Finally, the dirty bums said they had another poor soul (sucker) to stay with, and they finally, thank God, left, leaving their mess behind them. Melissa and I began the clean-up duty. We started in the bedroom. The sheets needed to be washed for sure. Just the idea of those two using the bed made my stomach turn. We were both chatting and in a happy mood now that the scuzz buckets were gone. We pulled the sheets back, and lookie here! The female pig had had her period, and the sheets were covered in blood! They were white sheets with yellow roses, and all we could do from being further grossed out was to make a joke and say now we had sheets with red roses on them. Through our feeble attempt of a joke, it made us gag. Thankfully, they never begged to stay again, and Melissa wised-up and never invited more guests. I most likely would've killed her had I seen another couple of vagabonds at our door.

I was becoming bored with living at the apartment, night after night working at the Showcase, making little money and being hungry. Besides, Melissa had a serious boyfriend she was planning to marry, and I knew she'd fly the coop before long. The only good thing in my life at that point was Brad, but since he lived at home, I couldn't very well stay there with him. I had to move again.

As an escape and for some time to think, I decided to go visit Auntie Shirley who now lived in that big city of Monticello. She had escaped too. Maybe she could help me decide what to do next.

Auntie Shirley had lived there in the city for a few years in a big house (a commune of sorts) she shared with her boyfriend, Keys (he played the piano beautifully), Keys' brother, Earl, another roommate, Mack, and another roommate, Rolland, otherwise known as Roll who just happened to be Freda's older brother I had somewhat known and had a crush on from seeing him at her house back in high school.

It was wonderful to be with Auntie again, and now that we were both adults out on our own, we got along famously. We always did get along well, but now I guess we were more on the same level. We had both grown up. She had grown up to be such a truly unique and loving aunt to me. She is now and always will be one of my favorite people on earth. *Quirky* is a good word for her, and *entertaining* would be another, and I wouldn't have her any other way.

Auntie Shirley and I had a good time together, talking, laughing, and reminiscing. Chatting away, she brought up the name of my secret heartthrob from my high school days, Max Parker. He was a friend of Keys' and the one I had loved from afar, one of the cool guys from Coolsville. Max never even knew I existed. Throughout all my high school years, I about peed myself at the sight of him. If he would've even spoken to me, I'm sure I wouldn't have been able to utter a word and probably would've melted into a pool of marshmallow cream. He was a diminutive little man, long straight hair, and always wore his signature oversized sweater and jeans. He always looked the same; don't think he ever washed that sweater. All part of the sheer awesomeness of Max.

Then Shirley told me an interesting and devastating fact about Max. "He's gay," she said.

"What?" That one I had drooled over for all those years…was gay? As you know, from the time of my dear aunties, I have nothing against anyone being gay. I now have lots of really good gay friends whom I love dearly, but in those days, nobody had come out yet, and even if a person was known to be gay back then, it was kept quiet. So at the time, finding out about Max, I felt betrayed by my own feelings I had been brewing for all those years.

While staying at Shirley's, Rolland and I were talking more and more. Still quite handsome and fun to talk to, I felt like I already knew him better than I did from those times at Freda's house a few years back.

One night, everyone who lived in the house had gone out or gone to bed. That left me and Roll. I was rather pleased with the setup. We sat in the living room, having a few drinks and having a nice conversation. Auntie Shirley had always loved animals and had a dog and two cats that were accompanying us that evening. I was sitting on the sofa. Roll sat on the floor. First the dog jumped up on the couch with me, followed by one of the cats. Finally, the other cat joined me, now completing the menagerie. As a joke, I said, "Well, come on, the rest of ya (meaning any other animals lurking around the place)." That was Roll's cue, and he came up onto the couch with me. Some passionate kissing took place, and that night, I went up to his room. I was totally bowled over by him.

He knew of my dilemma with the Melissa situation and asked me to move in with him in the big house in the big city. Perfect solution. Wow, me and Roll, my heart-throb from the past. Perfect.

I went back to the apartment Melissa and I had shared, got my stuff, and was packing when the phone rang. It was Dad. He seemed quiet and sounded serious. Then he said, "I have bad news... Jim died."

How could that be? He had been clean for months. I said, "What do you mean Dad? How can he be dead? Are you sure?"

Dad then explained the story he had heard. Jim had been at a party at someone's house, then had passed out on the living room floor, and when they tried to rouse him, he was dead.

I was stunned and felt sick, to say the least. What a sorry shame. Jim had kicked his addiction, and for what? For absolutely nothing. He had tried, succeeded, and failed. Some people just can't leave the stuff alone. A nice friend I could never speak to again. What the hell? Goodbye, poor, lost Jim.

A-Do A-Ditty, I'm Movin' to the City

What a trip living in the big city with Roll and all the other residents of the house. We didn't live right in the city proper; we lived on the fringe of the city, close enough to enjoy all the city had to offer but without the hustle and bustle, sirens wailing in the night. But it never got dark there at night, always a greenish glow from the lights of the city, rather ghoulish and haunting.

The giant old house consisted of a large living room, dining room, which featured an upright piano, an old-fashioned granny-type kitchen, a small dingy basement with an old wringer washing machine (that was "fun" to wash clothes with), and the upstairs which had four bedrooms and a bathroom and an attic that housed a pool table.

Shirley's guy, Keys, his brother Earl owned the house. Earl had the largest bedroom by all rights and barely ever came out of it. He was a quiet guy, not much to say, and kept to himself. Roll and I had a small but comfortable room. Auntie and Keys had the room next to ours, and another single guy, Mack, had a room that he liked to entertain the ladies in now and again. Also, as I mentioned, there were our roommate pets. The dog, Dandy, one cat, Piggy (ate everything), and the other cat, Felix, plus some other unwelcome "pets," which were a handful of bats that congregated up in the large attic. Nobody, including Earl, paid any attention to the bats. We never tried to get rid of them, just left them alone to do what they did up there in the "belfry" where they slept by day, hanging upside down from the rafters. Ick.

Speaking of bats, one night, Roll and I were sound asleep and I heard a whirring noise. I sat up in bed to listen, and *whoosh!* A bat swooped right over my head! I covered my head and let out a few noises myself, gasping in surprise and horror. Roll woke up and quietly said, "What's wrong, sweetie, are you having a bad dream?"

I then loudly replied, "Heck no! there's something flying around in here!"

No sooner had the words come out of my mouth, *whoosh!* The bat dive-bombed us again!

Roll got out of bed, clad in only his undies, and reached under the bed for a small baseball bat he kept there (Did he think he would be attacked by bats or some other intruder?). Baseball bat in hand, he took a few swings. As I hid beneath the covers, I pictured him there in the middle of the room in his undies with bats tangled in his really long hair, and then what would he do? The bat kept circling, and Roll dove back into bed under the covers. Maybe he pictured the bat caught in his hair too. We lay there under the blanket, sweating in the heat of a hot summer night, afraid to do anything but to come up with a plan. The whirring continued, and when we dared to peek out, we saw the demonic creature, claws scratching on the windowsill, trying to get out. Finally, the dumb bat figured it out, and away he went. Roll and I lay there, giggling and talking about our midnight visitor, unable to sleep after the freaky and comical event.

I got a job at a factory making pies. They were the little mini snack pies. The company also made potpies. We only made the crust portion of the pies. It was a small operation and only employed about a dozen of us.

A tall guy named Dewey would come around the corner with a tray of golf-sized balls of dough. These would be flattened in a machine operated by me and another woman. When we ran out of doughballs, we hollered out, "Doughballs!"

And here Dewey came with another tray. Hollering out "Doughballs" struck us funny at times, depending on the amount of sleep we had had the night before or if we were in a jolly mood that day. Then someone came up with the idea to call Dewey, "Dewey Doughballs." How childish, but I liked that job and the people I worked with.

Roll had a job driving a forklift at night, and the only way I could spend any quality time with him during the week was to set an alarm for 4:00 a.m. I was happy to be sitting on the bed, awake, waiting for him to come home from his shift. That's what I call love. We always had our best times together at 4:00 a.m.

I almost forgot to mention the early morning music, most times way too early. It was Keys living up to his nickname, playing the piano. I loved it. My favorite was and always will be piano music of any kind. It was a lovely way to wake up until…the singing began. Auntie Shirley and Keys singing their hearts out…out of tune, that is. They sang "Nothing Would Be Finer," "It's a Grand Old Flag," old songs like that. They were having fun "yodeling," and it was funny, but I wished Keys would have just played the keys, that's all.

Roll had been yearning to go back up north, back to the woods that he loved most. That man would've been happy to live in a tent in the woods for the rest of his life with his only companion being a dog. He loved to party and socialize, but deep in his heart, he was Daniel Boone. At that point, I was ready to move on too. It would be nice to have our own place and to see a dark night sky again with a view of the stars.

Auntie Shirley still owned my grandma and grandpa's house in Utopia. My oldest cousin had lived there for a while but would soon be moving out. She said we could rent the place from her.

Before long, we moved into the old house of memories and made it our own. I got a job at a bar downtown in North Haven, taking the bus four nights a week to work, and the last bus home. We didn't have a car at the time, so I relied on the bus for everything. It was a pain, especially when I loaded up Roll's big satchel with loads of dirty clothes, got on the bus, and went to the laundromat. I then sat at the boring place for a few hours, washing, drying, and then folding the clothes back into the satchel and then back on the bus for home. I hated it.

The bar I worked at downtown, Cha-Ching (sounds like something in Vegas), was a crazy place. The guy who owned it would get some big hokey ideas in order to attract a crowd. One being all the waitresses, including yours truly, would wear a "fetching" costume which consisted of a football jersey, black pantyhose, and black heels for Monday Night Football on the big screen. Charming. Didn't all the old pervs just love that! On those football nights, I was summoned by the jolly bartender I had become quite fond of a huge guy—older with a wild sense of humor—named Buddy. He asked so sweetly, "Will you please deliver this tray of drinks downstairs to the guys?"

With about ten drinks, I had to make my way in heels down a steep set of stairs to where a bunch of shady looking characters sat with the boss/owner. They got all quiet when I came down to deliver their drinks. What were they up to down there in the dungeon? And no tip from the creeps. I hated going down there just to be stared at in my embarrassing getup. The upstairs crowd consisted of a wide array of customers, good and bad, and quite a few foreign men from far-off lands. Since it was a port city, there were always some wayward sailors who couldn't speak English who were ready to entertain you with their odd customs and curious ways.

Enough was enough. Between that costume of sorts, the clientele, and the basement drinks delivery, I left that job. Shortly thereafter, I heard the boss man got busted big-time along with some of the other thugs from the basement gang. He had been running a small mafia-type gambling saloon in that basement. Serves all those creeps right.

I was out of a job, and whatever money we had was down to nil. And some of the money we had left Roll had spent on booze for when his friends came to party. Roll hadn't worked at all, and it was getting old, and I was so hungry. I flipped out one day and was screaming at the top of my lungs about how pissed off I was with the whole situation. I rarely lose it, but this was one time I really did. Roll just didn't seem to give a damn about anything. I started grabbing one shoe at a time and made a hell of a racket hurling them down the stairs into the kitchen below. It was like a scene from a sitcom, but not funny.

Finally, when I was to the point of starving, I called Grandma Lil. In tears, I told her we had no money for food. It was the only thing I could do. Roll was way too proud to call his mother and ask for help. I could hear the distress in Grandma's voice, but she said they'd be over with some groceries. I felt so small and stupid when Grandma and Grandpa showed up with a few bags of groceries for us. I thanked them repeatedly and hugged Grandma, hoping she would feel my gratitude.

Things got worse, and we couldn't pay Shirley the rent. We weren't even eating. Shirley despised Roll for being a bum and not working and not paying her. Soon we had a summons to go to court. Yup, Shirley was taking us to court. She wanted her money. Okay, try squeezing blood out of a turnip.

The day came, and we went to court. The judge was brief and said no more than "Pay up." Afterward, Shirley pulled me aside and said it had nothing to do with me and that she wanted Roll to grow up and be responsible. She was right, and I felt sad because it drove a wedge between my Auntie and me and a wedge between Roll and I.

I should've run away then and there, but I still loved Roll and would remember when we had had our happy times back in the city.

Since we had nowhere to go now, Roll ate his pride and asked his mom if we could stay with her and the family temporarily back in Small Town. Fine. I didn't have to go to school there. Yes, she said we could. But he didn't want to impose too much and asked if we could live in the hayloft of their barn. Yes, the barn. Are you kidding me? By day, we hung around the house, but come nightfall, we headed out to the hayloft where our bed was. And our clothes. And our earthly possessions. It was a brand-new barn his parents had just built; no animals yet, but it was still a barn…

Even though we lived in a barn, he still went out drinking with his friends. Long after I went to sleep in my hayloft bed, he was still out whooping it up. One night, very late, I heard him climb the ladder, and he got into bed after leaving his jeans in a clump on the floor. A few hours later, I heard rain. I opened my eyes, and there was Roll, standing in the corner, peeing all over his jeans. I said, "What in the hell are you doing?"

He replied with a slur, "Number seventeen."

I flipped over in bed utterly and completely disgusted. Drunk as a skunk he was.

Roll and I finally came into the house to sleep in October when I begged for warmth. Asshole.

Aah…a warm bed at last. Since there was little room with all the family living there, I slept in the top bunk of the girl's room. I didn't mind, except for when they blasted the stereo at night. *Boom, boom, boom* with the bass. We stayed for another month or so and we both got jobs at a food processing plant in North Haven. After a few months, we managed to save enough money to get our own place. At last. Things would be better now with money and our own home. Rented, but ours.

We found an inviting farmhouse to rent in the next town over from Small Town. An old Finnish lady owned it but lived in another town far away so she'd come to stay now and then upstairs in her apartment. We had the downstairs. Her name was Hilma, and she was a warm and humorous lady.

Roll and I traveled back and forth to our jobs in the food processing place. All was fine, but the drinking still continued. Sure, I drank right along with our friends when they came around, but Roll would drink every day like he couldn't go without it. He didn't even act or seem drunk. He just drank. All the time.

It Was Only a Dream

I was invisible. Standing outside of an apartment building, I noticed a group of kids approaching. There was gravel around the outside of the building. I decided to test out my invisibility skills and simply walked across the rocks. It made a crunching sound and left indentations from my feet, rearranging the terrain. The kids couldn't see me but heard the crunching and saw the gravel moving. They started screaming and hit the trail, not knowing what sort of paranormal scene they had just witnessed. It was all very amusing being invisible.

Nothing Lasts Forever

Grandma Lil and Grandpa Henrik had a few really good years together until, as Grandpa tearfully told it, "Lil said she had a headache and went to the bathroom to get some pills (aspirin), and she didn't come back. I went to find her, and she was on the bathroom floor. She was gone." It really broke my heart when Grandma Lil died. She had always been so sweet to me, and I always felt so loved by her from the start, way back from the "precious, precious" days.

I remembered that I had something very special to remember her by, a treasure she had given me a few years prior to her death. She called me into her bedroom one day, opened a dresser drawer, and withdrew a small white box. She turned to me and opened the box. There in the box lay the loveliest, most delicate necklace. It was very old, the design reminiscent of the late twenties perhaps. It had a small imperfect pearl dangling from the bottom. She then spoke, "Your Grandfather (the one before Henrik) gave this to me on our wedding day. If I give it to you, what will you do with it?"

Without missing a beat, I gave my sincere and logical answer. "I'll wear it on my wedding day, Grandma."

And what she said next has stayed with me ever since. She said, "Bless your heart, it's yours."

I'd gladly go back and relive that precious moment with my sweet grandma all over again. And I do in my mind and in my heart.

A few years later, when Grandpa Henrik was eighty-one, he passed away. I couldn't believe it. It seemed to me he'd go on forever. I told Auntie Shirley about my disbelief of Grandpa's passing, and she said, "Nothing lasts forever. My gosh, he's not a tree!" Words of wisdom, and she was right.

The very last one of my wonderful grandparents was now gone. Grandpa Henrik's funeral was to take place at Hill's Funeral Home, owned by a family of brothers. Our family had been to the same funeral home so many times (between the grandparents leaving us, a few old aunts and uncles, and some family friends that came to their premature demises for various reasons) that we knew the mortuary brothers by their first names. Honestly, throughout my childhood and teenage years, I sometimes felt like I belonged to the "family of death." They should've put a revolving door on the front of that dreaded funeral place, for heaven's sake.

Each time, we had the same awful singer for the funeral service. I surmised years later that when people are grieving, they really don't want to be bothered with details too much. So it probably came down to one of the Hill brothers asking the grieving family who they would like to sing at their loved one's service and the grievers saying, "Well, gee, we don't know, do you have any suggestions?"

One of the brothers offered a consoling answer by saying, "We do have an excellent baritone singer that we normally call on to sing any songs you'd like to hear at the service." Done.

And here's what you got: All would go quiet, and a man dwarf would waddle out (no, I have nothing against dwarves). There was a small platform he would step up on, and he would begin to sing. Always "The Lord's Prayer" in his wavering vibrato. "Ourrrrr Fatherrrr…which art in heavennn…" The whole song from the terrible beginning to the terrible end with the warbling vibrato. If you didn't feel bad enough in the first place, you felt wiped out by the end of his version of the could be beautiful, should be comforting classic hymn. Thank God, literally, that someone else stepped up and sang at Grandpa's funeral that day, and it was a song about going to heaven on a train. Very fitting since Grandpa had worked for the railroad for years. Not a warble was heard.

I Do

Roll and I decided to get married. To this day, I think I must've been on another planet when I said yes. I knew it, I knew it. I should not be doing this. But in a ridiculous dumbass stupor, I went right ahead. Things were getting planned, and I guess I was too caught up in the plans to back out. A few bad omens came to pass in the days leading up to the big day that should've warned me... The day before the wedding, our sewer backed up all over the basement floor. Stink-o-rama! We were to have the reception/party there. Now what? We managed to clean it up and fumigated the best we could, closing the basement door behind us.

On the morning of the wedding, big black clouds filled the sky, and it was looking ominous. The wedding ceremony was to be held on the deck of Roll's mom and dad's house. The whole day would be enjoyed outdoors, but maybe not if we were going to get a thunderstorm. The day was doomed for sure. Suddenly, an hour before the wedding, the clouds parted, the sun came out, and it turned into a glorious, bright, warm day. That made me feel better. Maybe this day and this marriage wouldn't be doomed after all.

The ceremony was simple and nice. Roll looked so handsome in his suit. Had I ever seen him in a suit before? I myself had found a dress that was perfect for me. The dress was simple with belled sleeves and a square neckline, floor-length, and I cherished my grandma's antique necklace I wore with her love. Roll's youngest sister had made me a halo of woven flowers from the woods to wear on my head, which I couldn't have loved more. Mom, Dad, and Vance were there along with a few relatives of mine and all Roll's family and relatives too.

This was turning out good. The reception went well, and everyone was having a good time. My old friend, Ally, was there who I had lost touch with, me moving back and forth, etc. So special to have her there that day.

Since Roll loved the great outdoors so much, one of his favorite things to do was to go camping. HIS favorite thing, not mine. Call me spoiled, too good for the great outdoors, I don't care. I like my luxuries. I like sleeping on a bed, I like heat, washing my hair in the shower, and cooking on a real stove. I do not like sleeping on the ground—wet, dry, or otherwise—unknown objects poking me in the back. I don't like freezing or getting rained on till I'm soaked through to my skin. I do not like washing my hair or bathing in a freezing cold lake, and I do not like cooking on a campfire, followed by washing the dishes in water that has been heated by the campfire. And then there's the mosquitoes. Oh, what fun we're having now!

I think I make myself crystal clear. I don't see the thrill of any of it. Okay, back to nature and all that, but it does not turn me on one teeny bit. Camping and country music, no thank you. However, because Roll loved his favorite thing so much away from everything and everyone (the only good part of the adventure I can agree on, being away from everything), I went along just for the vacation factor. It would be the only form of vacation I got.

We went somewhere way far north out in the sticks, a beautiful spot next to a lake, and it rained nonstop for the three days we were there. It was so cold all we could do was to swaddle ourselves in warm clothes and rain gear. Finally, thank God, it was time to pack up and go home. On the way home, we passed a lake with some resorts, and I noticed quite a few dollhouse-looking cabins at the side of the road. In the sweetest, most convincing voice I could muster, I asked Roll if we could stay at one of those warm, welcoming cabins.

Normally, he would ignore my request and just drive on by, but maybe he was sick of being wet and cold too, and my idea seemed inviting to him. He pulled into a cluster of cabins and actually rented one. Now you're talkin'! When we got into the cabin, which was two rooms, one with a bed and the other was a small bathroom, Roll then admitted to being cold and would like to take a shower to warm up.

A few minutes later, he came out of the bathroom, towel wrapped around his waist. He did a sort of side step, and the towel fell to the floor. As he bent over to pick it up, his butt had come in contact with a small wall-mounted burning hot heater. As he tried to stand up, he lost his balance, which caused his butt to remain there longer than it should have. "Yow!" he yelled out.

I went to have a look, and he had actually been branded by the heater, his butt bearing the heater's brand-name in red letters: Sears. Hilarious, but not funny. He was in pain. The rest of the evening was spent with him face down on the bed, me running back and forth with cold rags for his burnt butt. That made for a good story to tell everyone when we got back home. We did have warmth, a bed to sleep in, and running water that night.

Still working at the plant, we arose at about 4:00 a.m. for the long drive about thirty miles down the hill to work. In the winter, it was especially hard to get up in the middle of the night, go out into the subzero temperatures, bundling into the car, literally wrapped in blankets at times. I would get so mad driving along through town on our way, noticing chimneys of houses with smoke pouring out… warm smoke. I imagined the people inside, snuggled in their cuddly beds. Ooh, I was so mad.

The plant itself was like a factory you'd see in a cartoon—workers scurrying about, machines pounding out a rhythm, conveyor belts conveying, the place all abuzz. The workers consisted of a strange group from young to old from all walks of life. The big boss, never there, was keen on hiring mentally challenged people, which was a good thing but made for some amusing scenes around the place. Some of the challenged were known to hide in the big freezers for some chilly sex romps amid the pizzas. One of the challenged ones, a tall skinny guy nicknamed Slim, would be in a bathroom stall and peer over into the next stall and simply say to the occupant, "Mornin'." One ancient woman worked there for the sole purpose of donating every penny she made to a TV evangelist.

For most of the time I worked there, I was in the Prep Room. It was where the bits and pieces for the pizzas were prepared. Lots of foods were made there, but the main thing being mass-produced was pizzas of all sorts. In the Prep Room, we peeled giant pepperonis and cut giant chunks of cheese into shreds by feeding them into different machines. I met a very unusual woman there whose name was Esther. She looked like a pretty country western singer and had long flowing platinum hair and a great big smile. And her amazing talent was she could yodel! Not that I'm a big fan of yodeling, but I'd never known a person before or since that could do real live yodeling. I would coax her into doing it every chance I got. She was a nice, nice lady, and I was always happy to be paired up with her.

The plant was in North Haven near to the downtown area where I had worked at the bar before. So at the plant, we had maybe some of the same foreign guys working there that I had dealt with at the bar previously. They couldn't speak very good English but managed to get by once they were shown how to work a particular machine.

All the tomato sauces were concocted in large chrome vats. At the end of the shift, the vats were emptied onto the floor, which in turn was hosed away down a drain. One night at the end of the shift, a dark-skinned man appeared at my side. After seeing the sauce oozing onto the floor, he said in his low sultry accent, "It look like human blood." True, but what a gruesome way to put it.

It Was Only a Gruesome Dream

I was in the basement of my childhood home, but I was my true adult age. The basement floor was about two inches deep with blood. I had done something horrific; my fault all that blood was everywhere. I just didn't know what had taken place beforehand to cause it. In my hand was one single roll of paper towels and thought to myself, *How will I clean up all this blood with one roll of paper towels?*

It Was Only Another Gruesome Dream

This time, I was in the upstairs of my childhood home. I was running through the house from room to room with bloody hands, again feeling as if I had committed a brutal crime. As I ran through the kitchen, I left a bloody smear across the refrigerator. I left bloody handprint smears as I dashed by walls and around corners.

*****

These dreams disturbed me greatly, and I wondered if I had some psychotic mental condition I wasn't aware of in my waking hours. Then it dawned on me one day it's that place I work—all that tomato sauce running down the drain in the floor. It didn't help that the foreign guy made the comment that the sauce looked like human blood! Once I had figured out what was causing the dreams of blood, I never had another one of those nightmares again. Thank God for that.

The very worst part of that job was that Roll and I started our shifts two hours apart (we only had one car, so we had to leave at the same time). He started his shift at 5:00 a.m., thus the freezing cold rides in the middle of the night to arrive on time. I started my shift at 7:00 a.m. I usually read a book or talked to someone in the cafeteria till I went down to my shift. The real trouble came when Roll's shift ended. He left the building and headed straight to the nearest bar, giving him a solid two hours to drink before he came back to pick me up. I drove home, thank you very much.

I was behind the wheel on a day when he got a bit more sauced than usual when I noticed a cop car in the rearview mirror. The red light went on, and I pulled over. The cop had pulled me over for something minor, but he saw Roll laid out between the bucket seats, torso in the backseat, legs in the front. The cop says to me, "What's with him?"

I said right back, "Oh, don't mind him, that's why I'M driving." I think the cop was happy with that answer. He let me go.

A Kindred Spirit

I met Rhonda through Roll's friends. She somehow was associated with them. How, I don't know, but when I met her, I instantly liked her. She was offbeat, a real talker like me, and we struck up an easy conversation. And we both loved stupid jokes, jokes in general, even bad jokes. I had found a kindred spirit. She was a tallish young woman with beautiful long legs that I could only dream of, and she had a style that was all her own. She didn't follow the crowd with her style or in any other way. She was also a talented painter, as I would see for myself, viewing her small art gallery that decorated the walls in her home.

I must say I envied her undeniable talent, and Roll was impressed by the art she had created. He made me feel like, why couldn't I be the one he could boast about for a talent like Rhonda's? I might've been jealous of Rhonda after seeing the light in Roll's eyes, hearing his enthusiastic praise, but I couldn't be jealous at all. Her work was good, and I admired it and just liked her so much.

Beyond her creative artistic flair, she looked at the world on a different level than anyone else I had known. I loved her for it and haven't known anyone since who had the same unique sense of the world around them. The most amazing thing we had in common was that we had near enough the same sense of humor that no one else seemed to get, except for her and I. We still do.

Speaking for myself, it's everything—whether it be a comedic movie, a TV show, a book, a comedian, or anything else the general public thinks is funny, I can't imagine why. It's made me wonder so many times why my sense of humor is different from the rest of the world. A simple everyday mishap or something not even meant to get a laugh are the things that are funny to me. It can be one single word or a line that tickles me. I've seen people flailing in their seats with laughter in a movie theater, for instance, while I sit there wondering what on earth is so darn funny.

Rhonda started going out with a good friend of Roll's, and we had so many good times together, the guys pairing up to talk about man stuff, her and I off together in another room, telling jokes as always and laughing about what was only funny to us. I would lose her for a time in the future due to circumstances of life but would find her again years later, picking up our great friendship like no time had passed. Always, I find "like no time has passed" as the sign of a really precious relationship, always meant to be. Thanks, Rhonda.

Daddy's Getting Married!

Meanwhile, back in Grandville, Dad was getting married! He had met a nice lady, and he was happy again. I was so glad for him and his new wife to be, Lauren. Dad wanted me to be there on his big day and sent me some money to fly down. I wouldn't have missed it for the world. I would've sold my soul to see this major event in his life. Good for him!

Lauren was pretty, funny, pleasant, and outspoken and had pulled Dad out of his cloud of sadness. It was the best thing that could've happened. Lauren was lucky too. Who wouldn't be to have my charming dad?

The wedding was simple and beautiful. Dad and Lauren were so happy, both of their faces beaming on their day.

I stayed at the house with them for a week or so and got to know Lauren. We talked for hours, and I felt overjoyed and relieved that Dad had found someone really good to spend the rest of his life with. She had come along just in time to pick him up and dust him off, and he was alive again, right back to his usual corny, silly self. It was wonderful to see him that way again after being so alone. He had been beside himself with grief after Mom had gone. Now he could start a new chapter with his new wife.

The Greatest Gift of All...Ever

At twenty-two, my biological clock was ticking, chimes going off on the hour. Roll was as keen as I was to make a baby. We actually planned the night we would create our new arrival, marking the calendar at the nine-month date—a brand-new baby for Christmas, our gift to each other.

Sure enough, I missed my period the next month and made an appointment at a clinic for women. The clinic performed pregnancy tests, gave out birth control, and did abortions. Most of the women were young and were dreading the result, not wanting to be pregnant at all, or they were there to say goodbye to the life inside them that they'd never know. My reason for being there was because I really wanted a positive result. Alice, a friend from work, had come with me. The test was done, and it seemed we sat in the waiting room for hours.

My name was finally called, and I was led to the examining room. It was true! It was positive! I was having a baby! I came back out to the waiting room. Alice stood up. "Well?" she asked. I smiled from ear to ear and, almost shouting, said, "Yes!"

We hugged right in the middle of the waiting room, but as I looked at the other faces in that fateful room, my joy was not shared. The other women looked at me as if to say, "You WANT to be pregnant?" Yes, I do. And I did. And I was.

Roll had been on a hunting trip the day I found out I was expecting, and when I got home, I placed a pair of baby booties on the kitchen table for him to discover when he returned. The very night we had planned to conceive, it had happened. Roll was ecstatic.

In the midst of my pregnancy, we moved to a tidy bungalow in Coolsville. I loved that house. This was the first place we lived that I felt was a real home. Well taken care of, the house just had a comforting feel to it.

I went through the usual symptoms of pregnancy, puking my guts out in the first few months, then afterward, craving bunches and bunches of green grapes. Toward the end, before the life-changing event would take place, I craved nothing but…you guessed it, sugar! And that meant candy. For many months, I ate very healthy as my body seemed to naturally know what it needed to do. I could not tolerate a cigarette, and when someone offered me a beer, I almost threw up at the thought of it. I did good until those last few months when it was all about candy.

During those last months, I had attended one of those house parties where the hostess was touting those expensive plastic containers or expensive cosmetics. All the silly games they play at those parties were played. One of the games, all the answers were the names of candy bars. I won.

Roll and I had discussed names for our baby. We could've found out the gender of our child-to-be but agreed that it would be more exciting to have a surprise at the time of delivery. We went round and round over the names. Since Roll had always identified with the Swedish side of him (his dad's heritage), he wanted a boy to have a good strong Swedish name. He was stuck on Agvald.

Are you frickin' kidding me? I wanted some sort of gallant name like Arthur, as in King Arthur. Don't think Roll even had a girl's name in mind, being so hell-bent on having his boy named Agvald. It may be a perfectly lovely name in Sweden, but that poor kid would have to go to school in America one day, and his classmates were going to have a field day with that very unusual name. I had picked Alexis for a girl. It just had a nice ring to it. We got into quite a few altercations over the naming, and it came down to the wire closing in on my due date. Roll wouldn't budge. I begged, I cried, I reasoned. No, Agvald it would be. I finally gave up but told Roll that I would be picking the middle name, and I knew what it would be: Urho, in honor of Vannie's uncle I had admired so much.

What could Roll say after I had given in to his choice of the first name? He probably figured that the middle name wouldn't be used that often and would only appear on the birth certificate. I just KNEW I would have a boy, and his name would be Agvald because I so didn't want that name. And Agvald Urho at that!

My time being pregnant wasn't without some crazy dreams…

It Was Only a Baby Dream

I had made a deal with some scientists to have a half-alligator, half-human baby. I then realized after the deal was made there was no turning back, but I really wanted a fully human baby.

The time came, and the baby was born. After it was delivered, I looked down upon my new baby and was horrified! It had green scaly skin and sharp pointy teeth! I started to cry and cry hysterically, and through my tears, I sobbed to the scientists, saying, "I don't want an alligator baby, I want a real baby!"

It Was Only Another Baby Dream

I was in the bedroom of our house, sitting on the edge of the bed. Roll was out in the living room. Suddenly, I felt like I was about to give birth. I instinctively spread my legs, and a baby came out—*plop!*—with no effort at all and fell onto the floor. *Plop!* Another one fell out onto the floor. *Plop! Plop! Plop!* Three more fell out. I calmly got up and went into the living room and matter-of-factly said to Roll, "I had five."

*****

Early one morning, I got out of bed. I had to pee. I noticed something odd in the toilet. I had lost the plug that is discarded before you go into labor. Roll called work and explained to the person on the phone, "It's all goin' on!"

We jumped into the car and drove down the hill, driving to North Haven, thirty miles to the hospital. Roll was so excited and nervous he drove to the wrong hospital. I told him to keep going.

We showed up way ahead of time now at the right hospital. As I would find out that day, I would have hours yet before we welcomed Agvald into the world.

Well, what a time I had. First a doctor came into my room and asked if it would be okay to have students come in to witness the ordeal. I thought it would be fine, my reason being how would they learn if they couldn't witness the whole process firsthand? My mistake.

Soon there were students of every sort in and out of there. I guess when my brother-in-law, Fred, showed up, they just let him in too. Another student perhaps? Fred came into the room, my legs up in the air spread apart as wide as could be. I just couldn't even believe it! The only thing that came to mind was, *Oh, sure, why don't you go get a bunch of people from out on the street and let them all in too?* My next thought, trying to calm myself, was, *Okay, he's seen it all before.* Next thought, *But he hasn't seen mine!* I totally wanted to climb right under the bed!

Things finally started happening, and Agvald was coming. They wheeled me into the operating room and got me started, Roll following closely behind. I made sure I got the big mirror to view the birth exactly so. "A little to the left. No, down a bit. Now over to the right a bit."

I wasn't going to miss a thing. I was reasoning again and thought, *This may be the only baby I ever have, and I'm going to see the whole thing happen from start to finish.*

A different young doctor, not mine, began. No time to wait for my doctor to arrive, but I really wanted him there. He had been with me through the whole nine months. He was an older gent, the kindest, most loving fatherly doctor. He had delivered Roll and all of his siblings.

Baby on its way, I pushed and pushed, and in walked my doctor. Relief washed over me, knowing I was in good hands now that Dr. Anthony was there to take over. "Push, push," I heard. Quite a few more times, I heard the command. The head was starting to come. And then, "Push as hard as you can."

I did push hard, and I pushed so hard I had to take a small breath to keep breathing at all. I took the smallest of breaths and could feel the baby suck back in. A few more times of the small breath and the baby retreating, and then they had to cut. A big cut. I got a shocking view in the mirror. a fountain of blood gushed out everywhere. I spoke up and said, "Wow, that's a lot of blood!"

Roll chimed in and said, "Sweetie, consider where they're cutting you." Yeah, right.

After the cut, the two doctors put all four of their big man hands into the opening they had made to pull the baby out. At that moment, had I had a gun in my hand, I would've shot both the men with the "helping" hands dead.

The baby seemed to come whooshing out, and Dr. Anthony proudly announced, "It's a GIRL!"

Hallelujah! There would be no Agvald! I had my Alexis. MY girl. My lucky day all the way around. My wish had been granted, and what a dream come true. As they gave me my new baby GIRL, what a perfect, beautiful baby she was. She had a head of dark hair like Roll and the sweetest little face to ever grace the face of the earth. I fell in love on the spot. Whatever had come before or would come in the future, she would always be the love of my life.

I stayed a week at the hospital, unheard of these days, but I feel it's the way it should be because once you get home with your newborn, it's up to you to figure it all out. You should bask in the help and advice of all the nurses that are there for you around the clock while you can.

It Was Only a Postpartum Dream

I was driving the car down a well-known route in Coolsville. I was doing at least eighty miles an hour if not more (I would never drive that fast!). My left hand was on the steering wheel, my right arm was holding baby Alexis (as if). As I sped along, driving with only one hand, I saw the turn I wanted to take coming up ahead. Not slowing down one bit, I cranked the wheel, careening around the corner on two tires, driving one-handed while holding Alexis in my other arm.

It Was Only Another Postpartum Dream

I was sitting on the bed with baby Alexis. I reached over for something on the bedside table. Oh, no! I dropped Alexis! As she fell, her head got caught between the bed and the table. She hung there by her head, suspended between the furniture, the poor little dangling baby.

*****

I had been home approximately three days when Roll decided he'd have a few friends over to celebrate the birth and arrival of Alexis. Don't worry about me who's just had a baby… There was all sorts of merriment out in the living room as I sat in the bedroom with Alexis, keeping her away from the party animals in the next room. As I sat there, crying, I shouldn't have been surprised that all the Neanderthals had come to our home to live it up days after I returned home. I was so not amused. They stayed too long, and I was relieved and thankful when they finally left. I had enough on my plate. All I wanted was some peace and quiet so I could bond in perfect harmony with Alexis.

Lexi—as we now called her—cried and cried till I felt like crying. No, wailed and wailed was more like it. She had colic and could wail for hours on end. Each time I tried to put her down, "WHAA… WHAAAAA." I once stood bouncing her for five hours straight. We had a wind-up swing for Lexi, and since she was still tiny, we used a long winter scarf tied around her waist to hold her in securely, one of the only ways we knew to quiet her. The only problem was the minute the swing ran out of time, her eyes would pop open, and the wailing would begin. Roll came up with a solution. When the swing was about to run out of time, Roll stopped the swing midair, gave the handle a quick crank, and let the swing go, not interrupting the motion. Aah, peace for a few minutes longer.

It was more than I could bear, the forever bellowing of my sweet baby. Roll would say, "It bothers you more than it does me. Go out for a walk." I'd take him up on it and would feel much calmer when I came back.

Thank God I had the book of baby remedies written by the most well-known pediatrician in America. I cherished that book as you would the holiest of Bibles. I consulted that well-written book so many times, and I'm grateful to this day for the famous doctor who wrote it. Just because you become a mother doesn't mean you know exactly what to do. Every problem, whim, and hiccup a baby could have was found in that informative and sometimes amusing treasure of a book. You all know the man and the book, and I thank the wise doctor. God bless his soul from the bottom of my heart.

As time went on and Alexis became a toddler, we had so much fun with her. She was a little imp as I had been and full of the devil, and she just got cuter by the minute. I loved her more and more with each passing day. And I loved Roll less and less. It was mostly the partying and his constant urge to bug me and try to pick fights with me. I did not want to fight with him. As the old saying goes, I'm a lover, not a fighter.

Once when I had refused to argue with him, he actually said, "Can't you just fight to fight?"

No. I didn't want to. I had seen how my mom and dad (the two that had raised me) had been together. They had been so together on everything. They never even raised their voices. They had disagreements but agreed to disagree, and that was the end of it. It was what I expected in my married life. It wasn't going in that harmonious direction at all. I decided I needed to talk to someone professional. Nearby, there was a group of psychologists I had heard of. I made an appointment and met Jayne. I didn't know what to expect on our first session. She made me feel very at ease, and soon, I was confiding in her, telling her all my problems with Roll. Sometimes we'd get so deeply into it that my head would be spinning after leaving the session.

All things were brought to light, including my childhood, upbringing, my hopes, my dreams, disappointments, and everything in between. The great thing with Jayne was she never told me what to do. She would ask me, "What are you going to do about it?" and "Why do you feel that way?"

I learned from those chats with Jayne that it's one thing to think something and a totally different thing to actually voice what you're thinking aloud. It makes it real when it comes out of your mouth in real words. So many times, after vocalizing a thought, I would say, "Did I just say that?" It really validates all those things you've never said.

At a meeting with Jayne one day, I told her I needed to go talk to Mom Lauren and Dad about the hopeless situation I was in with Roll. I was seriously considering leaving him. She asked me, "When will you get your ticket?" Bless her for making me do things. I was known to be a procrastinator, and I could put things off forever. I told her as soon as I got home, I'd make the arrangements. And I did. And Lexi and I flew off to Grandville. Mom and Dad met us at the airport and were both teary-eyed to see Lexi since they hadn't seen her since shortly after she was born.

Alexis and I stayed for a week, and I talked it all out with Mom and Dad, explaining that it was over for me and Roll. They asked questions about the whole situation, wanting to make sure I was sure. I was.

Back at home again with Roll, I told him that I couldn't go on and we needed to part ways. Our biggest concern was Lexi and what we were doing to her. We both cried for her sake, but we both knew that it was the end for us. Shortly thereafter, Roll moved back into his mom and dad's.

Jayne still comes to mind as one of the most helpful and influential people in my life. She helped me find my way when I couldn't find it myself and gave me courage when I had none left. I owe her so much gratitude for helping me realize so many things about myself. It's one of the best things I've ever done for myself, having those life lessons with Jayne. Jayne, thank you for giving myself back to me.

Ta-da! It's Me, the Divorcee!

Now I needed a place to live, and new townhouses had just been built in Coolsville. If I could get into one of those, it would be perfect. My old friend, Faith, lived in the existing building across the parking lot from the new one I was hoping to get, and Vannie lived right down the street. A new place and old friends nearby—love it!

Bingo! I got in! The place was brand-new and modern. It had a small kitchen with new appliances, large living room, and upstairs were two nice-sized bedrooms and an ample bathroom.

The townhouses, old and new, had been built for single moms and low-income families. Way too many kids around there, but one thing for sure: Lexi never had far to go to find a playmate…or ten.

Soon I had a few new friends there too. Patty was two doors down, Brenda two doors away in the other direction, and Ivy was right next door. Ivy had two teenage girls who could babysit for me. Also, Ally's mom, Nina, and Ally's brother, Josh, lived on the other side of the complex, and Josh could babysit also.

My new friends I had made were all so different, and I loved them each for their differences. The one who's remained my friend through thick and thin is Ivy, a tiny little woman who is quite spiritual who I've always loved for her kind and nonjudgmental personality. She doesn't stand on a pedestal and preach her deep beliefs; she doesn't have to. Her beliefs are in a sacred place inside of her. I feel special around her, enjoying her company and our conversations.

Brenda was an energetic, fun person and was always up for a good time. She had a little girl who was a year older than Lexi, and they played together but rubbed each other the wrong way most of the time. Brenda and I would have to break it up between the two kids, sometimes ruining the good time the two moms were having.

Patty was something else, period. She was a wild one and had an array of bikers at her place most nights of the week. Her boyfriend, Eddie, was there most times, and he worshiped her and would do anything she said. But when Eddie wasn't around, it was party time with the bikers! I got to know all the various characters, and they were a scream.

Patty had a daughter named Crystal. She was twelve years old, a pretty girl, but the poor girl had been burnt as a toddler, terrible burns scarring her arms and legs. She was even missing a few toes. Crystal had been playing with matches. Dealing with Patty as a mother who could be demanding and curt, it was tricky for Crystal to live up to what Patty expected of her. Crystal got away with nothing. As much as I liked Patty for her unconventional ways, I did feel sad for Crystal at times. However, Crystal could be as boisterous as Patty and would give it right back. You go, Crystal!

I got a job at a local nightclub as a waitress. The Flamingo sounds fancy. It wasn't. Since it was the "in place" to be, Brenda and I would sometimes go there on my nights off, checking out the guys and the bands that played on the weekends. What happened to the cool guys from Coolsville? We didn't see any cool guys at all. Guess all the cool guys had all flown the coop for cooler destinations.

Brenda and I would sit at our favorite spot at the curved part of the horseshoe-shaped bar, a perfect view of the door to critique the clientele. Since we lived in the north woods, most of the guys wore the same "uniform." Plaid flannel shirt, old worn-out jeans, and shit-kicker boots. The ensemble was often topped off with a baseball hat sporting a chainsaw advertisement on the front. Charming. They would probably be laid out in their coffins one day looking like that.

Canada not being far away, somehow, we'd picked up on saying, "Eh." As Brenda and I sat watching the door, the "lumberjacks" would start to arrive. As the first guy came in, we'd say in unison, "Eh?" If it was two guys, it was "Eh, eh?" Three, "Eh, eh, eh?" It was pitiful and hopeless. Rarely did any of the men who came through that door give us one ounce of hope.

But there was one guy who walked through the door from back in the high school days—Jimmy. We began by talking, got to know each other more, and then began going out, and then became a couple. He was so nice with a kind open face. He was good with Lexi and got such a kick out of her antics. And he was very generous. He spoiled both Lexi and I, and who wouldn't love that?

After Jimmy and I had been together for quite some time, I thought it best to have something done to prevent a surprise pregnancy. I already had Lexi to take care of and didn't need another kid. If I wasn't married and became pregnant, even worse. Besides, by the time I did perhaps marry again, did I want to start all over? The thought of nine months with the ups and downs of a pregnancy for starters didn't thrill me, and then what if I had another colicky baby? Could I do it again? Did I want to? No. I had my perfect little girl, and she was enough for me. Could another child even compare? All the answers came to me as no.

I came to the conclusion that I would get my tubes tied. Excuse me for not remembering the technical term for this procedure; I was twenty-four. I thought surely my doctor would tell me I was too young to make this monumental decision. But when I told my doctor what I wanted, she just said, "Okay." I asked her why she didn't try to talk me out of it since my friends had said the doctor would turn me down because of my age.

The doctor then said, "When women come to me requesting this operation, they've given it some thought and their mind is already made up."

Okay, then. I went in and had the op, feeling that it was one of the wisest choices I had ever made. After the op, I was brought to a regular hospital room to recover. The woman in the other bed had just had her fourth child. As we conversed, I hoped I didn't have a look of bewilderment on my face when she told me her husband's name: Freddy Johansen, the gorgeous model-type guy from years ago that had strolled into the Coffee Cup Cafe. It's unreal how things come full circle in your life.

Well, well, well. Freddy was married to this very nice plain-Jane type, and they were very religious to boot (obviously Freddie had changed his ways). I didn't see that coming. Freddy came to visit his wife and the new baby one day, and he either didn't recognize me or pretended not to, maybe remembering the drunken girl he dropped at her door and never saw again. He was a man of God now, and maybe he had put everything in the past behind him. I hoped he was having a happy life. I wished him all the best. We were adults now.

As great as he was, Jimmy drove me crazy. He would chase me around all the time, not literally, but he felt he had to keep tabs on me wherever I went. He had nearly all of my friends' phone numbers, and he'd call every single one of those numbers until he located me. When he finally found me, he would say something dumb as a reason for the call. He'd say something like, "I think I left the lights on at your place" or "I heard there's a party at so and so's this coming weekend." He just had a burning desire to know where I was at all times. If I was out and about on my own or with friends, he'd show up wherever I was.

I was out with friends at the Flamingo one night. A whole group of the girls and I were sitting at a big table, having drinks and laughing it up. Suddenly, Jimmy's head popped in between me and whoever sat next to me. I literally jumped at his surprise appearance. He would say his favorite greeting, "What's happening?"

Oh, for heaven's sake!

Despite all of his detective work tracking me down, Jimmy was one of the kindest, most loving people I have ever known. He was so agreeable and laid-back. It was a welcome relief after the rocky relationship I had with Roll.

Jimmy's mother was one in a million. She was well into her eighties and sprightly as could be. She had been a reputable doctor in her day, and some of her medical findings could be found in a well-known medical journal read by physicians the world over. She was a smart little lady. At about four feet, she was cute as an elf and feisty as a pit bull. Even though Dr. Szyko could come across as very serious and stern, Lexi and I both got along well with her for her kindness and her humor. She had some interesting habits and mannerisms that only the doctor we knew and loved possessed.

Where do I begin? She saved everything. Her huge dining room table had become her desk with a giant assortment of receipts, paperwork, bills, letters, warranties, pamphlets, snapshots, newspapers from years gone by, and God knows what else was under that mountain. Maybe better off not knowing. I think all of her notes, papers, and all the items on her dining room "desk" came from being a doctor with all the papers and pieces of info that must entail.

Dr. Szyko kept labels she had used to mark containers for leftovers. After she had eaten the leftover carrots she had stored in the fridge from the night before, she saved the piece of paper and the tape that was used as the label and put it aside to use again until she had more leftover carrots another time. Heaven forbid she'd waste a scrap of paper or a small shred of tape.

A thick tablet of paper was kept next to the phone with every name of every person Jimmy had ever known, so if the Doc needed to contact Jimmy, she'd start at the top of the list and keep on going till she found him (and I wondered where Jimmy got the detective habit).

Dr. Szyko also displayed certain behaviors that were comical in the least. She was known for helping herself, stealing food and treats at parties and other functions. She would spy a bowl of a nut and mint mixture and, opening her purse, would tip the whole bowl of treats right in to snack on later. She would proudly announce she had been to a funeral and had taken part afterward in the procession, calling it the "funeral parade."

Jimmy carried a small step stool around in his truck, so in the event he brought his mom somewhere, she could hoist herself up into the vehicle. Jimmy had left the stool at home once, and so Dr. Szyko ordered him to give her a boost up. He grabbed her under her armpits for the hoist. He tried to shift her several times. It wasn't working, and getting exasperated, she said, "No, no, Jimmy, push me on the butt!" Not one to mince her words.

Dr. Szyko thought nothing of answering the door in a pair of pants and her bra. It was summer, it was hot, and too bad if she wanted to cool off in her bra. I think that came from her years of doctoring also. Just seeing all those bodies for all those years partly dressed, feet in stirrups, all bits of anatomy hanging out for her to examine or completely naked, a body is a body—everyone has one, so what was the big deal answering the door in your bra?

I thanked her at the time, but I send another thank you to her now, as she surely resides in heaven, for the loan that enabled me to go back to school all those years ago. Also, thank you to Dr. Szyko for being so sweet toward Lexi and I and for being one of the most colorful people in my life.

A few times, Jimmy and I took a break from each other, probably at my request due to his favorite pastime of tracking me down. On one of these breaks, I had a few dates with a guy named Gary. It didn't last long with Gary because it was clear to me that he was still in love with his ex-wife. He would moan about what a pain she had been, sounding to me like childish tantrums she had never outgrown. But for whatever reason, he still carried a torch for her.

On one of our few dates, Gary asked if I'd like to go with him to hear the band his brother played in. The band was playing in a nearby town, and it sounded like a good time. Gary came to pick me up, and as we drove along, Gary informed me that his brother played in a country band, Gary not knowing my complete and utter hatred of country music. "How un-American can she possibly be?" you're asking yourself. I'm not un-American at all. I just loathe country music and everything associated with it.

Besides detesting the music, I can't stand cowboy boots, cowboy hats, plaid western looking shirts with the pointy pockets, string ties are the ugliest thing ever invented, and square-dancing attire? Pa-leassse. The closest I can get is maybe a bit—a small bit—of country rock. But the old favorites, the twangy stuff especially, well, to be truthful, it actually hurts my ears. And the message in the music, nine times out of ten, includes depressing woes which would go good with crying into your beer. Plenty of people live for country music. They can boot scoot as much as they like. Unlike them, I will not be doing any fancy footwork to any of the heartbreaking twang.

When Gary mentioned the band we were about to see played country, I told him nicely, "Not my thing" but that I could and would deal with it for tonight. I then told Gary that if and when I heard "The Green Green Grass of Home," I would promptly leave the premises. That's where I draw the line.

When we got there, Gary found a table up close to the stage so his brother could see that we were there to cheer him on. I was having a nice time with Gary, having a few drinks, chatting between songs. We had been there for about an hour, and what should I hear? The song about the green grass. I stood up, pulling my jacket off the back of my chair, and headed for the door. That was it. Gary had been warned, and he followed me out. What choice did he have? I'm outta there!

I got tired of the nightly shenanigans at the Flamingo caused by the dumb drunken lumberjacks. I needed to think of what to do in the future. I decided to go back to school. Maybe college or a vocational school.

Having decided on the vocational school in North Haven, I was accepted and began my classes. It was a long drive, especially in the winter, but it didn't stop me. My dear friend, Ally, babysat, which was all I could've asked for. I couldn't have had anyone better to look after Lexi.

School was great, and this time, I wanted to be there (not like it was in high school), and I was learning all aspects of the fashion/retail world. I had taken a two-year course, and when you have a three-year-old to manage on top of it, it was a lot. I would feed Lexi dinner each night, play with her for a bit, put her upstairs in bed, and then crack the books, "burning the midnight oil."

On one big study night, after getting Lexi settled, books and papers covering the kitchen table, I began the arduous task. I heard a small voice from above. "Mommy!"

I called up, "Yes, Lexi?"

Lexi called back, "Can I have a drink of water?"

Okay, I went up the stairs with the water. Lexi was tucked in again, and I was back to the books. Again, "Mommy!" This time it was, "Can I have a hug?"

Hugs given, and back to the studying at hand. No sooner did I start in again, and once more, "Mommy!"

Enough was enough. I was losing my cool, now ready to blow my top. I practically shrieked back, "What? What do you want?"

A small sweet voice said from on high, "I love you." All that for that. I returned the sentiment, and then she finally went to sleep. Ya gotta love 'em.

At the end of the second and final year at school, a class trip was planned to go to New York City, fashion capital of the world. Mom and Dad helped me with money for the trip, THANK YOU, and Roll would take Lexi.

It was the most exciting, invigorating time I'd had to date. We saw all the sights and the lights and did everything amazing there was to do there. The two teachers that had planned the trip had put together an awesome itinerary.

But it all came to a screeching halt as soon as we landed in the cold north woods. What a letdown. The time I had at school ended too, and it was sad to say goodbye to all the fun girls and women I had met and gotten along with so well.

Most weekends, Roll took Lexi, and they stayed at his mom and dad's where Roll was living. It was nice that he wanted to spend time with her, and she had plenty of playmates there with Roll's sister's kids when they visited Grandma and Grandpa. That was fine until she came home all revved up, from being all go, go, go with her cousins. It took Lexi a few days to calm down and settle back into our quiet life together.

Roll came to get Lexi one weekend and said they'd be driving back to his mom's via Wood Ridge Park, stopping along the way somewhere to enjoy the beautiful day (Wood Ridge Park, the one with all the cliffs and s-turns where I'd almost lost my life years ago with BAD CHAD). I didn't like the idea. It scared me. In my mind, I pictured Lexi getting too close to the edge, Roll not being able to catch her in time. I was probably just being paranoid. Off they went. Then I fell asleep.

It Was Only a Dream

Grandma Lil and I were in a huge basement that looked as if it were underneath a mall. Grandma Lil was carrying Lexi who was a tiny baby wrapped in a pink blanket. Not much down there in the basement area. Cement walls, cement floors, and lots of empty space. There was a line of people behind Grandma and I. I was in the lead, then Grandma, and a variety of about ten or twelve people behind us, men and women of different ages. Whatever direction I went, they all followed. It was almost like a children's game of follow the leader. If I went to the right, everyone went to the right, left, or wherever I led them.

Up ahead, I could see a ladder. At the top of the ladder was a small platform and then a ladder going down on the other side of the platform. The ladder was in the middle of the floor, plenty of space to pass by on either side. For some unknown reason, I needed to lead the group behind me up the ladder. I started to climb. Grandma was right behind me. Using one hand to climb the rungs of the ladder while holding Lexi in my other arm, I got to the top and asked Grandma to hold Lexi so I could turn around on the platform in order to climb down the other side.

As I turned around, Grandma had lain Lexi on her back on one of the rungs of the ladder. I couldn't believe what I was seeing: My baby lying on her back, teetering, balancing on the rung. I screamed, "Grandma! What the hell are you doing?"

And just then, down Lexi went. She fell and fell and fell. I flew down the ladder as fast as I could humanly go. There lay Lexi, motionless, still wrapped in the blanket. I gently opened the blanket, fearing she was dead. When I peeled the blanket away, there was my beautiful baby, looking up at me, smiling like nothing at all had happened. She was just fine.

I woke up then, sweating, heart pounding. How completely symbolic. I was so worried that something would happen when Roll and Lexi left for their adventure to Wood Ridge Park. Just the thought of it is what had sparked the dream. But really, everything was fine all along. Whew!

Tons of Fun

I was having tons of fun with Vannie and Faith. I'd walk to Vannie's with Lexi, and she played with Vannie's girls, or sometimes I'd go see Vannie myself when Lexi was with Roll.

One snowy, stormy night when I was on my own, I called Vannie and said I was coming to visit. She said, "Oh, no! It's too dangerous out there!"

I said, "It's just snow, and I'm bored. It will be an adventure." I put on all the winter gear I could find and started out. It was only two blocks away, but I trudged. The snow was so deep already. I got to Vannie's front door, opened the screen door to knock; the wind blew me off the front porch, and I landed on my butt. We had a good laugh about that.

I stayed at Vannie's for a few hours and decided to head home. More snow, thigh-deep. Halfway home, I was huffing and puffing and thirsty. I sat in the snow and ate a handful of the newly fallen snow. I started trudging again, and a snowmobile approached. *Good*, I thought, *I'll get a ride*. No. The snowmobile buzzed by. Thanks. I barely moved. The snow was even deeper and so thick. I finally reached the row of townhouses where mine was located, and since I was so worn out, I came up with a great idea. The back doors of each townhouse had a small attached porch with a railing. I climbed up and held onto the railing of the first porch, grabbing the rungs one by one, stepping sideways until it ended. I jumped down and went to the next railing (saved on the huffing and puffing).

I did that repeatedly until I reached my door at last, which was buried in snow up to the top of the door! I started digging like a gopher with my hands until I had cleared the door enough to get in.

The minute I got inside, the phone started ringing off the hook. I answered. A nearly hysterical Vannie asked, "Are you okay?"

"Yes, yes, I'm fine, but it was quite an adventure."

Faith and I, one weekend when we were without kids, decided to get together one night at my place. In our nightgowns (may as well be comfortable), we had a few drinks, talking and laughing, watching music videos on TV. We had a favorite video we had waited for. It featured an unbelievably good-looking singer who sexily slunk around for a while, then slithered across a bed, singing something like "Love me in the night." He finally ended up on the floor and proceeded to slink around again until the end of the song. And the music was good too…

Being a bit buzzed, we cranked up the volume and were literally screaming with delight. We stayed up till all hours, then Faith went home, crossing the parking lot to her place.

Next day, Jimmy called me and asked, "Were you having a party last night? I came to the door, and all I heard was loud music and screaming." I think he felt left out of the wild party I hadn't invited him to. I explained that it had been Faith and I in our nightgowns, screaming at the video. All was innocent. No wild party or orgy going on, Jimmy.

Jimmy had a friend that Faith went out with for a time. It made it nice that we all could go out for dinner or dancing. Faith's guy's name was Seth, but he went by Ziggy. Ziggy played in a band, and we would go see him play. One night, a bunch of us were there—a group of Jimmy and Ziggy's friends, their girlfriends—the whole gang. At one point, Faith and I had left the table to use the ladies' room. When we got back to the table, Ziggy was on a break and was sitting in Faith's chair. Faith politely and girlishly asked Ziggy, "Can I have a knee (meaning, could she sit on his lap)?"

Not missing a beat, Ziggy exclaimed, "How about a wee-nee?"

Everyone at the table roared with laughter. I thought Faith would be embarrassed, but she joined in, roaring along with the rest of us.

It Was Only a Dream

I had been out somewhere, maybe with friends, had a few drinks, and was now home in my two-story house (it looked like no house I had ever lived in). I had just closed the door, and I heard a knock. I opened the door, and there stood a guy I had never seen. For some reason, I let him in. Once inside, I knew in my mind he was going to kill me.

I told the mystery man I was going upstairs to the bathroom.

Lexi was a baby in the dream, only three or four months old. I crept into where she was sleeping. I was so petrified I was barely breathing, and I whispered to her to be quiet. I was going to the neighbors to get help (We had no phone, and like she could understand what I had told her at four months old...oh, sure). Somehow, I snuck out of the house and started running like hell. Then I realized the guy was on my heels! It was starting to get light outside. I ran and ran. I came to a steep gully, ran down, started to go back uphill, the fiend still after me. The incline was slick with mud. I just kept slipping and sliding each time I tried to get momentum. I finally managed to get moving again, and he was right behind me.

I saw a house with some lights on. Thank God. I pounded frantically on the door. A man let me in. His wife was sitting at the dining room table, drinking coffee. I was hysterically trying to explain that someone was after me! Just as I got it all out, I looked up, and beyond the dining room, there in one of the small diamond-shaped windows of the back door was the face of that evil man!

Somewhere Out There

I had seen an ad several times on TV for the same adoption agency I had always known I was adopted from. Each time I saw it, I thought maybe I should write down the phone number that came across the screen and use it to see what information I could get about my ancestry. I never had a longing desire to know such things as many people do. I had always been content with the amazing parents that raised me. Over the years, it popped into my head that maybe one day, I'd go on a search to find where and who I had come from.

The commercial came on a few more times, and one day, I decided to write down the number and then call. I was nervous and still didn't know if I wanted to know as I dialed the phone. But I made an appointment. The lady I spoke to said they could give me non-identifying information—no names, places or dates. Okay, it was a lot more than I had, which was nothing. I had to drive to Monticello to hear my story, and it seemed a longer trip than usual, my mind dreaming up all sorts of scenarios of what I might learn.

I was led into an office where a professional-looking lady sat waiting for me behind a desk.

We introduced ourselves, and she asked me if I had any preconceived notions of what could've happened or if I had any particular expectations. I told her no, it could be anything, anything at all. To me, having been adopted, you've got to be honest with yourself and know that you will need to accept whatever you find out. You may wonder and even dream up scenarios as I had done, but until you know, you just don't know. The counselor, Jan, then said she had met people before me, sitting in the same chair as I sat now that had told her about visions of running in a field of daisies toward their birth mother. I thought to myself, *Get real, people.* If you set yourself up like that, you may be in for a disappointing result.

And then Jan opened THE folder. She proceeded to give me an explanation of what had happened. My birth mother hadn't been married when she got pregnant with me and felt she didn't have the wherewithal to raise me on her own. I also had a sister who came before me with the same father. She said that my mother was English and my father was French and German. My mother had come to America, given birth to me, and went back to England. My father was a serviceman, and that's how they had met when he was stationed in England. She described my mother by saying she had a pixie-ish appearance, and people through the years had said that to me! I had come from a long line of short people on both sides. Gee, thanks.

My father played the piano (my favorite instrument, always), my grandfather (mother's side) grew a vegetable garden, and my grandmother (also mother's side) had knitted mittens. Jan smiled and said that in the time I was born as the paperwork was prepared, they liked to tell a story (such as the vegetable garden and mittens) not like today when you'd get strictly facts. Before Jan left the room to make a copy of my story for me (less the names, dates, and places), she warned me not to view THE folder or she would ask me to leave (There must've been additional information in it). Why I didn't look at that folder the minute she left the room, I will never know. I guess I was shell-shocked at what I had just heard and was lucky to get what I got. I'm sure there wasn't a hidden camera in the room. I was a good girl and didn't spy.

Now I had to get into the car alone with nothing but my story and my thoughts. My head was spinning with all I was trying to absorb. I had to remind myself I was driving and to concentrate on the road. With all this new information to ponder, a thought occurred to me: I pictured myself up in the rafters over a stage with a play taking place below. All the players were members of my newly found family going about their everyday lives. I could see them, but they couldn't see me. That's exactly how I felt.

The other thought that came to me on my drive home that day was, *I have a sister, I have a sister.* I had longed for a sister all my life and always felt the emptiness of not having one. I had watched a soap opera in my teens, featuring two sisters that always seemed to be in a crisis, and they'd cry and cry in each other's arms. Each time they'd cry, I'd cry too, wishing for a sister I could cry with for whatever reason. Not that I didn't love Vance. I did and do, but he was a boy, and you just couldn't have those intimate girl times I so had wanted to have. Here, the whole time, there was a sister somewhere out there…

Off Again, Lexi in Tow

I had taken the summer off after leaving school. I just wanted to relax and think of what to do next. I knew I wanted out of the north woods altogether and felt that Lexi and I should start a new life somewhere else. But where? Where could we go where it was safe and I knew someone to help me get started again? Yes, we'd go back to Grandville, four hundred some miles away. Mom and Dad were there, and some of my friends from high school were still in the area.

When I called Mom and Dad and told them the plan, they were all for it, and Mom said they would put a deposit down on an apartment for us. Jimmy reluctantly and sadly helped us move. That was the thing with Jimmy. He loved us, and even though we were moving away from him, his heart was so big that he still wanted to help. It was because it's what I wanted.

At one point, Jimmy and I had talked of getting married, but the longer it went on between us, the more I knew that he would follow me around day in and day out, and I couldn't live like that. I did not want to get divorced ever again. The man I would eventually give my heart to in the future would have to be exactly the right one. Sometimes I felt with Jimmy that his sole purpose on earth was to take care of me. Like God had sent him just when I needed him most and that he was there to see me through. And that he did. Jimmy and I would talk on the phone after I had moved to Grandville, but long-distance relationships rarely work out, and we both moved on with our lives.

Lexi and I had moved into a small ground floor apartment which was close to the schools and to Mom and Dad. I got a job at a large department store at the mall nearby, doing displays. Each morning, I brought Lexi to Mom and Dad's where she caught the school bus, and they also generously paid for Lexi to go to an after-school program where I picked her up when I got off work.

In first grade, Lexi started at her new school. One evening, she began to cry and tearfully told me that she had sat on a swing by herself during recess, and what she said next broke my heart. She said through her sobs, "I was all by myself, and no one would play with me."

My heart fell, and guilt came over me for dragging her away from what she had known. I called off work the next day, and Lexi and I spent the day together. We talked, and I assured her things would get better. And they did. Soon she had made a few little friends, and she'd be okay. Thank God. I couldn't live with myself seeing her so upset in her new environment.

It Was Only a Dream

I was located behind a rustic cabin.

There were other people there, my mom being one of them. I think they were visiting someone who lived there. I was sitting alone on the back porch, enjoying the nice day. A car came down the alley, which was no more than a rugged dirt road. The car was barely moving, crawling along. Another car came up behind the first one, also driving very slowly. Even at a snail's pace, the second car banged into the first one. The first car looked really smashed into, even though there was no speed involved.

A guy fell out of the first car and lay motionless in the road. I jumped up and ran to help. As I approached the injured man, his head turned toward me and then fell off! And the severed head's face was tattooed like a clown! It scared the hell out of me, and at the same time, I felt so sad and sorry for the guy. He was dead, whether he had a clown face or not.

I ran as fast as I could, out of breath when I reached the porch. Mom was standing there. "Mom! Mom! Oh my God, Mom!"

What Have I Gotten Myself Into?

The job I found was at a well-known department store, and my boss was a nice, young, chatty woman. At first, I was getting along pretty good until I discovered that me and my new boss didn't see eye to eye. It was my first job doing what I had gone to school for, and I knew what I was doing. And I really did. However, some bosses like the authority to have it done exactly their way and no other. She would give me a task. I'd ask questions to make sure I knew the instructions. When I completed the job, she'd always come to inspect. I had always done it wrong (according to her since she knew EVERYTHING), no matter what I did. She'd page me overhead, and when she finished scolding me, she'd hang up on me!

Every day, every day, we went round and round. It was all I could do to get out my front door in the morning, knowing what I might face. Some days were perfectly fine when she was happy. It was the not knowing, the trepidation of it all. I went to work, walking on eggshells. Some days by the time lunchtime came around, I felt I couldn't take it for one more minute. I'd go to a pay phone out in the mall, not to be heard, and would call Mom, crying and distraught about the terrible day I was having. Then I had to dry my tears and go back, acting as if nothing had happened. No way was I going to let the boss see me upset. *Don't give her the satisfaction*, I thought to myself.

I don't know how many times I did a big presentation/display, went off to lunch, and returning to my completed display, it had been totally changed. By her. She had to have it her way. It was disheartening to say the least. She knew it all, and I knew nothing.

I have never had a boss before or since that was as utterly as hard to work for and with. Thank you, God, for that.

There were a few bright spots at the job, and those were some of the truly awesome people I worked with. A few of them took pity on me, knowing what I had to deal with and with whom.

Thank God for Jeanie...

My absolute favorite person to work with was the advertising person who had her desk in a corner of the studio—Jeanie. She was so down to earth, and I felt comfortable with her from the start. She had a great sense of humor and had a joke to tell every day. I would visit her at her house on occasion, and I always had the best time.

And Mandy...

Shortly after I had gotten to know her, Jeanie told me her daughter was moving back to town, and she knew that her daughter and I would hit it off. Along came Mandy, and we did hit it off! We were a lot alike and would sit on her porch every Friday night, talking and having "a few drinkies" as she liked to say. She was a single mother with a small cherubic-faced girl named Jaynie.

Mandy had a hard time of it with Jaynie's dad and decided to start her life over again too. I could sympathize. Another lifelong friend I wouldn't trade for the world. She's a salt of the earth type and will tell you straight exactly how she feels. And she's a giddy sort too, full of fun. One of my favorite memories of Mandy is just so typical of her:

Mandy called and said she was coming over. I had been cleaning the house that day, music blaring to keep me going. When I had finished the chores, the music still on, I began to dance around the living room. *Knock, knock.* Still mid-dance, I answered the door. Mandy came through the door, whipped her purse on the floor, and started right in dancing with me, like she just couldn't hold back. Only Mandy would do that.

At about the same time, I met Serena. A girl I worked with was getting married, and she invited me to her wedding shower. At the shower, I sat across from a young woman, Serena, and we began talking and getting along very well. Another lifelong friend was made that day.

Serena was her own person, much like Mandy. Serena was married to a nice guy, Ed, and they seemed quite content with their free and easy lifestyle, not having any children. They had a beautiful spacious home which Serena had decorated in her own unique style. Serena loved art, books, and anything a bit out of the ordinary. This gave us a lot to talk about since I like those same sorts of things. Serena and Ed had some extraordinary parties in the rec room in their basement, especially for Halloween when Serena went all out, making ghoulish looking drinks and food. The house was decorated to its full extent with skulls and candles on each stair as you made your way to the party room downstairs, which was also expertly done. Serena was all about throwing a shindig to the max.

Soon Mandy, Serena, and I became a diverse trio of friends together. Each one of us was so different from the other, and we had some lively and, at times, heated discussions because of our differences. We also laughed a lot and were happy to have new friends in our lives.

And Layla...

A professionally dressed young woman in her office-type blazer showed up one day at work. We were introduced, and her name was Layla. She was about my age, very pretty, and Italian looking. Within a few days, we were getting along like a house on fire. She had so much energy, it almost wore me out just being around her. And she was funny and spazzy as hell, really fun to be with.

As we got to know each other, I found out that she was married to a successful businessman, no children, and lived in a gated community. She had traveled near and far and seemed to have it all. I couldn't even imagine what it would be like to be her. I was barely keeping me and Lexi alive. But the thing I've always loved about Layla was her down to earth-ness. She could've come across like someone superior but never did. She was and still is a fabulous person in every sense of the word.

She invited Lexi and I to her house one Saturday, and when we drove up to the gatehouse, they actually called the resident you were visiting before they let you in. Lexi slid down the front seat, hiding, embarrassed to be in such a luxurious place in our old beater of a car. I found Layla's house out of all the grand houses, and she appeared at the door, smiling her beautiful smile. The house was huge and rather empty. It looked like a show house, staged to be shown as if it were for sale. Even the kitchen was bare: no toaster in view, not a blender or a coffee pot. So bare, it looked like a strong wind had come along and blown everything away. I mentioned this to Layla years later, and she said she really never wanted anything so big and daunting to live in, but her husband, Dwight, thought it an impressive place to live.

Layla spent money like it was growing in her backyard. Since we worked together, I knew how much money she was earning. It was Dwight who had megabucks. And what was his was hers. We would go shopping, and she didn't bat an eye as she whipped out her checkbook and wrote out whatever amount she needed.

Her mother was coming to visit, and she wanted to freshen up the guest room. We stopped by the bedding department one day after work, and in less than two minutes, she found a beautiful pricey bedding ensemble. Layla had to have all the matching items, grabbing off the shelves like she was going to a fire. Bedspread, sheets, bed skirt, pillow shams, throw pillows, curtains (she had curtain rods at home), and then she threw the whole pile on the checkout counter, wrote a check, threw it at the saleslady, grabbed her bag of goods, and we left. The whole picking and choosing and paying in total took about five minutes. Amazing. I was stunned. She hadn't even checked to see if the bedding was on sale! I have never seen anyone spend money like that before or since.

Another time, we went to a big artist's show. We walked into a large tent full of artsy unusual earrings. It was a sight to behold. We were both oohing over the wonderful variety on display. Almost immediately, she had chosen two pairs at forty dollars each. She then asked me which ones I had an eye for. I pointed at a pair and said, "These are nice." She snatched them up, and off she went to make her purchase. One hundred and twenty dollars for three pairs of earrings! Again, picked and purchased in a matter of five minutes! I was dumbfounded. Then she fished my pair out of the bag, handed them to me, and said, "Here, you liked these." Wow. Just wow.

The point of the money-spending scenarios? Layla was so very generous and always shared her wealth with me. She knew my situation and did so much to help me. She would give me a bag of clothes and tell me they didn't fit or didn't look right on her, knowing I couldn't afford to have new things like she could. A lot of the clothes she gave me still had tags on them, and I'm sure she just bought them for me. I would've liked her had she never offered me so much as a cup of coffee, but for her to be so giving and kind, the whole Layla experience was beyond words.

Christmas time was upon us, and she called and said, "Get ready, we're going to the grocery store, and Dwight and I decided that's going to be your Christmas present from us. Get whatever you need." The best gift I could've wished for…and she knew it. At the store, she told me that her husband had a hand in the shopping gift. He had told her that times were tough for his single mother back when she had raised Dwight and his brother on her own, so it was a good idea that Layla and I should go for groceries. I was ever so grateful to both of them and called Dwight when I got home that day to thank him too, tears in my eyes.

Dwight was generous with Layla, and she told me tales of trying on clothes at a real salon in some exotic location when they were on vacation. She'd go into the dressing room and come out to model for Dwight, him seated in a comfy chair, sipping champagne. Well, that sounded like something from the TV show about the rich and famous. La-dee-dah.

At work, we had each other's backs, dealing with the everyday surprises we got just being there for eight hours a day. I would entertain Layla with my singing of Ethel Merman's "Everything's Coming Up Roses" and another old country western song, "I Fall to Pieces." For some reason, I can imitate the voices of the women who sang these two songs to a T. Layla would scream with laughter, and it did my heart good to know I could at least make her laugh at the very least for all she had done for me.

When Layla wanted time off from work to go on a vacation to somewhere tropical, off to Canada to a concert or wherever her heart desired, all she had to do was say the word, and her time off was granted. Boss lady aspired to be in the same category as Layla and thought it was fabulous, just fabulous when Layla would tell her where she was off to. Pissed me off royally. Not that Layla was off to another fabulous, just fabulous location but that it didn't quite work the same for me when I would request time off. Since bossy knew that I had nowhere to go on my time off for lack of cash, her comment to me every time I requested the time off (time I had coming) was "Well, I'll have to see, we're so busy. Very busy." Never just "Okay, that will be fine." She held it over my head that I had no money and was struggling bringing up Lexi and had bills to pay. *Shitty* is the word that comes to mind.

Things began to deteriorate between Layla and Dwight. Layla wasn't into playing Queen of Sheba, and Dwight had high expectations. He was also known to gamble and drink too much at times. Layla had never been a drinker at all, and it can be trying to deal with the person you're married to, talking nonsense when they come home sloshed (Tell me about it, I know what it's all about). Poor Layla. She filed for divorce and, in the meantime, escaped to my house. We were together almost every day. We talked, we cried, we laughed, and for once, she needed me. I couldn't help monetarily, but I could listen and offer comfort and was glad to help her through it if all I could give her was support.

Layla moved into a fashionable apartment after the divorce and seemed a bit lost with the oversized furniture from the her previous residence now swallowing her somewhat smaller living space.

We still did lots of things together, and one thing we loved to do was go to psychics, psychic fairs, fortune tellers, card readers and the like. Layla was really into that sort of thing, and I was intrigued by it all. We were told things by various mystics that were believable and some not so believable. It was fun and interesting to compare notes afterward. She called one Sunday and told me she had seen an ad in the paper for a meeting in a neighboring town all about chakras, auras, and finding your soulmate. Interesting...

We drove around in circles for a time, trying to find the address and didn't know to look for an apartment building. Finally, we had the right address, opened the door on street level, and climbed the stairs, not knowing what we'd find when we reached the top. The door was open to an old spacious apartment. Chairs were set up, and quite a crowd had gathered in front of what looked to be an altar of sorts.

The meeting began. A woman stood at a lectern and began speaking of being bathed in violet light and white light. Hmm... Then she said there was a cult of people living out west somewhere underground (?) that were all part of this enlightening movement. Heavy stuff and a bit freaky. The speaker then started to chant, and the group of believers, in unison, joined in. Something like, "I am, I am, I am. O God Almighty, I am, I am."

Layla and I looked at each other without saying a word but "psychically" thinking the same thing: *Get the hell out!*

We endured about fifteen more minutes of the rhythmic chanting, squirming in our seats, ready to beat it when the chance arose. This cultish group of strangers were dead serious in their endeavors to find light in their lives. Too much light for us. The chanting finally ceased, and Layla and I couldn't find the door fast enough. We tore down the stairs and jumped into the car. Layla hit the gas and drove away from that crazy apartment-shrine. That was a bit way too weird for either one of us, and we talked and laughed about it all the way back to the safety of home. Fine to believe what you want to believe. Who were we to judge someone's beliefs or ideals? But really, it was just weird. All these years later, I can pick up the phone, dial Layla, and upon her answering, I chant, "I am, I am, I am," and hysterical laughter ensues.

And Incredible George

One day, there was a new guy working in the cosmetic department. He was extremely tall and very chic. I hadn't caught his name. The phone rang back in our studio, and it was the new guy, asking me how to program an electronic sign he wanted to use. I told him I'd be out to help. We were trying to get the sign to work, and I was explaining what to do. I looked up at him, all six-foot-ten of him, and said, "Who the hell are you anyway?"

He replied with a deadpan look, "Who the hell are YOU?"

I introduced myself, and he told me his name was George. We both laughed then about our first words to each other and have been friends ever since. He was so charming, funny, and genuinely nice. I fell for him. A bit younger than me, but what a catch. We then met up for lunch out in the mall, eating our sandwiches and chatting. He was hilariously funny, just what I needed to break up a mostly miserable day. He was also going to cosmetology school to become a hairdresser, and one day, he said, "If you ever need your hair done, I'll be happy to do it for you. I need the practice and won't charge you." Yay!

Throughout our lunches and talks, I wondered if he might be gay, just by some of the things he'd said. Never knowing anyone gay, I couldn't decide. So I asked him to come over and cut my hair. He agreed and showed up with a guy I had never met (maybe he was gay). We sat at the kitchen table for a few minutes, and George said, "Let's go wash your hair." We went into the bathroom, and before the water was turned on, he said, "That guy out there? He's the one I want."

So the truth had come out. I think I was one of the first people in his life to know. Then a worried look came across his face, and he said, "Do you still like me now?"

I was surprised and not surprised and said, "Don't worry, I still like you."

He had the biggest smile on his face and looked totally relieved.

George and Ramone, the guy that he wanted, moved in together, and the real fun began. George would call and tell me to get dressed up. We were going out on the town. We went to some wild and crazy places. Gay places. And I had a blast with my two gay friends. It was odd at first, and I felt out of place, but as I became more accustomed to the gay world, I felt right at home. There were some real colorful characters out there, and they were all so friendly and funny and quite gentlemanly. The best thing about my experiences of going out with George and Ramone is that I felt completely safe with them. If George saw me talking to someone he didn't know, he'd saunter by and casually say in my ear, "Are you all right?" He would stand just outside a unisex bathroom and wait till I came out. Nothing would happen to me on his watch.

Afterward, we might go to a late-night restaurant and have something to eat. Then we'd head back to George and Ramone's apartment. Ramone would shuffle off to bed, and George and I would sit there for hours, solving the problems of the world. We became closer than any two friends could be.

And Lexi, now at the age of nine or ten, was enamoured with George and Ramone. Sometimes they would take her with them shopping or out to eat. I trusted them with my life and Lexi's too.

About two years later, George called and told me he had heard there was an opening at another more upscale store in the same mall where I worked. He said, "Get your butt over there, girl, before the job is gone!" He knew I was discouraged working where I was. Oh, to have a new job where I might be appreciated a bit more! Hopefully a lot more.

I went to the other store directly when I got off work the next day and made an appointment to speak with who would be my new manager. *Please, God.* I was to meet him in two days' time.

The day came, and I went to the store's main office, stating that I had an appointment with the visual manager. "Oh, you're here to see Beau," the lady behind the desk said. She phoned him, and I waited nervously. I so hoped that this would be my ticket out of the torture chamber.

Beau appeared, walked up, and shook my hand, introducing himself. He said, "Follow me." We walked through the store, having a casual conversation. He was trying to feel me out to see what I knew, get my opinions on certain parts of the store, and told me what the job would entail if he chose me. I had a good feeling that day with Beau. He was cute as could be, smart, friendly, and had a soft Southern accent and, again, with one of those smiles that could've provided lighting for the whole store. The smile always got me. And he was gay. Wonderful. After hanging around with George, I was much better at determining the traits and mannerisms of gay men. And since I had loved all the gay guys I had met through George, I was hoping I'd get a call real soon from Beau offering me the job, just knowing we'd get along.

As I left Beau, I said, "I feel really good about this."

He said, "Me too."

I was hoping and praying as I drove home that day that he'd be my new boss.

It Was Only a Recurring Dream

I'm outside of a house. It's not just a big house. It's huge. It's sort of a Victorian-style farmhouse—white, made of wood. It has a giant wraparound porch, and under the porch is a giant dog as big as a dinosaur, similar to Clifford, the dog from the children's stories. Instead of a big red dog, he's a big white dog. That's how enormous the house itself is. The dog fits under the porch. The dog is friendly and doesn't scare me. Sometimes I go into the house, up the back stairway. I go to the same room each time. The room is empty, except for five to seven people seated on the floor, having a quiet party.

Oh, Happy Day! When Beau Washed My Blues Away

The call I had been hoping and praying for with all my soul finally came. Beau said, "Welcome! When can you start?"

It felt amazing to go into work at the hellhole the next day and announce that I would be leaving in two weeks. I had now worked there a total of ten years. Totally trapped between looking after Lexi, paying the bills, and trying to keep things going, I felt I couldn't leave my crappy job for another job for the two weeks it would take to start getting paid again. Money was that tight. I think boss lady wanted me to stay and said she would talk to the store manager to see if they could offer me more money. No way in hell! If she would've offered me a million dollars an hour, I would've turned her down flat. I had a new job, a new boss, and a whole new outlook on life in general.

May wonders never cease! I was actually having FUN at my new job with Beau. We became more than boss and employee; we became friends. I've never worked as hard at any job before or since, and I've never had so much fun. Beau was a riot, and we laughed through most days as we ran through the store, absolutely sweating bullets from the nonstop work, work, work.

Someone had left a flatbed cart on the elevator as Beau and I got in to ride one day. Suddenly, he jumped up on the cart, arms flung out as if he was surfing, and began singing, "Everybody's gone surfing..."

Close to Christmas, Beau had found a secret hiding spot behind a wall. It was deemed a fire hazard, but it was a good place to store some Christmas decor. Since the stash place had no doors, Beau put a ladder up against the wall to climb to the top. Another ladder was set against the other side of the wall to climb down as to gain access to the hiding spot. Beau climbed the ladder, got to the top, carefully flipping one leg over, then the next. He looked down at me from the other side of the wall and said, "Come on!"

I climbed up and got to the top and had a problem. Way too short to flip either one of my short legs over the top of the wall. I said, "Beau, it ain't gonna happen. I'm too short!"

I got a typical Beau comeback, "Just throw those tits over, the rest will follow!"

I nearly fell off the ladder. People probably heard us throughout the store. We were laughing so loud! It was always like that at my new job with my new hilarious boss and friend.

Hanging out a lot together now outside of work, Beau and I went out to eat, we went dancing, grocery shopping, or we may go to the park and swing on the swings and talk. I was falling for him and had to constantly remind myself, "You can't have him, he's gay." He was a different version of George. Beau helped me more times than he knew. He was an excellent listener and would always advise me by starting with, "This is what I would do…" He was a dream boss and a dream friend and was almost fatherly with his advice. Good advice.

It Was Only a Dream or Déjà vu

One morning, before the store opened, I was busy fixing things that had been messed up by customers the previous day. I could hear music playing, coming from the inner halls of the mall. People came early in the morning to walk to the music. My favorite old song came on: "Ferry Cross the Mersey" (the song about Liverpool I had heard all those years ago, falling asleep at Glam-Gram's house). Suddenly, I was right back in the bed at Grandma's. Everything in real-time around me ceased to exist.

I could smell the coal furnace. I could feel the nubby bedspread. And I could see the orangey glow through the window shade I had seen so many times in my childhood. The feeling lasted only about a minute, but the feeling was so strong I felt I was instantly back in the bedroom at Grandma's. Almost as if I had blacked out and gone back in time. It was that wonderful song I've always loved that transported me back that day.

*****

Beau had some good parties at his house. He and his boyfriend, Dennis, would host some unforgettable get-togethers. New Year's Eve being the event of the year, everyone was there eating, drinking, and joking. Mostly drinking. Then it was storytelling time. Beau spoke up and said to the guests, pointing at me, "Did you know that she was a Las Vegas showgirl back in the day?"

I had a few myself and couldn't think of a comeback.

Beau then said, "Come on, why don't you tell everyone about it?"

Normally, I would've run with it and made up a load of crap just to play along, but I could think of nothing. So I casually replied, "Oh, Beau, you know I don't talk about that time of my life anymore."

We would laugh about that for years to come. What was even funnier was most of the people at the party believed it and, the day after the party, asked Beau if he would tell them all about it. Yes, Beau was full of it.

After I had been at the job for approximately two years, Beau got promoted. He was moving away to another state. Good for him, not for me. I was crushed that my crazy wonderful friend and boss was leaving. We would keep in touch, but it wouldn't be the same (but Beau would remain a very good friend for years to come; of course, I had no way of knowing that at the time). Beau left. I cried.

And then a scary thing happened. I took his place and became the manager. Scary because so much was expected of me at that store. The store manager was a stickler, and anyone who didn't live up to his expectations was called on the carpet. Yikes! The "bigwigs" would show up, sometimes unannounced, and then there was hell to pay. It all had to be perfection. Honestly, if there was a piece of lint on the floor, it was like the end of the world. Did I really want to put myself in this new position? On the other hand, if I didn't at least try, then I'd never know if I could've done it. I found out in a hurry that it was way too much. I was losing sleep at night for a job! No way it was worth it.

I then had a stroke of luck. The phone rang at work one day, and another guy I had worked with under Beau also, Phil, said, "Come work with me at my new job. They need another person and they pay more money." He didn't have to tell me twice. I got a new job with Phil.

This job was different altogether for the fact that we traveled, Phil and I out on the road, which covered a few states. All the stores were part of a chain. They paid more and they weren't anywhere near as finicky as where I had been. We had real creative freedom, and no one hovered over us. And our boss loved what we did. The stores we visited may not have been the Ritz, but who cares when you're treated well and paid decent money for what you do? Phil and I packed his truck with props and supplies, drove miles, chatting, smoking, and drinking coffee along the way.

I liked being on the road. I met lots of interesting and amusing people at these various stores, one being a guy named Harvey. Harv, who was a genius at what he did, was very creative and would tell the most entertaining tales. I wasn't able to see him much, only when he was sent from the store he worked in to assist us. He would tell us a funny story with a serious look on his face, and by the time he got to the conclusion, we were screaming with laughter. We kept in touch over the phone outside of work, and he remains a good friend to this day. He's also been a great help to me and an inspiration in my life. Thanks, Harv.

My Best Girl

Lexi was now a teenager, and she was such a good kid. She had an old soul for her age and had lots of friends, girls and boys. Before she went out with her friends, I asked her to please call me now and then just to check in so I would know she was okay. And she did almost to the point of "Okay, already," but I was glad she did. Every half hour or so, she'd call and inform me where she was. I gave her my trust, and she never let me down. She was responsible and would call if she felt uncomfortable, finding herself in a situation that may not be the best. She had been at the roller rink once with a friend, and I got a call from her, asking me to please come get her. Her friend had taken off with some questionable guys in a car to go drink some beer. Lexi wasn't up for that, stayed behind, and called me.

She had a best friend she had met shortly after we moved back to Grandville. They were friends all through school. Her friend, Tina, was into everything. Lexi was the voice of reason. Not that Tina listened to reason, but Lexi tried to save her so many times. Lexi would say Tina had an addictive personality. She said, "If you give Tina a bottle of booze, she'll drink it all. If you give her a bag of weed, she'll smoke it all. Anything she can get her hands on, she'll do it till it's gone."

Years later, Lexi told me a chilling tale that made my blood run cold. Tina and Lexi had gone to a rough and scary dump of a town one night, a place well known for crimes, drugs, and God knows what. Tina was driving. They pulled up to a shabby house, and Tina went in. Lexi waited in the car. Lexi assumed Tina had gone in to buy some weed. Tina came back out to the car and pulled out a small packet. It was crack.

Lexi was speechless. Tina offered some to Lexi, and Lexi replied, "No, that's okay." Just as I had years ago when someone had offered me heroin, and was terrified. I was never so happy to know I had raised a kid with enough sense to turn down the offer from her messed up friend that day.

On a brighter note, Lexi had some friends I totally enjoyed, nice girlfriends and a few boyfriends too. Some boyfriends were serious, some not. One particular serious one I wasn't thrilled about. I just didn't think he was good for her. They'd sit in her room and talk, and when I opened the door, they'd both sat there, crying. What the hell? I asked Lexi what had been going on in there after Joe-Schmo had left, and she said he was having problems at home. His Dad was a real bear. Well, that's sad, but I really didn't appreciate him dragging down my normally happy-go-lucky kid.

One of her nonserious boyfriends was the son of my long-lost boyfriend from high school, Miles. How odd and wow at the same time.

The Angel (Auntie Angel) and the
Loveable Devil (Uncle Charles)

Quite often, all of us (Dad, Lauren, Lexi, and I) would go to visit Auntie Angel and Uncle Charles. When we visited the most, myself as an adult (Lexi was between five and fourteen) by then of course, my cousins had long flown the coop.

Auntie Angel, Dad's sister, was called Angel because my dad as a small boy couldn't pronounce Angela but could manage Angel, and his name for her stuck. And it couldn't have fit her better. She was angelic, and everyone loved her. She was just so sweet and loving. She was a beautiful person through and through.

Living only a few states away, when we arrived at Auntie and Uncle's house, they rolled out the red carpet. They lived in a big sprawling house with a swimming pool in the backyard, and we ate beautiful food, laughed, and sang the whole time we were there and totally enjoyed ourselves. Yes, I said we sang. My dad's side of the family is the most "singiest" family ever. It's almost to the point of silliness. Auntie Angel would sing, "Dinner is ready."

Dad would sing back, "What are we having?"

It's contagious, and soon, we were all singing.

On that note (get it?), one of the highlights while we were visiting was to go to a popular discount store (just the girls—Auntie, Mom-Lauren, me, and Lexi). Auntie would drive and could barely see over the steering wheel. She had an old cassette tape of her favorite, Wayne Newton, and the minute we left the garage, we'd be listening to the crooner himself. Then she would sing along in her soft sweet voice to "Danke Schoen."

Funny, both Auntie Angel and my dad got the same serious glazed-over look on their faces when they sang. Auntie would sway her shoulders and bob her head as she drove along. And we loved it. It became a thing after the first time, and every time after, we would request that particular tape. Not that we were in love with Wayne but because we loved her car dance and hearing her sing.

Now Uncle Charles marched to his own drummer. He did and said whatever he felt was his right to do. It could be awkward at times, but he was just so lovable we took him for who he was. He once dove into the pool, losing his trunks in the process, and then he just got out of the water and roamed around for all to see. I didn't see that show, but fine with me; just hearing about it was enough.

I do remember a comment of his one time when I was about twelve when he'd come to visit. And I wanted to die of embarrassment. We were at the dinner table at Grandma Lil's, and someone asked about my cousin, his daughter, Beth. He said, "Oh, she's fine, doing well at school, growing up into a young lady. She's got two little nubbins now (breasts)." I wanted to die three times and crawl under the table, I being the age of getting my "nubbins" too. I couldn't believe my ears.

As I got older and got to know my Uncle Charles and got used to his peculiar ways, I also realized what a sweet guy he was. Once when we were on one of our visits, Lexi, being a little child at the time, fell and scraped her knee. He immediately scooped her up in his arms, hugging her close, speaking soothing words, then ran off with her in his arms to get the necessary bandages and ointment.

When Vance and I were younger, we got to see our Auntie, Uncle, and cousins a few times, not nearly enough. Whether they traveled our way or we went to them, it didn't matter. We just loved spending time with all of them. The oldest was Martin who Vance and I couldn't get enough of. We almost idolized him. We just thought he was the grooviest.

Then came Beth, a year or two older than me, and Andy, who was my age exactly. Beth and I got along famously, and Andy and I always were fond of each other. We seemed to have the same sense of humor. It was such a nice blend of our two families coming together as one big happy family on those memorable occasions. I am so grateful for those fun-filled reunions.

Dad's Brother, Bert...the Rest of the Story

You can't imagine how shocked I was when I found out what really happened to Uncle Bert, the uncle I had never known. It wasn't until I was in my mid-thirties when the truth was told.

Mom had told me Dad was going to sell some of his old army memorabilia on the Internet (Dad having been in the army just before he and Mom number one were married). He had a big old army-green trunk I had always seen as a kid hanging around in the basement. The old metal trunk was filled full of stuff—no interest to me years ago—but I remembered some of the items it contained: lots of newspaper clippings, a few medals, pictures, and the like.

Having gone to Dad's to pay a visit, he told me of his plan to get rid of the long-ago memories. He no longer felt the need to keep the moldy old stuff. We headed down to the basement, and there sat the open trunk. In conversation, Dad's brother Bert came up, since Bert had also been in the army. I asked Dad, "What really did happen to Bert?"

Dad replied, "You know."

I said, "No, I don't know."

Then in a voice barely audible, Dad said, "He killed himself. You knew that, didn't you?"

I then told Dad that I had always thought Bert had somehow been killed in the line of duty. I was stunned and saddened for Dad, now knowing the terrible truth. I looked into my dad's teary eyes and said, "Oh, Daddy, I'm so sorry. I never knew."

Then Dad told me that his beloved brother had drunk himself to death, saying, "After he came home, Bert just couldn't handle what he had been through overseas."

Two of Dad's siblings had taken their lives.

I pieced it together in my mind that of course I wouldn't have known what had happened to my would've been uncle. Bert had died before I was born, so what was Dad going to say to me as a child? "Oh, by the way, your uncle drank himself to death." So it was never spoken of, and I had come to my own conclusion.

My Awesome "Cousin" Jake, Again

One boring day, Dad called and said he had a letter for me that had been delivered with my name on it in care of him.

"Who's it from?" I asked.

"It's from Jake," Dad said.

Jake? It had been years since I had heard from my cousin Jake. The last I had heard was that Jake had joined the service and then been married. Now a mysterious letter had turned up. I jumped in the car to retrieve the letter. It was so good to hear from Jake; more than good, it was great. He now lived out west, long out of the service, then had been married, divorced, and that was it. He also had put his phone number in the letter, so a few days later, I gave him a call. We then talked back and forth quite often for a month or two. He had a great idea. Would I like to come visit him? Yes, I would. What a good escape from my blah job and blah life in general. Lexi was old enough to stay on her own, and she was all for the idea.

There he was, my old friend, cousin Jake. He hadn't changed much and still had his welcoming smile and twinkling eyes. We had a really good time for the week I was there, going for dinner, riding through groves of towering pine trees, and talking nonstop. I couldn't remember the last time I had so much fun. He was a total gentleman, and I was treated like a queen.

Sitting at a table in a restaurant one night, he was telling me about what had happened since we had seen each other last. Then he asked, "Do you know why I went into the army?"

I said I didn't.

He then said one of the most shocking things I've ever heard. "I had to leave because I was in love with you."

182

I suddenly felt choked up and blurted out, "I have to go to the bathroom!" And I ran away from the table. I needed a minute to absorb what I had just heard. The old saying, "Knock me over with a feather," comes to mind. I sat in the bathroom, not knowing what to say when I went back to the table. I could have cried just imagining how he must've felt all those years ago. I hadn't had a clue whatsoever.

I took a few deep breaths and went back to the table. He asked if I was okay, and I asked him to explain. He said he told his mom how he had felt about me. Then he said his mom and my mom (number one) talked about it, and they both agreed that it would be just too weird for all the families involved if something serious were to happen between Jake and I.

Is this a soap opera? I was shocked. My mom had never said a word to me. Jake's mom was maybe made aware through Jake that I had no idea of his deep feelings for me. Maybe the moms agreed to leave well enough alone. Believe me, if my mom were still alive, we would've been having a conversation. A big one. I think Jake was relieved to have the old secret dilemma off his chest at last. I felt sad that he had felt trapped by his own feelings, enough to join the service.

Another bomb that went off that same week with Jake was him telling me of his adoption I had never known about. What had happened when he was born was that his mother had been very young and had passed Jake over to her parents to raise as their own (his grandparents). He knew no different till he was sixteen, and somehow, his then girlfriend had found out and, in turn, informed him. What a shock for him. So now the woman he had known as his sister was really his mother. All his other brothers and sisters became his aunts and uncles. Now that is a soap opera!

As I said previously, do not play with children's feelings. It's a lot to swallow down the road. It must bruise your trust to the limit. This was old news when Jake told me this twisted tale and was now fine with it at this point in time. He and his real mom had made amends, spoke often, and got along well. So he really wasn't my cousin at all.

Time to leave, and I hated to go back to my normal life as I had such a nice time with Jake. As I was about to get on the plane,

Jake threw out an idea that I could pack up, grab Lexi, and move out there with him. Not a bad idea, I had to admit. Maybe we could be together for real now that we were adults. Or if not all that serious stuff, then we could be friends as is and take it from there. Either way, it would give me and Lex a new start. The only trouble was, how in the hell could I possibly move hundreds of miles away? With what money?

Jake never said anything about helping me to get there. Was he going to help? Or did he think I would just pick up and move out? Without me coming out and saying, "Got any money?" I was stuck having no funds for such a venture. It was awkward. I guess we talked on the phone a few times after I had gone back home, but then the phone calls ended, and I never heard another word ever again to this day. Did he get mad or feel hurt due to my staying put? What was I to do? I really need to find Jake again, not to rekindle anything but to clear the air and be friends again. I'd really like to know what he's up to now. I sincerely hope he has a good and happy life, my "cousin" Jake.

Still My Best Girl

Especially being a single mom, I couldn't have wished for a better child, teenager, and then a young woman to call my daughter.

To start, she is a beauty. As the saying goes, "Beauty is in the eye of the beholder," but she really is. As a baby, when wrapped tightly in a blanket, she looked very much like a Native American papoose with her dark hair and dark shining eyes. As a little girl with hair so dark it was nearly black, her dark eyes, and my very white skin, she was often referred to as Snow White.

Lexi was a witty child and came up with some silly and endearing comments as children do. I recall some of the more memorable ones:

I tucked her into bed one night, leaning over to kiss her goodnight, her enchanting face looking up at mine, and she said, "Mommy, you have such big ear loafs." (I most certainly do not)

She once wanted to play a board game with Roll. Roll told her he didn't know the rules and that she would have to teach him. Lexi picked up the dice and explained, "First you wiggle the diamonds (shake the dice)."

Lexi went through a stage of promising to be your best friend if you granted her wish for something she wanted. When she begged me for something, making her sincere promise to me to be my best friend, I would usually say, "Best friend or not, kid, you're stuck with me anyway." Like the promise was a magic wand, wish granted. Yeah, not the way it works for moms. We had stopped at a gas station; I was going to run in quickly. Lexi was to wait in the car. The window was rolled down just a few inches next to where she sat in the backseat, just enough for her to fit her little lips and call out, "Mom, if you get me some gum and candy, I'll be your best friend!" Sometimes her ploy worked, sometimes not.

One of my favorite tender memories was of her taking a bath and quietly and sweetly singing a charming song about two people in love that were missing one another. I stood behind the bathroom door, listening, and it was pitch perfect, sung with so much feeling in her innocent child's voice. It nearly brought me to tears. I was so touched.

At about ten years of age, Lexi added a few instigators to her little group of friends, and I dreaded when they came to visit. One particular friend and Lexi liked to mix up a concoction they called witch's brew. They did this at our apartment after school and before I got home from work. They were old enough to be on their own for a time, but not too old to get into mischief. Witch's brew was made up of everything in the kitchen cupboards and the fridge. You name it, everything went in to the biggest bowl they could find. The brew not only looked disgusting; it was totally inedible. Like I had the money for them to be wasting foodstuffs. I had to threaten them with something major to stop the little witches from making any more of their brew.

Lexi also had a friend, Consuela—Connie for short—who was a likable girl and also a mini comedienne and a trickster. The girls were approximately fourteen when Connie came on the scene, and they've remained friends ever since. Connie, the girl who could only get a few words in between all the giggling she was famous for, was a good girl and a nice girl but always the one who played harmless tricks at school to get a laugh.

Connie had borrowed the most expensive pair of jeans Lexi owned. Lexi had loaned them on the sly or I wouldn't have allowed it. Washing day came, and the jeans were washed and dried. As I pulled the pricey pants from the dryer, I gasped at what I saw—red, greasy, smeary swirls all over the designer jeans. Connie had left a tube of bright red lipstick in one of the pockets, and now they were ruined.

Grandma Lauren had purchased the fancy pants for Lexi, and did I have money to replace them? No.

I absolutely wanted to throttle Connie and told Lexi never again to loan any clothes to Connie or anyone else. Connie still came over, giggling from the time she came through the door till the time she left, and I still liked the likable friend.

Lexi did normal teenage things—had friends, boyfriends, and did well at school. At one point, Lexi and her group of female friends collectively decided that boys were worthless and dumb. They joked that they would all become lesbians and stick together as the superior sex; to hell with the lesser sex. That same year they had given up boys, they ditched all those dumb boys and went to the prom together. Who needs boys to get all dressed up and go have fun? Girl power.

Not your average teen girl, Lexi didn't have to have all the latest clothes, a face full of makeup, and all the extra trimmings that a girl her age would more or less demand. She had friends like that, but not her. She was content to be herself and was a modest girl who didn't show off by wearing anything the least bit revealing. No short skirts, no low-necked tops. She's always been that way. I'm modest myself when it comes to bathroom privacy of any sort, wrapping a towel around myself from shower to bedroom, but aside from that, I've been known (as a younger woman) to wear some hip and somewhat sexy attire. Being a petite young woman, I could, so I did. Not my Lexi. As her mother, fine with me. She had enough boys interested in her just the way she was.

I tend to make Lexi sound like a model child, but she had a smart mouth as a kid, and she got in trouble when she spouted off. I chased her up a flight of stairs when Vance was over visiting after one such incident when she had used a snotty tone with me. Vance, the smart-ass, commented as I came down the stairs out of breath, "Geez, sis, I didn't know you could move that fast!"

As a teen, Lexi gave up testing me, and we became best of friends. Kids these days don't seem to know who's boss. They're catered to, coddled to, and bowed down to, like they're the ones in charge. You don't need to be a dictator parent day in and day out, but you do need to instill the fact that there will be consequences for actions that are not acceptable. Plain and simple. And trust. That was one key to our success as mother and daughter. I trusted her to do what was right. She was expected to be responsible for herself, and for the most part, she was.

Lexi turned out good. Every parent's prayer answered. I had done it myself with little outside help. I take a bow on behalf of myself and the smart and beautiful young woman I'm proud to call my daughter, my own.

She was right there with me through thick and thin (more thin) and held me tight through my darkest times. We laughed with sheer joy and cried for each other when things didn't work out right. At times, she was more of a mother than I was to her, wise beyond her years.

From the very first day I looked into her eyes until now, she's been my best girl. When I've called her my best girl as I have many times through the years, she almost always says, "Mom, I'm your only girl."

I always reply, "I know, but you're the best girl in the whole world."

It Was Only a Dream

Me and Lexi were running along the path in the woods behind my family home in Small Town. We were running a race. When we were halfway up the path, Grandma Lil stepped out from behind a tree. She asked, "Are you guys having a race?"

I said, "Nah," whacked Lexi on the back, and we tore off running again (this was definitely a visit from Grandma Lil years after she died, just making an appearance).

Stan—Is He the Man? (of My Dreams)

For quite a few years, I had been writing to my pen pal in England (it was before computers came into existence). His name was Stan. Stan, the nice man. I had found Stan in an ad in the back of a famous music magazine. I had been so bored when I first moved back to Grandville, reading the magazine from cover to cover out of boredom one night, when I came across the ad. It stated you could write to people in other countries, men or women. One of the countries was England. Since I had always had a fascination with England, that's the country I picked.

I must explain the fascination. The only thing I really knew of my heritage was my nationalities—French, German, and English (Mom and Dad had told me that much). And way before I found out all the adoption agency info, the English part had always intrigued me. I was always into anything to do with England. I felt it was the most predominant part of my genes, not having a clue why.

From the first time I had heard my song, "Ferry Cross the Mersey," to seeing the fab four on TV as a kid, to Twiggy who I had idolized, and then all the English bands we heard from across the pond, England was it. A few times throughout my life, a few people had asked if I was English, sure that they could hear a trace of a British accent when I spoke. Even at a young age, if someone had asked me if I had a choice of anywhere I'd like to go in the universe, you guessed it—England. It really is in your genes.

So when I thought of who would be fun to write to, in what country, it was Stan in the UK. We wrote back and forth for years. I got on with my life in the US, Stan got on with his in the UK. But it was such a welcome surprise when I saw a letter waiting for me with his handwriting on it. We wrote of our lives, families, friends, and jobs; interests, hobbies, hopes, and dreams. I felt it was such a good way to really get to know someone. Okay, a person can write a load of bs as well as they can verbally speak it, but things don't happen as fast as they can in person. And that's fine taking your time with the opposite sex. I know myself, at times, I've delved into relationships and situations before I took enough time to think it through the way I should have. And I know plenty of people who've done the same. Time is a good thing.

Stan's letters kept me going through difficult times at work, through loneliness, and just plain boredom. At one point, Stan's letters stopped. My heart sank. What if something happened to Stan way over there? How would I know? What if he became ill? What if he got amnesia? What if, God forbid, he was killed? I couldn't get the thought out of my head and wrote a heartfelt letter to Stan, expressing my concern. I wrote that I had become quite fond of him and requested that he please write back as soon as possible to let me know all was well.

About a week later, I got a letter from Stan apologizing for the delay. He wrote that he had just been busier than usual. He also said that if anything were to happen, his sister would get in touch with me. He had told his sister about me. Really? Wow. Usually, guys keep stuff to themselves. And something happened after that letter. Things got more serious. The letters took on a new feeling from both sides of the pond.

Another year or so went by, and then the long-distance phone calls began. It was like heaven to hear Stan's voice. He had a soft silky voice and a light British accent I had no trouble understanding. I'd hang up the phone and melt.

He Is! The Man of My Dreams

Calls went over the ocean between the UK and the USA, and then back again for a few years. And then a few more. Letters flew back and forth, some heartwarming cards and small tokens of affection, be it Christmas time or for no reason at all, but for the feelings that were slowly brewing. When I was away from home, traveling for my job, I would call Stan from the hotel; it made the work trip a bit more bearable, and listening to Stan's voice made him feel nearer since I was on the road, farther from home than usual.

I had a surprise call from George one day. Now the interesting thing is George had left for Miami a few years before and had met a new guy who happened to be British. What were the chances of that? Funny how even though George and I were far apart in distance, our lives were running in parallel ways.

Before long, George had flown off to jolly olde England. Both George and I were involved with Brits. Who would've thought it? George was calling from the UK (we had kept in touch the whole time through his moves, first to Miami, then to Britain). George told me he wanted to see me and so for my upcoming birthday, he would send me money for a plane ticket to fly over to the UK. I was overjoyed, to say the least. How wonderful and generous of my awesome friend, George.

I then rather timidly said to George, "I don't mean to sound ungrateful or that I'm taking advantage of your amazing offer, but as long as I'm coming all that way, I must meet Stan."

He knew about Stan and said that would be just fine. When I hung up, I immediately called Stan and told him my fabulous news.

Stan was ecstatic and suggested I come to him first for a few days, then he would be happy to drive me north to where George was living. Perfect! And exciting!

This was it! I would finally meet Stan face-to-face after approximately nine years of writing, talking, dreaming, and imagining how we'd be together in real life. To have time off work for two weeks, I had to call the main boss at headquarters. I knew her quite well and really liked her, and I actually said, "I must go, Gina, this could be it!" I had told her all about Stan.

Lexi was excited for me too, and she liked Stan more than anyone else I had ever dated. Once she had answered the phone, and since our voices over the phone are so alike and have fooled many, Stan thought he was speaking to me and said, "Hello, dahling."

Lexi replied, "Stan, I think you want to talk to my mom." Lexi and I had a good giggle on that one and pretty much all of Stan's other quirky British sayings, pronunciations, and quirky quirks in general.

Time off granted, there was no holding me back, and away I went.

*****

Stan picked me up in London, and it was a good two hours' drive to get to his house in a place called Weston Super Mare, right on the shores of the Atlantic Ocean or "by the sea" as Stan would say.

Sitting in the very same car with Stan! The scenery was just what you think it will be in England—lush green rolling hills with plenty of sheep romping in them. From the freeway (called a motorway), I could see castles here and there in the distance. This was getting better by the minute!

When at last we pulled up in front of Stan's, it was just what I had pictured—a tidy row house with lacy curtains in all the windows. Stan had told me, "Unless you're well-off, row houses are what your average Brit lives in." It was obvious by the rows and rows of them where the term row houses had come from. Inside it was a bit old-lady-ish. It really did seem as if an elderly lady lived there, not a bachelor.

Stan had informed me in one of his many letters that he had never been married and had fathered no children; believe me, I was very pleased to learn that important tidbit. No baggage—unheard of in this day and age, most people having been married and divorced maybe several times.

Stan and I had a perfectly splendid time going to the beach, having drinks at the pub nearby, talking and laughing till we were nearly hoarse. We sat out on a patio, seaside, eating fish and chips, and told stories of our childhoods which were worlds apart in comparison. As I had hoped, we got along even better in person. The whole first experience had been like something from a movie. The breathtaking scenery, the quaintness of jolly olde, and especially getting to know Stan in his lovely environment.

Too soon, it was time to go north and spend the rest of my time in England with George and his significant other, Miles. It was a long way up, and I was glad of it—more time with Stan. We found George's place; inside, it was painted every color of the rainbow. Really a funhouse atmosphere. Stan wasn't sure of where I had taken him. George invited Stan to stay for a few days, knowing I would love it and knowing that Stan had taken some days off work.

I could tell George approved of Stan for me. Not that I needed George's approval, but it was nice that George was protective of me (as he always had been on our previous escapades going out on the town all those years before).

Then the dreaded day came when Stan had to head back home and get back to work. We went outside to say goodbye, and we kissed and hugged and didn't want to let go. A single tear slid down Stan's face, and he said, "I don't want to go."

He really did have feelings for me. I tried to put on a brave face and asked why he couldn't come visit me next back in America? We agreed to call each other every day till I left George's, and of course, I would call him the minute I got back home. Stan then reached into his pocket and handed me a small jewelry-sized box and told me to open it on the plane on my way home. How thoughtful. He then reluctantly got in his car and drove away, not looking back. He was so upset. Me too.

George had planned for all of us to go to a festival after Stan left, so we got into George's car, and then I cried.

George asked, "Are you okay honey?"

I replied through my tears, "I don't know… He's such a good person, and I would be dumb to ever let him go." My mind kept going back to Stan's pitiful face when he left. I had never seen any man before him actually cry for missing me, and in that moment, I knew I had a keeper.

I managed to have a good time at the festival and for the rest of the week with the guys. The plan had been for them to drive me in their car back to London. Change of plan: The car conked out, and they would have to take it to a garage to get it fixed. The car could just about make it as far as the bus station, but not the whole length of the country practically, to the airport. To make things worse, on the day of my departure, my period arrived. Great. What else could possibly go wrong?

Boarding the bus for the hours-long journey, I was in no mood for any of it: journey, sadness, and especially "my little friend" that conveniently made an appearance at exactly the wrong time. I read a book, tried to sleep, and was mostly bored and very nostalgic as I watched the lush green scenery go by, having to leave it behind in this enchanted place. I was headed back home to what? Nothing. The only heartwarming idea I could think of was Lexi there waiting with open arms and ready ears. Other than my Lexi, there wasn't a damn thing.

I felt soggy (you know where) about halfway through the bus ride, and I began looking around for a bathroom. I needed to check out the situation before it was too late and I had a pool underneath me on the seat. No. No lavatory, as the Brits called it. Surely there was a facility on the bus for a long trip like this. But maybe not. I was in a foreign country, after all.

After what seemed an eternity, the bus driver made an announcement that we were approaching the airport. Someone got up in front of me and started to go down some stairs right inside the bus! The bathroom I had so desperately wanted to find! It was UNDER the bus! What kind of a damn place/bus is this? No time now. Someone was occupying the bathroom, and the bus was coming to a stop. By now, I didn't know if I had a big red spot on the butt of my pants or not. Oh, I did not need this.

I just knew upon standing, I'd feel a whoosh, and that would be it. I then had a good sneaky idea. I rummaged in my purse and dug out a pad. When no one seemed to be looking, in ten seconds or less, I stood up and stuffed the thing down the back of my pants, shoving it a bit forward. There. Luckily, I had a longish jacket on that would hopefully hide whatever may have happened. The minute I got into the airport, I made a mad dash for a bathroom and got the mess under control. Leave it to me. I shouldn't have been surprised because I was prone to having "that time of the month" at always exactly the wrong time—any big event, birthday, Christmas, swimming party, dance-a-thon, shopping trip, or any outing of any sort. Oh, the joys of being a woman.

I was aboard the plane when the stewardess came and asked if I'd like a drink. No shit. I requested a G&T that I had become fond of during my stay in the most beautiful of places I was now flying away from. Damn it. I drank it down in two seconds flat. I suddenly remembered my present from Stan. I quickly dug it out of my carry-on and opened it. In the small fancy box, there lay the most stunning necklace I had ever laid eyes on. It was a dainty Celtic cross made of rubies, my favorite (and also my birthstone). Stan had remembered that. Well, that did it. I began to cry and cry, and I couldn't stop. The stewardess was at my side then and, seeing the state I was in, asked if I was all right. All I was capable of was to nod my head yes.

Not two seconds later, she appeared again with another drink. And then another and another. I then had a notion that she must've thought someone died for the way I carried on so.

Completely wiped out after the bus ride, the plane, and all the tears, as the plane was landing, I was teary-eyed again. Now Stan was many thousands of miles away. When would I see him again? The magical kingdom of England was only a memory. Now back to my work-a-day life. I wanted to scream at the top of my lungs, "Shiiiiiiiittttt!"

Goodbye Lexi, and Hello Stan

On the phone, I cried again as I thanked Stan for the precious time we had together. How can everything be just perfect one day, and then the next, so deflating?

Things went back to normal. Blah describes it accurately.

Finished with high school, Lexi was now going on to art school, taking the train into the city each day. She was in her element and meeting all sorts of interesting people in the process. I had told her that it would be totally different from high school and that she would like it so much more. Like me, there came a point when all she could do was to get the hell out and leave her less than "beloved" alma mater behind. I was very happy that she had found her niche in art.

Stan and I continued our talks, letters, and cards. Then the happy news came when he told me he was coming to visit me and Lexi on our turf. He also said he had a surprise for me... Mom was sure it was an engagement ring! I didn't want to get my hopes up, just to be let down, but I secretly wished for the ring that Mom was so sure of.

Lexi was excited to finally meet Stan in person: they had talked on the phone several times. Mom and Dad were anxious to meet him too, and my friends really wanted to meet him and to hear the accent they had only ever heard on TV.

The day Stan arrived, I had put a big Union Jack he had given me on the front window of our apartment. Everything was ready. I met him at the airport, both of us smiling from ear to ear. I noticed he was carrying a large box. Could that be my surprise?

We got back to the apartment, and I could hardly sit still. I hadn't slept a wink the night before. When all of us had settled in a bit, Stan brought the mysterious box to me and proudly said, "Here's your surprise! I carried it all the way over here just for you."

I thought to myself, *Too big of a box for a ring*. I opened the box. "Oh! It's a cake!" Nice gesture, but not the surprise I had hoped for. And as I cut into the cake, nope, no ring baked into the cake either. Drat. But maybe in time, the ring would come; for now, we'd make the best of the time we had together.

And we did. And it was a blast and a dream come true having him by my side once again. Everyone was completely taken with my Englishman, most of all me. Lexi, Mom and Dad, and all my friends knew I had found myself someone special this time. Especially Dad. Dad had been telling me for years that he knew in his heart I was going to find someone good. He knew of my discouragement after some of the "winners" I had been out with before. After hearing his "I just know" speech quite a few times already, I would just reply, "Thanks Dad" or "I hope you're right" or sometimes all I could say was, "Yeah, yeah." I figured he was just being his kind and gentle self. Dad had been right all along. I had finally found "the one."

Once again, the time I had with Stan flew by, and it was good-bye time. It wasn't AS heart wrenching this time. We were on another level now, and even though he'd be in the UK and I'd be in the US, there would come a day when we would be together for good. And it would be sometime in the near future...

We talked on the phone more than ever before, and during those chats, we agreed we needed to be together forever. But who would go where?

In the interim, Lexi was about to finish her two-year course, expressing to me her desire to move to Colorado where a friend of hers had been living since they had graduated from high school. It was time for her to spread her wings, just as I had all those years ago.

It's the natural way of things to want to get out there in the world and see if you can do it like a real adult. I hated to see her go, my best girl, my reflection who had shared her whole life with me. She was off to "see the world."

197

And since Lexi was going on her new adventure miles and miles away, I decided that I would go on my new adventure even more miles away.

Yay! I'm Off to the UK!

I ended up having a few rummage sales and giving some of the bigger things to friends. The rest of my belongings were sent overseas in what seemed like at least a hundred boxes. I was off to the place I had always dreamed of with a loving man waiting, humble abode, and the picturesque view I would see in every direction.

We entered Stan's/our little granny-looking house, and on the dining room table was a "Welcome Home" cake and flowers. For me! Stan carried my suitcases upstairs. I could tell he was very happy to have me there with him at last, and he seemed just a bit nervous; the last woman he had lived with was his mother. I followed him up the stairs, getting familiar with my new home; our new home.

Stan said during one of our many chats that he had put a canopy over the bed. I had asked him to describe it, and no matter what he said, I couldn't visualize what the heck he was talking about. *Must be a British thing*, I thought. As we went into the bedroom, there it was. Oh no, it was ugly. There was a pole approximately two feet long that stuck straight out over the bed. Draping down from the pole were two panels of lace which hung down about four feet on either side. It reminded me of the same sort of thing you'd see hanging over a royal infant's bed. I'm sure Stan had hung it for the new lady of the house. He had tried to do something pretty for me. Not wanting to hurt his feelings, I didn't say a word. The very next day, he didn't say a word either, and it was taken down. I think it must've been the look on my face.

As I looked around further, I could see I'd be making some changes to my new residence. A lot of it had to do with clashing colors and patterns. The place itself was clean enough; it just needed a woman's touch. One feature of the house that was outstanding were the stained-glass windows—a big one on the front door and three small ones that ran along the top of the picture window in the living room. All the colorful windows were in the pattern of a sunrise in red, yellow, orange, and a bit of green. Stan had said a lot of the houses had them back when, but everyone thought they were too old-fashioned, so they tore them out and replaced them with clear glass windows. I told Stan no way we were getting rid of our gorgeous windows.

We had a bigger bathroom than anyone else in our adjoining row of houses and a bigger kitchen. The occupants of the house, before Stan bought it, had extended the otherwise smallish house, so we had plenty of room. There was a long narrow backyard, which is always called a garden in England. A backyard can be void of any plants or flowers whatsoever, but it's still called a garden. Ours really was a garden, and it was delightful. As a typical Brit, Stan had done an excellent job planting cheerful, colorful flowers and flowering trees. I loved to see him out there in his flat cap and wellington boots (called wellies), digging and planting. Since I had never lived anywhere to have a garden, I didn't have the first clue, and even if I did, gardening isn't my thing. That was Stan's forte.

Soon I got to meet his family, all of them living only a few streets away. He has a small family, and as I met each one, I felt so lucky to be so welcomed. There's his sister, Vera (two years older than Stan), her husband, Clive, and their son, Pip. Clive's sister, Elizabeth (Liz), lived nearby also with her live-in boyfriend of many years named Harry.

But my absolute favorite was Stan's mum. Mum was a slight, elderly woman, quiet as a mouse, and I could tell she was taken with me from the start. And I with her. Stan had started a tradition with Mum years before of showing up at Mum's door every Saturday with fish and chips as a little treat for her. So now it was the three of us gobbling down the delicious lunch. Mum would always have a pot of big fat disgusting peas ready to serve with the fish. Ick. I politely would say, "No thank you" as she neared my plate.

After we had eaten, we all sat in the living room and read the newspaper. Mum wasn't much of a talker, but a few words were said, and she was happy for the company. When we were out on the front walk, leaving, in her cheery old voice, she would call out from the doorway, "Cheerio, Mr. Cheerio, Mrs."

I think I gave all of my new extended family a buzz just for the fact that Mum's son and Vera's brother suddenly had a woman companion and an American at that! They were all very kind to me, and my brother-in-law, Clive, liked to lovingly tease me about MY accent! I let him have it right back, and we got along famously.

Stan and I went to all his favorite haunts, and I was seeing some incredible things. Storybook villages, the quaint seaside with its colored lights hung along the shore that shone and reflected in the water by night; and, oh, that glorious country side. Sometimes seeing the old thatched roof cottages, churches, and castles, I felt like a character in a Dickens novel or that I was in the midst of an old Victorian movie. In England, you no longer eat gruel or roast boar for dinner; it's up-to-date for the century in which we live, but if you go off the beaten path, the landscape is what dreams are made of. It was almost too much to take in at times. An overload of stunning-ness.

As he got ready for work, I found I couldn't talk to Stan too much or he would run late for his job or forget something. He wasn't used to dealing with another person there morning, noon, and night. He also would just leave at times with no goodbye. I would come downstairs and call for him. Where had he gone? A few minutes later, he'd come through the door, newspaper in hand. I asked, "Where did you go?"

His reply, "Went round to the paper shop."

I had to tell him that he needed to inform me when he left the house, adding, "I'm here now and I need to know where you are." I had to repeat it a few more times before he got the hang of it. All new to him.

The best thing between Stan and I was that we completely loved being together, even if it was staying at home, playing cards, talking, and joking into the wee hours of the night. We did everything together, and since I couldn't drive there (everything being the exact opposite of how I had learned to drive years ago), Stan dutifully went grocery shopping with me every weekend, and some of our best times were at the grocery store. It was all new to me, and I asked him endless questions about some of the odd and unusual items on the shelves. What in the hell was a Christmas pud (short for pudding; sounded like something dirty to me)?

Then there was the oven. It's all centigrade in the UK. What? I had to make a conversion chart for myself in order to use the damn oven. And no clothes dryer in my new residence. No way. That would never do. Most folks there drape their clothes over the radiators to dry them in the winter or hang them on a clothesline in the milder weather. Clothesline, fine, but no radiators for this spoiled modern American girl! You could smell the people who had used the radiator method. Smelled like a sour dishrag coming toward you. I would not smell like that and did not want Stan to smell like a dishrag either. Stan bought me a dryer. I was so overjoyed I told Stan that if I didn't marry him, I'd marry the dryer.

After I had been there a few months, I began to wonder if and when Stan and I would be married. It had been our plan for quite some time. I think Stan was a bit nervous never having been married before, and a few of his friends had been burned by their ex-wives, so he had heard all the horror stories about ex-wives taking their husbands "to the cleaners."

We did set a date, and we were to be married in the register office in the middle of town. We had to do the best we could with the money Stan was making. I wasn't allowed to work yet. There's a waiting period of sixth months, if I remember correctly. We couldn't afford to have anything lavish, but we still wanted it to be nice and pleasantly presentable.

Vera and I went shopping to find a suitable dress for the important event. I found a dressy royal blue suit with pretty pearl buttons, and Stan rented a handsome suit complete with long-tailed jacket. How very British. Flowers were ordered, and the one thing Stan wanted more than anything for our day was to have a professional wedding book made, like the one my mom and dad had—old-fashioned, thickly padded, with large glossy pictures—something that would last forever.

The only sad part of our upcoming wedding was no one was coming from home. It does cost money, and no one had the money or could get the time off from work to come. Mom and Dad sent a heartfelt card with a touching verse, and Dad wrote a personal letter, beautifully written, wishing us the best of everything. Also, he wrote that in spirit, he and Mom would be there with us every step of the way. In the card was a gift of money, but the sincere letter would've been enough; it was priceless. The one person who would be there for me from my past was George. Since he lived in northern England, he and his partner would drive down, and he'd do my hair!

An old stone fortress of a place in the downtown area was where the ceremony would take place. As we all gathered together, the officiating woman sanctioned to marry us said the words for us to repeat. When it was Stan's turn to repeat the part about my "lawfully wedded wife," he nervously repeated "my lawfully leaded wife." We heard stifled chuckling behind us. The short ceremony went off well, and afterward, everyone followed us back to our house. There were toasts and hugs, and Stan's Mum was grinning ear to ear, so happy to see her son finally happily married.

At the airport the next day, off on our honeymoon, Stan asked, "Would you like to know where we're going?"

I told him I would, and he said, "We're going to Cyprus."

I started to laugh and clap my hands, "Oh, goodie! Where is it?" How the heck did I know, being from America and for not paying attention in geography class? He then explained where it was, and it sounded good to me, wherever it was.

It was absolutely good. Palm trees swaying, the ocean, the sun, and best of all, my new husband. How much better could it get? We swam, we ate exotic food, we shopped for funny souvenirs, and I'm sure people could tell we were newlyweds by the light in our eyes and the constant smiles on our faces. Our honeymoon was glorious.

Back to our love nest, lovebirds that we were, taking a very late flight, it was around 2:00 a.m. As soon as I presented my passport, the man behind the desk said, "Come with me." Uh-oh. I was taken into a small office and asked some basic questions. "How long have you been here?" and "Who are you traveling with?" The officer then said I needed a visa to travel and that I could be sent back all the way to the US, but they would allow me to go back to England to sort it out. I knew I needed a visa, but I still had more time in which to obtain it. Not good enough; they didn't want to hear it. Stan and I were sure that at 2:00 a. m., they had nothing better to do than to give us grief. Nothing like coming to a screeching halt after our time in paradise.

To get help with the immigration predicament we faced, we went to talk to a solicitor (attorney, to me). Caroline, our attorney, was doing her best to find a way around the dilemma. Stan and I went back and forth several times to her office, and about two months later, a letter came one day stating that we must travel to Wales to meet with an immigration officer. And we could not take our solicitor with us. It was a government matter, and Caroline was a private solicitor, and evidently, the two would not and could not mix. Great. The letter included a list of paperwork and documents we were to bring with us. All very annoying and nerve-racking.

In the midst of worrying and gathering every piece of paper available, the most terrible and sad thing happened. Mum died. Poor lovely Mum was gone, and Stan was devastated. His dad had passed away about ten years prior, and Stan could barely mention his dad without getting teary eyed. He had truly loved and had looked up to his dad, and they had been best of friends. And now Mum. Stan's parents were now both gone.

Our meeting was in two days' time at the immigration office. It was a dreadful stressful time all the way around. The immigration office waits for no one, and Stan just wanted to get it over with, even though his mum had just died. It would take a few days before the funeral took place, so there was time to go take care of the immigration matter.

At the office, Stan was called in first. He was in there a long time, about an hour. I sat, nervously waiting for Stan, then it would be me next. Stan finally came out, stood before me, and I asked, "How was it?"

He said, "Not bad."

Before another word could be spoken, I was called in. A middle-aged man sat behind a desk, but he didn't seem threatening and was actually quite pleasant. He asked every question in the book, like when were we married, how many rooms in our house, did I have children and how many, and did they come to England with me? On it went; how long had Stan and I corresponded before I came over?

Finally, he wanted to see documents. I had brought a few cards and letters with me from Stan with dates stamped on them to prove how long Stan and I had known each other. The officer said he was satisfied with both of our stories and that he would now try to find a legal way around it. *Whew.* He said, "What would be the use of you flying back to the States just to get your passport stamped, only to turn right around and come right back? It would just be a bunch of unnecessary time and money."

Thank God we had this reasonable man to deal with. He told me to go out and wait while he tried to work some magic. And *poof!* He did! He came out and told Stan and I he had found a single paragraph in an enormous book that would set things right. All that for that. We thanked him and I hugged him because the whole fiasco could've been so much worse.

We now had a heartbreaking funeral to attend. It takes much longer to go through all the arrangements for a funeral in England. From the time a person dies till they're actually buried is at least a week or more. Vera phoned a few days prior to the funeral and said she and Liz were going to the "chapel of rest (funeral home)" to see Mum, to say goodbye before they closed the casket and had the funeral. Would I like to go? None of the men had the fortitude to view Mum's body, so the three of us women were on our own. I agreed to go. I really felt the need to see Mum one last time. I had only known her for a total of eight months. I was going to silently make her a promise that I would do my best to take care of her son.

Vera, Liz, and I were taken into a small room at the funeral home. As we entered the room, I must say I was a bit shocked at what I saw. There Mum lay in an old-fashioned coffin, the type you see in old western movies with the head of the coffin wider than the bottom, an elongated diamond shape. I hate to say it, but it was the type of coffin a vampire would be in. The cover of the coffin was leaning up against a wall and had a gold plaque with Mum's name and birth and death dates. The old-fashioned coffin would have been enough to make me question what century we were in, but Mum had been wrapped in a shroud. The shroud covered the whole opening of the coffin, her whole body, with just a hole big enough for her face to be seen. They definitely did things way different here in England…

It's fine. Different countries have different customs, but having been to so many funerals and visitations in my past, I had never seen a deceased person laid out quite like this. But the saddest thing that day was poor Mum had a bruise on one side of her face they couldn't quite cover up. She had fallen when she died. Poor Mum, lying there with her now expressionless bruised face.

Jolly Ollie and Gregarious Grant

Down the street, Stan informed me, lived two gay guys. Stan had no clue about anyone gay. He referred to them in British slang terms. He said he had always heard gay men called either "poofs" or (and this one is cringe-worthy) "shirt-lifters!" I then had quite a conversation with Stan starting with, "No, no, no!" As a lot of straight men imagine, they think a gay man will make advances toward them. I told Stan that gay men like or love other gay men, and why on earth would they want a straight man? I firmly defended my gay friends, explaining that they'd always been good to me, taken care of me, and loved me unconditionally. The record had been set "straight."

My next words were, "I'm going to walk down to their house and introduce myself." I had passed by the guys out on the street several times previously, and hellos were exchanged; it made me realize that I had really missed my gay "boyfriends" from back in the US.

When I reached the guys' house, they were sitting out on the driveway in lawn chairs, enjoying the sun. I walked right up and introduced myself. Instantly, the more smiley of the two exclaimed, "You're American! You know, we're gay." Like it was their nationality. Ha! But the way he said it, it was almost like an apology as if he thought I'd turn around and run away! Then he loved what I said back.

"I know, that's why I came down here. I have lots of gay friends back home and wanted some here too!" The ice had been broken.

The jolly one was named Ollie, and his partner's name was Grant. They both lived with Ollie's mom, Doreen, and Ollie's sister, Ruby, lived right next door. After that first meeting, we saw a lot of each other. Ollie was fascinated with all things American and asked endless questions about how Americans live, what they eat, where they go on vacation, what we watch on TV, the weather, our money, and he was delighted to know the answers and even more delighted now that he had a real American friend.

Grant, on the other hand, was a laid-back sort of fellow and smart too. He would interject now and then, but mostly, he was a listener with a good sense of humor and had a way with clever anecdotes, sayings, and subtle jokes.

The two moved out of Doreen's and got their own place, inviting me over for lunch many times. One day, Ollie called and asked if I'd like to come for lunch. I asked, "What are you having?"

His reply, "We're having spaghetti on toast, mashed potatoes, beans, fried spam, and a fried egg."

What? I told him, "I'm sorry, Ollie, I just can't eat that mixture. Can I just have the spam, toast, and an egg?"

Both Ollie and Grant are sweet, funny, and kind. They were the first real friends I had in the UK, and they remain good friends of mine even now. Kiss, kiss, love you both—more than you know.

Gifts, Gifts, and More Gifts

Things eventually calmed down after we got the immigration issue resolved and said goodbye to Mum. Stan and I went about our life, still happy but with a tinge of sadness not seeing Mum or not being able to do our Saturday ritual anymore. I was bored as could be at home every day, but it was nearing the time when I could look for work.

There was a small high street (shopping area) nearby I could take the bus to, and I decided to go look around for something to do. I entered a gift shop, and a middle-aged blonde lady said hello. She asked if I was looking for anything special, and when she did, I could hear it in her voice. She was American!

Then we really started to blab. We exchanged our names and where we were from back in the States and carried on like we were old friends. She said, "So what did you do in America? Work in an office?"

I said, "No, I've always worked in a store."

"Really?" she said. "Would you like to work here?"

I told her I would, and she said I could start the following week. Wouldn't Stan be surprised!

I started working at Gifts Galore, and that was a perfect name, the owner and my new boss, Betty, had given her shop. From floor to ceiling, there was an unbelievable variety of giftable items for any occasion under the sun. And then some. It was a tremendous trinket treasure trove extraordinaire. The small shop held an array of items—statues, vases, urns, artificial flowers and plants, figurines, dolls, dollhouses and tiny furniture to go with them, toys, teddy bears, jewelry—including belly rings and nose rings—fountains, outdoor statuary, and a scattering of end tables, nightstands, dressing tables, and chairs. I probably have forgotten half a dozen other wares. You couldn't bring a baby stroller or a large handbag in with you—"You break, you buy."

The women I worked with at Galore, young and old, were some of the loveliest women I have ever met, especially two young women in particular. The first one was called Sal who was close to my age, was rough around the edges, and had a mind like a trap, especially when it came to numbers, and that was a good thing since that's never been one of my strong suits. She had a typical west country gravelly accent and was full of the devil and funny as hell. She liked to drink on the weekends and could drink any man under the table. But Sal had a soft side few people would ever know. She was the first one to help if anyone had a problem or had been hurt in any way. She was a kind, crazy, true character, and I enjoyed her and loved working with her.

Another young woman a few years my junior, Livy, was a gem, stepdaughter of the boss, Betty. I've always thought she was most like a friend from back home. We could just really talk about stuff, and she also had a great sense of humor in a different way from Sal. One day, Livy and I were just chatting away at work; it had been a slow day, and we had already completed a crossword puzzle together. We were that bored. Betty always had us put a few bigger items out on the pavement (sidewalk) in front of the shop each morning, her attempt at attracting customers.

One particular morning, Livy and I had placed a giant stuffed Easter bunny in a chair right outside the front door. Glancing out the window, I saw a man come up, pick up the bunny, and start to walk away. All I could do was suck a deep breath in. Without saying a word, Livy then saw what I had been unable to verbalize. Livy hollered, "He's taking the bunny! He's taking the bunny!"

Livy dashed out the door after the guy with the huge bunny. I went outside to see what was happening, and I saw Livy grab hold of the bunny and yank it with all her might out of the thief's arms. She yelled at him and said, "What in the hell do you think you're doing?" Go, Livy!

We came back in to the shop and started talking and laughing about the incident that had just taken place. It was funny now, but not so much a few minutes before. Suddenly, Livy gasped and said, "Oh my God, the whole thing will be recorded on the camera, let's go watch it!"

In the stockroom at the back of the store, Betty had set up a TV that was connected to a few cameras in hopes of catching thieves, and there were plenty of them around. Thieves abound in England. And also, those cameras, we felt, were set up to watch us too. Not that Betty thought any of her workers were stealing but to spy and make sure we were busy putting our best selling skills to use. Livy and I rewound the tape, and there was Livy on film, exclaiming at the top of her voice, "He's taking the bunny! He's taking the bunny!" We watched that recording at least ten times, laughing hysterically with each viewing. It was similar to that old TV show with the hidden camera. But the bunny was safe, sitting there in its chair out in front, like nothing had happened.

I stayed at the gift shop for about a year, but I wanted more. I thought I'd try to get into a more upscale store. It would be further away, and I'd have to take the bus, but it would be more of a challenge and more money. Taking the bus some twenty miles away, I went into a large "la-la" department store and got an interview. The manager of the job I was to interview for was on vacation, so another general manager was to conduct the interview. I was to bring some mood boards depicting examples of what I thought various modes of fashion were. Really? I never thought the job I had done all those years was important enough for mood boards.

Armed with the boards I had pored over, I sat in an office with a young manager lady and another young woman who was so tiny and delicate she looked to be about twelve years old. The twelve-year-old person was who I'd be working with if I was lucky enough to get the job. Her name was Sophie, and though she didn't say much, she seemed congenial enough. I knew I could get along with her. The woman conducting the interview had a script she was referring to and kept asking me dumb questions like, "If the store was on fire, what would you do?" It was all very silly, and it was obvious she was the wrong person to do the interview. She knew nothing about the job I was there for.

I then had to go out to the sales floor and dress two mannequins to prove I knew what I was doing. They tried to trick me by giving me one mannequin with crossed legs, which to get a pair of pants on the thing, you had to put the pants on backward first, pull them up, twirl them around, and then they ended up in the right position. *Yeah, you're not gonna trick me*, I thought to myself. Sophie stood nearby to judge my work since the real boss wasn't there, and we chatted as I worked. She talked more now that we were on our own, and when I finished, she told me she thought I had done a good job. I wish Sophie could've just given me the job right then, but she informed me that they would call when the real boss came back. I had done what I could.

The Okay Job in the "La-La" Store

A few weeks went by, and having heard not a peep, I called the store and politely said, "Remember me?" The next week, I got a call, and a meeting was set up to meet with the manager I would be working for. Put me through the wringer, why don't ya? I already had the interview, mood boards, dressing mannequins—now another meeting?

I met with the young woman manager at the store's in-house cafe for coffee and a chat. Her name was Beverly. Seemed okay, and I felt comfortable having an informal meeting. Again, at the end of our talk, she said she'd let me know.

Another week went by, and I thought, *What the hell? What is taking so long? Do they want me or not?* Finally, I did get a call and got the job!

It was a large department store, upscale like the one I worked in with Beau. The usual tasks were assigned, and they were picky about the way things were presented, similar to the store where I had worked with Beau. But Bev was almost too laid-back at times, and some days, she would actually say, "What would you like to do today?"

Never in my working life has a boss ever spoken such words. I used to think to myself, *Should I reply, "Gee, I'd like to hang out and drink coffee and smoke cigarettes today?"* Other days, she would give Sophie and I a wad of money to go buy magazines so we could spend the entire day making mood boards. What was it with the mood boards? We couldn't grab the money and run fast enough. And we got paid for cutting pictures out of magazines! What a job! If that's what you want to call it.

For a time, it was only Sophie and I, and we became very good friends. It was great working with someone I hit it off with again. We created some fun windows together, sometimes getting in trouble from the visiting bigwigs for pushing the envelope beyond their boring taste. Just after Christmas one year, it was time for the White Sale, so Sophie and I decorated a window with New Year's Eve in mind. We brought a big luxurious bed into the window and dressed it with our most expensive gold and black bedding ensemble. Next, we dressed a female mannequin in black sexy lingerie and her mannequin partner in some black silk boxer shorts. We put black masquerade masks on them for the New Year's Eve theme. Those in the upper echelon paid a visit and went to view the windows. They were appalled by the party-going mannequins; it was all a bit too kinky for them. The masks came off.

We had to work with the props that had been there for years, so we really had to dream up whatever would work with what they had given us to use, which wasn't much. We had to make things and use old bits and pieces that we recycled ourselves. It was quite a task, but Sophie and I plugged along and talked and laughed our way through trying to create something out of nothing. You'd think a big "la-la" store like that would be overflowing with all sorts of implements to use within the store and in all the big windows we had to fill. No.

Soon another young woman, Kai, was hired, and she was Finnish! What were the chances of that? She couldn't believe it when I told her of my years in Small Town with all those Finns. Her and I had that in common, and she laughed about the fact that the only Finnish words I knew were swear words. Ha! Loved her too, but she was hell-bent on working her ass off, and we could barely get her to stop long enough to eat lunch.

Then another young woman was added to our team, the store manager picking her off the sales floor because he said she looked "creative." Thanks. There are lots of different elements you need to know to be able to perform your duties as a visual merchandiser. There are all sorts of basic rules about balance, proportion, color, composition, and the like. If someone comes into the job who is hired to portray the look of the store, not having any clue of these elements, then the ones who already know these components have to do the best they can to teach these parts of the job to the unknowing.

And finally, to round off the team, a young "pup" named Mick was added. At first, Mick was our helper and helped us haul stuff and would do prep work. Slowly, he worked into a full-blown team member. He had an eye for the job and had some schooling for design. He was a slight elfish-looking young guy. Had he been a bit taller, he would've been a good candidate for modeling. He had a style all his own, so fashionable with his unique dress sense. He was a an agreeable young man and a good fit for the team, and we really appreciated him.

At some point, someone in some head office somewhere started to send us new props to use, and the beauty of it all was that we could use them how we saw fit. Now we were having a way better and more fulfilling time doing our jobs. We got some amazing things to use in our twelve windows. A few windows were smaller, but at least eight of the twelve were huge, most of them facing the main street downtown. We did a world traveler-type window once that we all agreed turned out exquisitely. We had been sent large maps of faraway places to use as a backdrop, interesting artifact objects, old crates and trunks, old postcards, and old suitcases. It had been a group effort, each person giving their suggestions, and when it was finished, we all went out on the street, looked in, and proudly admired our job well done.

Another time, "the powers that be" wanted us to create a garden party in the window. We had topiary urns with roses, a wrought iron table and chairs complete with a tea set, strings of pastel pennants (called bunting in England), and tiny strings of white lights delicately draped from the ceiling (now this is typical; any tiny lights in England are called fairy lights, even for your Christmas tree!). Our garden party window was delightful and made you want to go right in and have "a spot of tea."

Of all my jobs doing displays all my life, the very best part was creating. And that's the way it was until the creative part came to an abrupt end when all the major department stores in the US and the UK either did away with windows altogether or started sending pictures of exactly how "they" wanted things to look. As I've always said when the new rules came into play, "Why don't they just get some robots or hire a bunch of monkeys to do the job?" Like the old song about the day the music died, that's how it feels. All the creative thinking, planning, and the act of actually using your artistic ability…gone.

Now you get a cookie-cutter version of in-store displays and display windows. Once that happened, the fun and excitement of the whole inventive job ceased to exist. Everything, store to store, has to look the same now. Continuity? More recognizable to your customers? I'd like to know who came up with that "brilliant" philosophy, and then I'd like to shred them to pieces. The world needs more art of all kinds, not less. Period. I think anyone, whether consciously or not, likes to see an interesting, amusing, or stunning store window. Having spent hours sweating in various windows over the years, I've found great satisfaction and a sense of pride standing back, looking at the finished product, viewing the scene I or a coworker or all of us together have invented on the other side of the glass.

Soon we heard that a new store was to be built on the other side of town. It was to be a multimillion-dollar store and the anchor store for a whole new shopping mall. And before long, we moved into the pristine building. However, I lost all my workmates and gained a new boss in the process. Since all the stores in the new complex offered a varying degree of goods for sale, it was an open door to new experiences for the young people I had worked with, and they were spreading their wings for new retail horizons.

My new boss was fine, this time a young man who didn't say much. He would give you jobs for the day, and that was it; most times, you never heard another peep out of him, and then you just left for the day. Since we moved into the new store even before it was completely finished, he and I spent a few days together painting walls of a big department within the new place (cheap labor getting us to do it). Since he had recently arrived, and he didn't say much, I thought our painting together would be a good way for us to get acquainted. I said, "So Barry, what kind of music do you like?"

Barry said, "All kinds."

I tried again. "Seen any good movies lately?"

Barry replied, "Not really."

I asked, "Do you have brothers and sisters?"

Barry said, "Two brothers, one sister."

I thought to myself, *What a scintillating conversation this is!* As time went on, he spoke a bit more but was always guarded and never relayed any information about himself whatsoever. But he liked me, especially because I was the more mature one of his minions, being old enough most times to be the mother of my workmates. I could take direction, wasn't moody, spoke my mind, and was on time (unlike some of my counterparts who may have gone out partying to excess and then feigned sickness; sometimes they had too many emotional problems that kept them from showing up for work).

I had some entertaining young ones to work with that came and went. They sort of looked up to me in a motherly way, and me being American, I was a novelty to them. They often came to me with problems concerning their love lives or perhaps they were deciding what exactly they wanted to do with their lives in general. They learned they could tell me things they maybe couldn't say to their own mothers; they couldn't shock me, and I wouldn't be judgmental. I listened and gave them the motherly advice they didn't want to hear from their own mothers.

A new guy showed up one day, Shelby, he was so very shy. My heart went out to him because he just seemed so uncomfortable around so many new people. He had moved from a small northern village and seemed so alone. I struck up a conversation, and I could tell he was grateful. In no time at all, we were chatting away like we had known each other for years. We got together for coffee and exchanged stories about our lives and loves. He came to visit at our house, and Stan liked him immediately.

Shelby was gay, and so was my boss, for that matter. I always find the gay guys to be a gentler version of mankind and have been drawn to them ever since meeting George all those years ago. I cannot count the times I've been accused of being a "fag hag," and I wear the badge with pride because some of my very best friends in life have been and are gay. Don't know any gay women besides ones I've met in passing, but I know plenty of gay men and love them. So call me a fag hag or whatever you want because I wouldn't trade my guys for anything.

It Was Only a Recurring Dream

I'm in an elevator, alone. As the elevator ascends, the cubicle itself starts to slowly turn within the elevator shaft; such an odd and unsettling feeling. I extend my arms, my hands on the walls on either side of me, in an attempt to remain standing. Sometimes I put my foot against one of the walls, trying to keep my balance. The small elevator room continues to slowly rotate. Sometimes in the dream(s), the cubicle starts to go sideways and keeps on going, and when the elevator finally stops and the doors open, I'm in a different town and have no idea where I am. I'm feeling totally confused, disoriented, and worried sick about how I'll get back home. I have no clue where to begin; I don't recognize any of my surroundings.

Over and over again, I've had various themes of these elevator dreams. Lexi and I were at an airport. I entered an elevator, thinking Lexi was right behind me, but no. The elevator did its usual tricks: rotating, going sideways, and when it stopped at what seemed to be a few floors up from where I had gotten in, I searched and searched for Lexi. I never did find her.

Sometimes the elevator doors opened, and I found myself on a moving sidewalk that moved like a conveyor belt. I rode the sidewalk endlessly all over town.

I had these elevator dreams for a total of five years, about a year after arriving in the UK. I was sick of the same dream over and over. I started to recognize while dreaming when it was about to happen, the dreaded elevator ride. I thought to myself, *Oh no, not this again*, and would begin to panic. The dreams weren't scary, just so disconcerting and annoying. I never knew where I would end up once the dreaded doors opened. Then I still had to get through the rest of the dream, roaming around, trying to figure out where in the world I was.

In the last of these dreams, I was standing at the bottom of a very long, tall escalator, and I could see an elevator waiting for me at the very top. I started to panic, but I said out loud, "No. I'm not going on that elevator!"

*****

The dream stopped the minute I spoke those magic words, and I've never had another elevator dream again. Looking back on those nightmares, I think I now know what they were all about. In real life, I really didn't know where I was. In my waking life, I was in a completely new and different country. And to add to it, every day at work, I rode on two separate elevators and a long, tall escalator.

Lady Fiona

I had a few good friends I had made in England, but one of the best ones was my friend, Fiona. We met at the cafe I went to every morning before I started work. I got to know all the regulars that came in for coffee each morning, one being a guy named Byron. He was sitting in a booth one morning with a pretty blonde woman. He introduced us. Her name was Fiona, and we made small talk, and that was it. The meeting in the cafe left my mind.

A few weeks later, sitting at the bus stop, the lady seated beside me struck up a conversation. I said, "Wait, haven't I met you before?"

She replied, "No, I don't think so."

Then it came to me. "Yes," I said, "I met you with Byron at the cafe. Fiona, right?"

Recognition came across her face, and then she said, "Oh yeah. Oh, him…" She told me that Byron had been pestering her, and she wasn't the least bit interested in him. We decided to sit together on the bus when it arrived. We talked all the way to my stop, which was her stop too. She only lived a few blocks away. We exchanged phone numbers, and that was how it all began.

She would come to visit me or I would go to her place to visit her. We took the bus downtown, had lunch, shopped, talked, and laughed. Fiona was so ladylike, unlike me. I'm not manly, just not the dainty type like Fiona was. As we talked more and told each other about our pasts, Fiona revealed some horrifying tales to me. She and her mother had been abused by her monstrous father. He would beat her and her mother. He once whipped Fiona with the cord from a vacuum cleaner! He killed her pet kitten, strangling it before her eyes!

Needless to say, she left home with her boyfriend at sixteen, not being able to run away fast enough. She and Roger, the love of her life, got married and had a son named Jacob (he was now a grown man and was a terrible kid; his name should have been Satan).

As a child, Jacob was a good little boy, and so Fiona, Roger, and Jacob made a nice happy family. Until Fiona faced the most heartbreaking devastation of her life. Roger was diagnosed with pancreatic cancer and died. She had mourned him ever since and would be heartbroken until the day she died.

A few years after Roger died, she met a guy named Gary. And he was a real "prize." He was a drinker, gambler, and womanizer. Fiona could not be married to this wild man, and they divorced.

Then there was her family, or lack of. Most of them were alcoholics and users, and she had distanced herself from them long ago. She kept in touch now and then with an older sister who lived in northern England where Fiona was from originally. Her poor abused mother had died and her disgusting father too some years before I had become friends with Fiona. So that left Fiona all alone. Her son had left and lived in a town miles away from her. He was married to a dreadful woman, and when Jacob and his wife had their first child, Fiona only saw her grandson twice in his first five years. Jacob couldn't be bothered to visit his mother or even pick up the phone. I never met Jacob, and it's probably a good thing or I would've ripped his head off for treating his own mother so badly.

Fiona had every medical problem known to man. She had severe pains in her legs and had a hell of a time climbing the stairs to her apartment on the top floor. It didn't help that her apartment was located at the bottom of a very steep hill, so she would walk along the flat street at the bottom of that hill until the incline wasn't as severe, then she would climb a small hill in order to take the bus to go to yet another doctor's appointment.

Because of her legs, Fiona couldn't manage to stand for any length of time and had left her job, not being able to bear the pain. Any job she had had, they had expected her to keep up. Besides her painful legs, she had some problems with her brain, which I had to remind myself of at times when she was forgetful. She had arthritis, and her eyes were failing her from a condition which was slowly making her go blind. To see her, you would never know the state she was in. Always meticulously dressed and groomed, out and about, men would approach her; some stared at her from across the street.

When I picked up the phone and it was Fiona, I heard her soothing voice, "Hello, sweet-art" in her northern accent. I could really get her going, and we would roar with laughter, me being more outspoken and saying it the way it is. It was good to hear her really crack up being the demure person she was. Because of her quiet demeanor, most people who met her thought she was rather odd, and a bit odd she may have been, but you couldn't find a nicer, sweeter, or more loyal friend than Fiona. I loved her for exactly who she was.

Travels with Stan

Back to my everyday married life with Stan… It was really fun, and we went everywhere together, whether it be wandering England's heavenly countryside, its cobble-stoned villages, or the scenic seaside. We also went abroad as the English like to say. Here's a list, and I'll touch on each place, my impressions as I took it all in.

Besides our travels in beautiful England, we went twice to Greece—or maybe it was three times—Spain, Portugal, Italy, Belgium, Holland, France, and Ireland. All were fabulous and so very different in their own ways. I can't say I have a favorite; they were all amazing and intriguing. I'd always dreamed of traveling, and my dreams came true.

Starting in the UK, I can't say enough for the sheer beauty of it all. And one of the dreamiest of places is a tiny hamlet near where Stan and I lived. I had a framed photograph I had fallen in love with that Mom had bought for me at an art show in the US of the very same village. I had sent over the picture that had hung in my apartment, not knowing the picture's exact location. I asked Stan one day, pointing at the picture, "Do you know where this is?"

He replied, "Yes, it's just down the road."

What a coincidence! A few days later, we were on our way. The road in was very narrow with trees bending in an arch overhead. We went down a slope, and there it was, the picturesque vision nestled in among the forest. Driving over a stream on a stone bridge, there were swans gliding along the water's edge. Was I dreaming? The cobblestone street beyond was lined with tiny stone cottages, many of them with ancient curved doorways that looked as though gnomes lived inside. A person of average height would have to duck to enter. There's not much there besides a post office, two pubs, and a really neat old church. In my wildest imagination, I would've never thought such a place could exist.

One year on my birthday, we went on a mini "holiday" to Southern England, and on the way back, Stan said, "I have a surprise for you." We drove way, way out into the countryside. This time, instead of trees making an arch over the road, it was overgrown hedgerows. We were so far out in the middle of nowhere I asked Stan, "Are you sure you know where you are?"

Yes, he was sure. Then I saw the sea in the distance, and next, we were on a cobblestone road entering a village. Stan said, "Here we are in Tintagel." He knew it was somewhere I had always wanted to go—a place of mystical wonder that had fascinated me in the pages of books. And it would prove to be all I had seen in pictures and more.

We got on a small open shuttle bus and went up, up, up and even further up; there it was in all its glory—the castle ruins atop jagged cliffs that overlook the crashing sea below. Hundreds of steep steps leading to what used to be the castle, I had the wrong shoes on that day for the adventure. I didn't care one bit. I needed to explore all the rugged rocks and ledges, the amazing view from way up top.

The remaining architecture included ancient doorways complete with a view through to the sea, and some of the rubble that remained was merely a fading outline of some long forgotten ghostly rooms dating as far back as the 1200s. Below the ruins, down at water's edge, is a large cave they call Merlin's cave, supposedly where Merlin cast his magic spells. What a truly invigorating experience!

Stan and I drove down to the coast in Cornwall, another Dickens-esque location. It reminded me of a town out of a seafarer's tale. Built on a hill, all the quaint cottages cascade gently down to the water's edge. During the day, we went down to the water, stopping to eat Cornish pies and creamy Cornish ice cream. Delightful.

We were staying at a guesthouse, which was someone's actual house, the owners renting out a few bedrooms. The first night we stayed, we realized the woman of the house had come into our room, made the bed, and had left the window open all day while we were out. It was chilly, to say the least, by the time we returned to go to bed. The next night, we were wise to it and hung out at the British Legion, biding our time, not in any hurry to go back to the cold room. The old folks (the only folks) there at the legion were enjoying themselves, playing bingo and singing along to old songs. Not very entertaining to us, but at least it was warm there. Finally, we decided to walk up the hill to our room, and it was so damn cold in that room we slept in all of our clothes! Stan came up with a new name for the place: The Fridge on the Hill.

Another scenic place in England (honestly, I could fill a whole book with all the stunning locations) is Stratford-upon-Avon, famous birthplace of Shakespeare. The buildings there are of the Tudor style. Beautiful. Once again, Stan had made the arrangements, and we stayed at an old crooked hotel built in 1402 or some such way beyond comprehension year. When we got to our room on the second floor, having had to duck down to fit through the door, it was something to behold. The whole room was off-kilter! I sat on the bed and looked across the room to where a small dressing table stood. The dressing table was leaning to the left, and I could see that the whole room was on an angle. How could this decrepit structure still be standing?

The town itself is filled with museums and gift shops all to do with Shakespeare. There are a few nice restaurants, and one in particular was magical. As Stan and I entered the White Swan, we immediately noticed the only light was candlelight. Candelabras, candlesticks, candle chandeliers, big candles, small candles, candles everywhere—very intriguing and romantic. Stan and I decided on fish and chips and ordered. As we waited for the food to be served, I overheard a familiar accent—Americans. A few tables over, there was a man and a woman. After our meal was delivered, we noticed the Americans were eating fish and chips also.

After the couple had finished their meal, the waiter went to their table and said, "Did you enjoy your fish?"

The woman exclaimed rather loudly, "Oh, it was WONNN-DER FULLL!"

I was totally embarrassed. Really, lady? It's fish and chips, not a prime filet mignon. "It was very nice, thank you" would've been satisfactory. I hate to say it, but I was embarrassed so many times by my fellow Americans while I was in England. The Brits already think we're loud and brassy, and they are correct. If Stan and I were touring a castle or at some sort of tourist attraction and heard a boisterous voice or voices? Americans. Tone it down, would you? It made me shrink away not wanting to be associated with the loudmouths.

One more place I must mention is Althorp, the stately manor home where Princess Diana grew up. I requested to go there for my birthday one year and thought it would be extra special that day since the princess and I share the same birthday, both July first, different years. The home and grounds are immaculate, and the museum of Diana's life is tastefully done. It was enlightening to see pictures of her as a baby through to childhood and onto adulthood until her life was so tragically cut short. There was a large room dedicated to her death that projected a film of her funeral. The floor was strewn with rose petals. Again, very tastefully done, but so very, very sad.

At the back of the grand house is an avenue of trees that arch over a walkway, leading you back to the pond with the memorial for the princess. On the path as I walked along, I felt that when I got there to see it, it may be just a bit too sorrowful to handle. I thought about turning back so as not to be emotionally destroyed, but I still needed to see it for myself and went toward the heartbreaking site. And I was pleasantly surprised at how I felt. It was peaceful, serene, and very calming; not dreary and soul destroying.

In the middle of the pond is the island where her remains rest in a white urn, standing tall in her memory. I experienced a quiet and reflective atmosphere and sat on a bench for quite a long time, remembering the beautiful, understanding person and princess that she was.

Stan and I took a trip that passed through France and Belgium, ending in Holland. It began as a bus trip from England, which then boarded a ferry, went a short distance, and then back on dry land again to France. The ferry part of the journey being a neat and new experience for me and landing in France first, we drove through emerald countryside till the bus stopped in Belgium. Only stopping for lunch and to have a look around in the middle of the village, it was very old-world-y with delicate Belgian lace in all the windows. Elegant stately buildings lined the main courtyard, and the cleanliness of the whole area was pristine.

On the bus again, we were en route to our hotel, which turned out to be a modern wooden structure set in a grove of pine trees, nice and peaceful, approximately thirty miles from Amsterdam.

The bus we had taken to the hotel was also scheduled for trips each day into the city. That night, Stan and I boarded the coach. Our tour guide announced that we could follow him through Amsterdam or we could go off on our own. He warned that he would lead the group through the red-light district and that it may not be for everyone. Stan had been there and seen it all before, but of course, I wanted to see the dimly lit, seedy, sex-driven streets I had only ever heard about.

Unusual in its architecture, the city's skinny, gabled canal houses lining both sides of the canals look as if they've all been horizontally squashed together by a giant. The canals are the main feature throughout this picture-perfect city where houseboats and long low tour boats can be seen gently floating by on a daily basis.

Leaving the bus, now on foot, our tour guide pointed out various landmarks and some of the more prominent points of interest along the way. Turning a corner, we were in the middle of it all—the promenade of prostitutes and sex shops. Hanging in the sex shop windows were all sorts of devices, trinkets, and toys, some of the gizmos unrecognizable. What in the world were these kinky curiosities? And how in the world did they provide pleasure of any kind? As we meandered through the avenue of all things orgasmic, behind a row of windows, we viewed every sort of woman (some actually men convincingly dressed as women) as they danced, pranced, posed, and some were seen, disinterested, talking on their cell phones. And surprisingly, it wasn't the least bit seedy, grungy, or dimly lit as I thought it would be. Though scantily clad, nothing was hanging out, no body parts on show. I had seen more on holiday around the pool. So everything everyone thinks about the red-light district is completely false. It was all quite respectable, considering what went on behind the curtains of those windows when the occupied sign was displayed.

Since marijuana is legal there, you'd think that would also be in your face, but it's very low-key, not in view anywhere. A large several-story building with a giant sign depicting a cricket is a well-known "den of highness" in Amsterdam, and Stan and I decided to have a look inside. Upon entry is a well spelled-out sign citing the rules of the establishment. The rules state that there is no liquor sold on the premises nor can you bring your own, and also, there will be no fighting. In other words, have a smoke and chill out. What could be more mellow than that? They were puffing like steam stacks in the den of smoke you could cut with a knife; no money necessary to get your high, just breathe for about ten minutes…

On a brisk sunny day, we went for a nice boat ride on one of the scenic canals. Aboard the boat were tables and chairs with a complimentary bottle of wine on each table and a small dish of cheese. I can't stand the smell or taste of wine, so I did not partake. However, Stan was game and started drinking the wine that was furnished on our table, having had nothing to eat that day. When Stan finished that bottle, he asked a woman at the next table over if she was going to drink her bottle of wine. She said she wasn't and handed it over to Stan. Two bottles of wine later, on an empty stomach, Stan was feeling no pain.

Once off the boat, he was getting a bit too chatty with people on the street, and I pulled him by the shirt sleeve several times to break up his drunken blabbing.

Time to head back to our hotel. We managed to find the bus, boarded, and sat down. I was not in the mood to hear Stan's ramblings, so I pretended to fall asleep, hoping he would do the same. After a few minutes, I opened my eyes, and sure enough, my trick had worked, and Stan was out. Thank God. Soon we were back at the hotel, we came to a stop, and everyone began leaving the bus. I gently woke Stan and helped him first to stand, then helped him wobbly-walk to the front of the bus. The bus driver stood at the bottom of the bus stairs, bidding everyone a goodnight.

Stan got to the bottom step and declared right into the face of the driver, "I'm Brahms and Liszt, I'm frickin' pissed!" I must explain: There's a whole slew of sayings in the UK called Cockney rhyming slang. Used in the old days in London, it disguised illegal dealings so those in authority didn't know what the criminals had in mind if they were overheard. A few examples of the slang are: Up the apples and pears means stairs. The old dog and bone means phone.

Stan tried every slang he knew on me when I first got to the UK, and I'd end up shouting, "Stop it! I don't know what you're talking about!" Also, pissed means drunk.

So after Stan made his profound statement in the driver's face, I wanted to die of embarrassment. I looked at the driver and rolled my eyes and then helped Stan in through the lobby, up the elevator, and into our room. Then I let him have it for being a drunken dumbass and made him promise to apologize to the bus driver the next day. Stan did as he promised and apologized for his "three sheets to the wind" behavior. When he came back to the room, I asked him what the driver had said. Stan repeated to me the driver's words, "Oh, it's fine, you were just having a good time on holiday."

Oh, pardon me, I had forgotten how much drinking (way more than in the USA) goes on in the UK, especially when you're totally enjoying yourself on holiday!

My last thought on Amsterdam was I felt as though I had visited another planet. Nothing is illegal. Hard to imagine there's a real place on earth like it.

And the last in my summary of vacations is Ireland. Aah, green and glorious Ireland.

Stan booked a long weekend in Dublin, and we flew from England to Dublin in thirty minutes or less. Once there, in a taxi, we went directly to the heart of the city. The taxi literally dropped us in the middle of the street, and the first thing we saw was a large glass, trimmed in brass case with a statue of Jesus inside. For sure, we must be in Ireland.

What a hoppin' place! I was expecting Dublin to be archaic, and rather peaceful. Granted, there are old buildings that have been there since time began, but the place was booming: restaurants, bars, shopping galore, lots of noise, and tons of people! And we came across more Americans than Irish.

All over the city are interesting statues of famous and not so famous characters; all have a plaque nearby explaining the story of the statue. The food is good, the people are friendly, and the place is always abuzz. Once you're away from the busy town itself and viewing the sumptuous vista, that's where you'll discover the Ireland that daydreams and legends are made of. It's even more enchanting than I'd seen in travel brochures.

...And We Went Abroad, Dahling

I cannot say enough about the beauty of Greece. Each time we went, I noticed how clean it was. Someone is always out in the street sweeping, washing, or cleaning something and everything. The Greek people are friendly and accommodating. From the first time we went till the final trip we made, it was exceptional.

Our first time in Greece, we got to our hotel by taxi; the driver drove up to no more than a door in a wall. Since Stan is the master itinerary planner, I wondered what he had booked for us. It was the right address, so we gingerly opened the door...and were astonished. It was spacious and elegant. Vaulted ceilings, marble floors, and potted palms decorated the lobby. After we checked in, we passed through a nearby door out to a pretty courtyard with a large pool surrounded by tall palms. Paradise. Good job, Stan! When we got to our room, second floor, our balcony was just above the courtyard—what a beautiful sight to wake up to.

Until I arose one morning, opened the curtains, and what I saw made my eyes pop! Directly across from our balcony at the edge of the pool sat a very large, very tan woman with her enormous brown boobs in full view. What a sight upon awakening. I never knew that when you travel around the Mediterranean, you see lots of bare-breasted women ...everywhere. Takes some getting used to. Now Stan, being well traveled, didn't seem to even notice. I asked him about it, and he said, "No big deal."

Really? Any man I've ever known, well, his tongue would be hanging out along with his eyeballs, not to mention the rising of his obvious trouser tent.

Spain—another stunning place to visit. Our most memorable trip there was a rather strange one. Fun and nice but strange. For some reason, we got to our hotel rather late at night, Stan got the key, and we had been promised a view of the sea. We got to our ground floor room and went inside. Oh! It was a small apartment with a living room, kitchenette, bathroom, and a bedroom. Very nice. I crossed the living room and opened the drapes to see what I could see. And to my dismay, right outside the front door of our apartment, was the kiddie pool! NO WAY! I had imagined having a nice mellow time, peaceful and restful, NOT tons of children screaming, crying, splashing, and being annoyingly noisy.

I said to Stan, "I cannot stay in this room with all those kids right outside."

Stan said he'd take care of it; he felt the same way. He tromped over to the office, and in a few minutes time, he was back. I asked him what had been said. He told me that he had walked right up to the desk and flatly said, "We can't stay in that room." The person behind the desk asked what was wrong, and Stan said we did not want to stay next to the kiddie pool and added, "My wife hates kids!"

I said, "Did you really say that?"

Yes, he had, and the person in charge said to stay in our room for the night, and in the morning, we could move.

The next morning, as promised, they said we could move to the other side of the complex. As we rounded the corner to our new location, we both sighed in relief. We saw a luxurious pool without a soul in it. And it was absolutely quiet. This was more like it!

The hotel consisted of a set of buildings, some of which held a restaurant, a bar with a huge dance floor, and some game rooms. The dance floor area got wild and rowdy every night. These holiday makers were making merry all right—drinking, dancing, and acting like idiots. Loud karaoke music could be heard throughout the complex along with singing, hollering, and a lot of raucous partying in general.

Stan and I poked our heads in one night, and we saw fat topless men, beer guts on display, doing their best dance moves; older women were reliving their youths in their short miniskirts and spaghetti-strapped tops. It was a free-for-all, and not one of them was going to waste one minute or one penny on their time away from their normal boring lives back home.

Since Stan and I were there in part to celebrate our anniversary, we wanted to have a special dinner one night. Stan went to wander on his own one day, and when he returned, he said he found a Spanish restaurant right on the beach—perfect for a romantic dinner to celebrate our years together.

Out of nowhere, a storm blew up, and the wind was howling that night. Normally, it was an open-air restaurant, but that night, they had to batten down the hatches—not quite as romantic, but we were going to have a good time regardless. All the waiters in the place didn't speak a word of English, and Stan and I don't speak Spanish. This would be interesting. The menu was also in Spanish, so we ordered a few things and hoped for the best. When the food came, two bowls of vegetables were put on the table, and great platters of meat were set before both Stan and I. Mystery meat for sure. Some looked like beef, some looked like pork, and some...who the hell knew?

With great trepidation, we began to eat. One piece of meat was a pallid pinkish blob that looked like innards, guts of some unknown beast, and it smelled...less than pleasing. In the mood for adventure, I said to Stan, "'Maybe it tastes better than it smells." I cut a small piece of the pink blob, popped it into my mouth, and started chewing. No, it tasted exactly as it smelled, and it was spit out immediately into my napkin. Gross! Almost to the point of puking.

Meal finished, we walked back to our apartment, laughing and joking about our dinner experience. Stan always finds a funny name for things, and he came up with "Meat on the Beach."

As soon as we got back home from our vacation (or holiday, as the Brits say), I got on the phone with Lexi to tell her all about our trip. When I got to "Meat on the Beach," I told her, "Guess what we had to eat? Pig's uterus!"

She exclaimed, "No way, Mom!"

I then came clean and said I had just made that up but that it could've been!

Portugal had some of the most tremendous scenery I had ever seen—glorious vistas for miles. Above the center of town, we walked way, way up a hill that overlooked the sea. It was extremely hot that day, and we were parched. We noticed some tiny old cafes, so we found the oldest most charming one and went in. An overly tanned, antiquated woman was serving the few customers that were crammed into the small space. In order to use the bathroom, I had to step over boxes of supplies in a minute hallway. Leaving the bathroom, I came face-to-face with the old woman, and she commented on the brace-let I was wearing. I thanked her for the compliment, and she asked where I was from. I told her America, and she said, "Me too." I didn't think I had detected an accent when she first spoke to me.

We struck up a conversation, and she said she was from New York City originally. Really. How much further away could you possibly get from the hustle and bustle of New York City to end up here, way up a hill in Portugal? I asked her if she ever went back home to visit (she had been in her cafe for thirty-some years). Her answer to my question made me feel sad for her. She explained that she didn't miss home whatsoever and that there was no reason to go back because everyone was dead anyway.

We chatted for a bit longer, and she seemed so interesting to me. Just to move so far away and be on your own in a country so different from where you'd come from was mind-boggling to me. Yes, I had done a similar thing, but by no means was I from anywhere as big as New York. And I now lived in a country with English-speaking people, and I wasn't completely alone as she was. I could've stayed there for hours talking to her. I bet she would've had lots of fascinating stories to tell...

At the hotel pool one day, it was hard to find an empty lounge chair. Everyone wanted to soak up the warmth of the sun. Suddenly, three identical topless Portuguese women were dashing about, trying to find three unoccupied chairs. From what I'd gathered, when most women go topless, they remain in a lying or seated position. Not these Portuguese triplets. They were all small breasted, and their lem-on-sized boobs were hard as rock, and their protruding nipples were like bullets! And as the three scurried around, they were all speaking

Portuguese to each other a mile a minute. I noticed the other sun worshippers trying to stifle their laughter.

One fine day, Stan said he'd like to explore the area beyond the hotel, and I was more than content to lay by the pool, headphones in place, a good book to read. Bye, Stan. I wanted to get some color to take back home with me, and since I was bound and determined to do so, I overstayed my welcome with my friend, the sun. Back in the hotel room, I was "hurtin' for certain." My feet were fried to a crisp. The rest of me was fine but my feet! I spent a good part of the night with my feet in cold water, making use of the bidet in the bathroom. Yes, a bidet. Most hotels abroad feature one of these cleansing items, to put it politely. Not meant for feet as a rule...but my feet were grateful.

Italy. What a treat. Enchanting. We stayed in northern Italy in a beautiful region known for its lakes and mountains. The hotel we stayed in was completely surrounded by jagged mountains with the lake below. It really was like a dream. And oh, it was hot. The Italians were some of the most congenial people I have ever met, and most of them seemed happy to be alive and were always smiling.

I was looking forward to eating some delicious Italian food, but the cuisine didn't impress me. Maybe it was the area we were in. Different regions have different ways of preparing food, but it was pretty bland. Sometimes Stan and I ate the fare included in the hotel package, and sometimes we picked an interesting restaurant to try. At the hotel, we looked at the menu, and they offered a soup before your main meal. I ordered the soup, and when it was put on the table, it looked like a bowl of tiny noodles floating in hot water. I thought, *Surely it's got to have some sort of flavor.* No. Hot water with noodles. Big deal.

I also read on the menu that they offered grape juice. It was printed as "Grapes juice." I wanted to try it, thinking of the many vineyards there, and assumed that it would be fairly tasty. What the waitress brought to the table was not "grapes juice," it was GRAPEFRUIT juice. Yuck. Not with Italian food! Those two flavors do not mix in Italy or anywhere else.

One evening, we thought we'd live it up and go somewhere fancy for dinner. Surely, we'd get a traditional Italian meal or what we'd think of as traditional Italian. No such luck. It was bland. No real flavor to it at all. How disappointing. The best thing to eat there was the gelato—creamy and delicious and so fresh. And anything made of amaretto. And the pizza was good too. Stay away from the "traditional" Italian food.

We saw a sign down near the water advertising a beach party featuring live music that was to be held later that night. Before the sun set, we strolled down to the event. There were lots of Italians enjoying themselves, enjoying the music. Many were dancing and, of course, they were all smiling. Surprisingly, the Italian rock band was singing songs in English. After a few numbers, I realized they had no idea what they were singing about. It was the slight mispronunciation of the words and the inflection of the words they sang. They must've listened to recorded versions of the songs and memorized the words as they heard them. But they really did a decent job of it. Then it struck me, standing in the midst of all these Italians, I was the only American there. Stan and I were possibly the only two people in the crowd who spoke English. It's a strange feeling to come to that conclusion. A stranger in a strange land. It wasn't frightening or anything, just an odd realization.

As we walked back to the hotel from the town center, ancient two-story houses with pastel weathered facades lined the narrow winding stone streets. Decorating the front of each house, colorful and fragrant wisteria climbed to each rooftop. The houses looked otherworldly to me, but if I lived there, one of the ancient and weathered houses would be the home I would live in without giving it a second thought.

Always, when we traveled to foreign lands, I would wonder who would live in a house like that. Whether it be a small shack up the side of a mountain, nothing but a door within a wall of a village, or a two-story weathered house with wisteria wafting in through the windows, it never ceased to pique my imagination.

It Was Only a Recurring Dream

I could draw a picture of this town, but I've never been to it in real life. It's that vivid. It's exactly the same every time. It's a picture postcard type of place with a bridge crossing over a river that empties into a lake in the background. The part of town I always end up in is on a main street on a hill. I start at the bottom of the hill and can't wait to go through all the curious shops lining the street, the type of shops I love with all those trinkets and treasures they hold. But each time I go, the town clock strikes five, and all the stores close. Damn it. Reminds me of the song we loved so much in the seventies. When she gets there, she knows… You know the one.

Hello and Goodbye

After moving back and forth, I had lost track of Joe-Joe sometime after high school. On the Internet, I somehow got connected with my old boyfriend, BAD CHAD. I mentioned Joe-Joe to Chad, and Chad said he spoke to Joe-Joe all the time. Chad sent me Joe-Joe's phone number, and bingo, in no time, I was speaking to Joe-Joe. I learned of his history during the years-long gap between us. He explained that he had been married and told me that his now ex-wife was crazy, he couldn't take it anymore, and they divorced. Now living on his own, he had a good job and belonged to an Asian musical group (being one of the few Americans in the ensemble) that played instruments sounding somewhat like wind chimes.

Through this musical group, he had met his fiancée who was a Chinese music professor. Joe-Joe had traveled to China twice to be with her, and she had come to America to visit him. He was really in love with her, and they had been going through the many necessary requirements to get her to the States; then they would be married.

One night, when Joe-Joe was to perform with the group, a good friend, also one of the musicians, said he had something to tell Joe-Joe after the show. The group played their various pieces and went off the stage. Joe-Joe found his friend backstage and asked what it was that he wanted to tell him. Joe-Joe's fiancée had been murdered by one of her students over in China.

Joe-Joe was beyond heartbroken and didn't want to live without his true love. He was managing the best he could to get through each day, even though his reason for living was gone. My heart ached for him.

About a year after we had found each other, Joe-Joe called and said there was a concert he was coming to see in England. The band he was coming to see was a great band from back in our high school days; it was to be their last ever event. Could he stay with Stan and I for a few days?

It would be amazing to see Joe-Joe again after such a long time had passed. He did come over and he stayed at our house, and it was a pleasure to see my old friend in person. But there was a sadness about Joe-Joe. It was nothing that he said; his light was gone. And he carried his loss like a heavy woolen cloak that weighed him down in sorrow. I felt I should have a magic phrase I could say or maybe some sort of mystical verse I could chant to take his sadness away, but instead, all I could do was be as calm and accommodating as possible during his visit. After he left, we continued our chats over the phone.

A few months after Joe-Joe's visit, my old friend, Joy (I had kept in touch with since my days in Small Town), called and said, "You were friends with Joe-Joe, weren't you? I was reading the obituaries, and I noticed Joe-Joe died."

I was completely shocked. I had just found him after all that time, and now he was gone forever. Why? I asked her what had happened, and she said she didn't know. Of course, they don't tell you why in an obituary. I got on the computer and got in touch with Chad again to see if he knew what had happened. He didn't know and said there was a backlog at the coroner's office and that Joe-Joe's autopsy wouldn't be done for weeks. I asked him if Joe-Joe had any medical conditions I didn't know about. Chad said not that he knew of. Joe-Joe hadn't shown up for work, and when the police entered his apartment, they found Joe-Joe; his pet cats had been found there with him.

After I came to grips that Joe-Joe was no longer on this earth, my thought was, *Well, now he can be with his love in a beautiful place. I hope they're very happy together at last in eternity.*

It Was Only a Recurring Dream

Always going somewhere on the bus. Over hill, over dale, but where am I going? I never quite know where I'm going. Sometimes I get off the bus and shop or eat. Been to some fascinating places, though. Sometimes I'm somewhere riding through the rolling hills of England, sometimes it has the feeling of Mexico, and sometimes the surroundings have a Vegas feeling.

I once visited a place out of the '40s. It was a dance hall-bar-restaurant. The building was very art deco with shining gold statues, old-fashioned milk glass light fixtures hanging from the ceiling, and a black and white tiled dance floor. There were very ornate curved doors everywhere with gold filigree trim. I felt as though I was in a movie. The place was magnificent. Across the street, I found an old-time hand-me-down shop. All the items inside were very unusual and odd curious pieces of the past. I picked up each object in the shop, examining each one carefully. I bought a hat. I had a nice time but had no idea where I was. Soon I got on the bus again with no idea where I'd end up next.

Other times, I get on a plane, never knowing where I'm headed, never getting to where I'm going. The plane sometimes drives down the street on its wheels like a car, never lifting off the ground. It makes me feel anxious not having a clue why I'm on the bus or in a plane in the first place, aimlessly riding around, not knowing where in the world my final destination will be. If there even is one.

Mom and Dad Fly Across the Pond

Besides showing Mom and Dad all of our favorite places in England, we took the short flight over to France. And what a fabulous time we had.

At the Louvre, Dad was staring in awe at the Mona Lisa with a total look of wonderment and complete bliss. Stan quickly captured the moment on his camera, and that photo will always be one of my prized photos, one of my favorite Dad moments that still comes back to me and makes me sigh.

What a spectacular place the Louvre is. Everyone, everywhere, should see it at least once in their lifetime. You could be there for two weeks straight and not be able to see all the treasures it holds. Thousands of magnificent works of art all gathered together in one magnificent place. It's more than words can describe.

Paris itself, the City of Light, is called such for good reason, as it seems to shimmer even in broad daylight in all of its decorative splendor. With gold gilt work all around you and streetlights shining through globes of crystal, it doesn't seem real. Pretty pastries in all the bakery windows fit for a king, the charming sidewalk cafes, just the feeling in the air around you. As you can see, I fell in love with the most romantic city in the world.

One lunchtime, we found a pretty sidewalk cafe in which to sample the taste of France. We had a hard time reading the menu in French (we couldn't read it at all) and asked the waitress about a few interesting food items…basically, what they were.

Mom pointed to an item on the menu and asked the waitress, "Can you please tell me what this is?"

The waitress, not knowing much English, collected her thoughts for a moment and then replied, "Hmm, how you say? She's pink and swims in the sea."

We thought maybe she was trying to describe shrimp, but we weren't taking any chances and we all ended up having sandwiches.

The Look on Dad's Face...

Since Stonehenge wasn't far from where Stan and I lived, everyone who came to visit wanted to see it. After taking our tourists there quite a few times, we'd stay in the car while our visitors went to view the ancient stones. Then usually, we'd take the guests on to Glastonbury, which is very mystical: Land of the Hippies (even in current times). The best part of seeing Stonehenge when we took Mom and Dad to see it was the look of ecstasy on Dad's face as Dad took it all in. He stood there in the same spot for quite some time, and then he quietly said, "I've been waiting seventy-four years to see this."

Another trip we made during Mom and Dad's visit was to the seaside village of Ilfracombe on the southwestern coast. It's a lovely little place, one of the many in England; they're all beautiful and heavenly. Like most seaside places, the tradition of stringing brightly colored lights along the shoreline was displayed here too. The first time I saw this sight, I absolutely loved the old-fashioned look of it. It made me feel nostalgic.

We all went out and about to see the sights during the day, and then after dinner, we would go down to the bar for the nightly entertainment.

On one of those nights, they had a DJ who was playing the hits from way back; the small crowd of people enjoyed it, mostly senior citizens. A more "modern" song about the YMCA came on, and all the elderly ladies knew exactly what to do. Arms raised, they spelled out Y-M-C-A to the song. Mom and Dad had never seen this happen before and joined right in. Dad especially was having the time of his life. Easily amused, he was having such a good time. We all were. Something so simple sometimes can be so much fun.

Dunster, a small village that surrounds you with wonder, was another place we wanted Mom and Dad to see. Mom absolutely fell in love with the feel of the hamlet, and I think she would've been happy to stay there for the rest of her life. The main cobblestone street comes to an end as it rises up a hill to a castle at the top, guarding its residents below. I was always swept away into the history from the past. At these types of places, you almost expect to see nobility in regal dress pass you on the street on horseback or a hunched over old crone coming out of a thatched-roof cottage. So many times. I was totally transported in my mind to illustrations of my childhood.

Mom, Dad, Stan, and I had a pleasant day having a cream tea out on the lawn behind an ancient pub. Cream tea, if you don't know, is a pot of tea, plain scones, a small bowl of strawberry jam, and another small bowl of clotted cream. Clotted cream sounds awful, but it is one of the most delicious things you will ever have the pleasure of consuming. It's a cross between butter and very thick whipped cream. Need I say more? The idea is to put the jam and cream on your scone, a scone being sort of like a buttermilk biscuit to us Yanks. But who cares about the jam? Just slather that cream on and call it a day. I digress…

The day was sunny, there were roses, and there was laughter and it was close to perfect. Cream tea was Mom's favorite, she had decided, and then requested it for the rest of the time they were in England.

I loved having Mom and Dad there to see all the beauty and wonder of where I now resided. It was a wonderful experience for all of us and one none of us will ever forget.

Ye Olde English Oddities

1) The So-Called English Language

There is a cornucopia of sayings and slang words in the UK. Two of my favorites: if someone is a bit dippy, they're "away with the fairies." Or if a woman is a known runaround, it might be said. "She's had more men than I've had hot dinners!" Instead of saying, "Don't get your pants in a bundle," it's "Don't get your knickers in a twist." Another one I loved was "She looks like mutton dressed as lamb (rough-looking woman who tried to doll herself up but didn't quite make it)." It seems I heard a new one every day...

Two mispronunciations that made me cringe and my ears burn every time—the word sixth pronounced as "sikth." As in May twenty-sikth. There is no k in sixth. The other word referred to a sliver of something. Example: "Can I have a tiny piece of pie (sliver)?"

Answer: "Would you like a small slither?" A slither belongs to a snake.

Depending on the region you lived in, you might say, "I weren't going." Or the very best backward sentence I ever heard was, "I've asked she to marry I, but her won't." What? WHO created the English language?

It's not all atrocious, though. Some of the lingo is absolutely quirky, such as calling someone of the male gender "his nibs." Or Ollie always calls a baby a "babb-ee." And always, always, Ollie, just as he hangs up the phone after saying goodbye, he says in a sweet voice to the air, "Oh, bless." I pause because I know he'll say it. So endearing, and it gets me every time.

A common greeting is "All right?"

Not "Hello" or "How are ya?" Nine times out of ten, you'll be greeted with, "All right?"

If you answer, "Yes, I'm fine," they didn't really want to know in the first place. It's just a salutation. Stan had this "All right" habit when I first got there, and each time I came into a room, he said, "All right?" Till finally, one day, at the top of my voice, I said, "I'm fine! Stop saying all right!" And thank God he stopped.

When we had moved to Grandville all those years ago, everyone there said, "Where's it at?" Cringe, cringe, and ears burning. In England, it's, "Where's it to?" Just as bad. Each country, region, and town throughout the world has its own way of expressing their particular language with inflections and pronunciations. It's just that when you go somewhere entirely different, it takes time to tune your ears to newly said words.

2)   Food

The thing about food in jolly olde: They eat all sorts of things in weird combinations. Not weird to any of them, but stranger than fiction to me. Everything is on toast. I came to the conclusion that a lot of the filling foods they eat came from back in times of war when food was scarce and they needed to survive. Since the olden days, and for years after the war, the Brits just keep on consuming stuff on toast. There are beans on toast (the icky tomato-based pork and beans from a can—yuck). There's heated canned spaghetti on toast—yuck. If you order eggs and toast at a cafe, you'll get eggs ON toast. That's not yuck, but you must specifically say you want your eggs separate, not ON the toast.

Also, everything goes on a baked potato (always called a jacket potato), those same icky tomatoey beans, egg salad (called egg mayo), coleslaw, chili, and whatever else they can think of.

They all eat brussels sprouts and parsnips like there's no tomorrow. Mushy peas look disgusting like guacamole but are delish. And stuffing, as in turkey or chicken, is always served as hard little balls that taste like dirt. Coleslaw is considered a garnish or is eaten on a sandwich, not eaten on its own as a salad. And if you order egg salad, ham salad, or a tuna salad sandwich, it means you'll get egg with lettuce and tomato—no mayo (which is way too dry). Ham and tuna, the same (salad meaning lettuce and tomato, not salad meaning the main ingredient mixed with mayo as we have). If you want the American version, you must order egg-mayo, ham-mayo, or tuna-mayo.

Food with funny names: Toad in the Hole, a covered-in-pie-crust dish with potatoes and veggies inside, sausages poking their "heads" out through the crust symbolizing the toads, I guess? The perviest sounding one ever is Spotted Dick (sort of a rolled dessert dish made from suet pastry, fruit, and served with custard). The ingredients sound gross, and then to give it a name like that... It is a bit spotted from the raisins you can see through the pastry.

As for fab food in the UK, you can get a giant piece of salmon that will cost half the price of what you'd pay in the States. And huge shrimp half price too. And no one anywhere has creamy treats as creamy and dreamy as you'll find in any bakery. And the granary bread is heavenly too.

There's an Indian restaurant on every corner in which the food is served mild or hotter than hell, depending on your preference. It's delightful and different. Chinese takeout (take away) is the same as the US, but don't expect gravy with your foo young; disappointing to say the least.

My all-time favorite, fish and chips, is found on every corner also. The F&C, as I refer to it, is served up as a good-sized piece of battered cod and an enormous portion of chips, which are like steak fries in the US. And you must have malt vinegar sprinkled on the whole works, a bit of salt, and you're in for a cheap and tasty meal.

And I must praise the melt-on-your-tongue chocolate. I once brought some American chocolate back from the US, and when I offered it to my workmates, some turned it down flat saying, "I can't eat that, it tastes like wax!" They'll eat canned spaghetti on toast, but they won't eat our chocolate. Go figure.

At times, it was hilarious when we had guests over to our house to eat. Brits are very unadventurous eaters, almost afraid of food unless they know exactly what it is. If you put something on the table they've never seen, someone will say, "What is it?" Translation: "I'm not eating that."

Now I could see if I was from a Third World country or somewhere where they eat all sorts of fishy things, insects, or groundhogs for dinner, but for the most part, food is pretty normal in the US, and lots of foods in both the US and the UK are the same. I sometimes wanted to speak to my guests as if they were children: "Just try it, you only have to take a little bite to see if you like it. Please?" At an informal get together, I had made sloppy joes. First, I heard the usual, "What is it?" But once they were brave enough to try it, the guests gobbled them down, declaring how good they were, never having heard of such a "delicacy" as sloppy joes. My comment to them was, "In America, you start eating sloppy joes the minute you come out of the womb!"

Another time, Ollie and Grant came for a backyard picnic, and I served seven-layer salad—pretty commonplace in the US. I brought it to the table in a long low dish. Ollie took one look at it and asked, "What is that?"

Of course, I said, "Salad?" Like, what does it look like? They summoned all their courage and tried a small amount…and then ate it till it was gone.

I had the girls from work over at Christmas time, and I had made a Mexican meal (Mexican food in England leaves something to be desired, but you could find most of the components at the grocery store). The girls liked the tacos and the rice, but Kai spotted the refried beans and asked what it was (of course). I told her, "Refried beans."

And I heard her whisper to Sophie, "Ooh, refried, no way." They wouldn't touch them.

After the main meal, I brought out a delicious strawberry dessert that anyone would dive into, but I noticed Sophie wasn't eating it. I said, "Sophie, don't you like your dessert?"

She replied, "I expected it to have a different texture, so I can't eat it."

I'm sure there's a name for the particular phobia: the fear of food.

3)   Lager Louts

Lager lout. Definition: Noun; a young man who regularly behaves in an offensive way, typically as a result of excessive drinking.

People in England drink. A lot. Then they go crazy and destroy stuff. Drink, crazy, destroy. It's bad.

It was the one thing about living in the UK that was shocking, appalling, and out of control.

My first "I can't believe it" experience of lawlessness was one night at home. I would read, sitting by the boiler in the kitchen for warmth. I happened to glance toward the window that overlooked the backyard, and through the curtain, I could see an orange glow. It looked like it was coming from the alley. I set my book down, peered through the curtains, and saw that something was on fire in the alley!

"Stan! Stan!" I shouted. "Something is on fire out back!"

Stan quickly appeared and went through the back door, down through the yard, and out through the gate to see what was on fire. When he came back, he informed me that a car was alight. This is a common occurrence. When Stan's car broke down one time on a main street, two days later, it had been stripped for parts and then burnt up too.

Around October and into November, there's a traveling night-time parade that comes through the area. It's called a carnival, and it's not a carnival at all. It's what I've always known as a parade. With approximately four hundred floats, it's spectacular! All the floats have hundreds of colored sixty-watt lightbulbs on them, and as they glide by, you can actually feel the heat radiating from all those bulbs. Aboard the floats are people in costume, there's music, dancing, and all the floats have moving parts whirling and twirling. I was amazed by the amazing sight, and the floats kept on coming and coming for hours into the night.

As Stan and I stood on the curb, hypnotized by the conveyor belt of wonderment before us, we noticed some young unruly guys a few steps away. They were taunting the entertainers on the floats and then falling back into the old folks sitting in folding chairs at the edge of the street.

Having had a few (too many) previously at some local pub, they were obnoxious and annoying everyone around them. Finally, the police came along and spoke to the louts very calmly and politely. The louts got right in the cop's faces and shouted from inches away, "Fock off! Fock off!"

I was completely stunned. I said to Stan, "Oh, if they did that to the law in America, they'd be on the ground and in handcuffs."

The hooligans were then escorted off the premises. Within minutes, the maniacs were back, starting right in with their annoying shenanigans all over again.

Even more shocking occurrences happened downtown. More pubs downtown = more trouble. Early one morning, as I rode the bus to work, I couldn't believe my eyes as the bus pulled into the downtown area. A large burger restaurant with huge plate glass windows had been totally destroyed. The previous night, some rowdies/louts had bashed in every one of those windows. Seven huge windows in total had been completely smashed just for the "fun" of it!

Another morning, the store I worked in, one great big window had been smashed with the intent of stealing the latest cell phone on the market. To go to all the trouble and on the main street of downtown just to steal a small item to show off to your deviant friends... The glass was shatterproof, so the jerks never did get their grubby paws on the item they wanted so badly.

Phone booths (called phone boxes) again all the glass smashed come Sunday morning, the result of some heavy-duty indulging the night before. And it didn't stop there; playground equipment, broken. Why? Gee, let's drink ourselves into oblivion and then go destroy stuff. What a blast! What was the point?

And then there was pee. Everywhere. On my way to the bus stop one morning, I actually saw a guy in broad daylight peeing against the wall of a small shop. He didn't try to be sneaky or even to go down the nearby alley! No, he just stood there, peeing. I was completely grossed out and disgusted all the way to work that day. Downtown at night, on the weekends, cylinders pop up out of the sidewalks so men have a place to pee. Again, disgusting, but at least it's sort of a private place to go and not quite AS disgusting.

Mayhem, to say the least, on a Saturday night downtown… Wow, it's a war zone. Stan and I usually went out locally and only went downtown once on a Saturday night, and I never wanted to go again after what I had observed. All the young ones were out in full force. And they were sloshed. There was fighting, screaming, there was puking, peeing, and some staggered out into traffic and were nearly run down. It was like hell on earth. I'd never seen such a state of complete pandemonium. Utter chaos. Are we having fun yet?

It Was Only a Dream

I went to a library. There was a reading group that was meeting in the library basement that evening. I followed the spiral staircase down a few floors to where the meeting was being held.

I got about halfway down, and there was a young woman standing on a landing. She had long dark hair and terrible dark circles under her eyes. She looked a bit ghoulish or ghostly. She handed me a pamphlet and told me about the meeting downstairs. The way she spoke was spooky, and it struck me that she was evil.

I carried on to the meeting. When I got to the designated room, it was full of people that were lined up against the walls on all four sides. I spotted a group of three to four individuals nearby and approached them. The person who spoke to me said in a quiet creepy voice, "Oh, we know who YOU are." Something was seriously weird and wrong from there on out. Then someone else said, "Oh yes, we know all about YOU."

As I went around the room, they were all eyeing me. I was in deep, scary trouble.

Another person approached me and said, "Here, have a look at these." They had been passing around pictures of me and my family. As I looked at the pictures, a family member or friend would simply fade away, disappearing right before my eyes. As I looked around me at all these strangers, they all had pale, haunting faces. I needed to get the hell out of there! They were all out to get me!

I started to run as fast as my feet would carry me. Up all those winding stairs, up each floor, nearly falling several times. I reached the outer door and felt I was safe now in the parking lot. There was my mom and dad! I ran to them, "Oh my God! Mom and Dad! Those people are after me!"

They calmly said, "Okay, honey, see you later." What?

I got into my car, which happened to be a station wagon. The backseat had been folded down, leaving a large bare space in the back. For some reason, that space was filled with white butcher's paper, like the paper you use to wrap dishes in to move house.

I no sooner got seated behind the wheel, and I heard the paper in the back of the car rustling around. Someone was hiding under that paper! My final thought was, *That's it then, they're going to kill me.*

Gorgeous George

There're two guys I refer to as Gorgeous George: My longtime friend, George, and George Michael.

My George, as I mentioned, is extremely tall, just under seven feet and extremely good-looking. Actually, there was a time when people would tell "my George" that he reminded them of George Michael (except mine is taller). George and I had kept in touch through my moving and his moving. He met a Brit named Hal somewhere along the way, and they moved together to the north of England of all things! George and I were both now in England!

George hated it there in the north and moaned to me on the phone about what a dreadful place it was. One day, he called and asked if it would be all right if he lived with Stan and I, just until he could find a job, rent an apartment, and then Hal would come to join him. He had arranged to view an apartment in the same town Stan and I lived in, but when he came to see the place, it was a dump in a bad area, and the landlord seemed shady.

George was at his wits end. I told George I'd have to discuss it with Stan. I really had no idea what to expect from Stan... I gently proposed the plan to him, and without a second thought, he said, "That will be just fine." May wonders never cease. I myself had a few reservations. For one, I thought George may go out partying into the night and come in at all hours. I wouldn't take too kindly to that, and Stan would've had a fit. But I really wanted to help my friend.

George moved into the spare bedroom, feet hanging over the end of the bed since we had no bed suited for a giant. Everything went better than I thought with our new guest-cum-roommate. He was so very helpful and was willing to do anything I asked of him. If I ran out of milk, George would jump up out of his chair and say, "I'll get it!" We had a convenience store nearby, and with his long legs, he could run, get the milk, and be back in no time flat. It was great to have him around for all sorts of reasons. I so enjoyed his company, and as Stan got to know him a bit more, he loved George too.

I came home from work one day, and George had done a fabulous job cleaning the kitchen. It was sparkling clean from top to bottom. To this day, I have never met a better cleaner than George. I could never in my wildest dreams clean like that.

And George didn't party at all! He was most likely saving money to be able to get himself and Hal established in our neck of the woods. He was a perfect roommate, and I was a bit sad when he told us that he was moving to an apartment nearby (Nearby? Yay!).

It was wonderful having George close by again, and I really grew to love Hal too, the two of them being totally different from each other. George is larger than life in every aspect, and Hal is quiet, calm, unassuming, and very sweet.

The thing about George is his storytelling ability. He is one of the most hilarious people I've ever known. And because of his towering stature, he says it the way it is. He'll tell off a stranger if he disagrees with their attitude or mannerisms, and what is the person going to do to George? George could sit on a person and kill him. It's so amusing to see George in action because people will back down every time. He'd make a good bodyguard.

Here are some examples of George's entertaining tales:

Living in northern England, when he had his salon, George had a call from the police one night. The salon had been broken into. George had been sound asleep. He flew out of bed in his pajama pants, got into his car, and tore down the street to his place of business. Once there, he could see a gaping hole that had been smashed through the plate glass window at the front of the shop. The criminal in question had stolen a few hair products. That was it? Break a window and break the law for hair products? Sad but typical.

The cops that were there, along with George, studied the footage on the closed circuit TV. The slimy little perpetrator was in full view on the screen, wearing a colorful patterned sweater. As George and the officers went out to the front of the salon, George spotted the thief just down the road. In George's words:

"I hollered out 'Oi! Oi!' and took off running after the slime. Here I was in my pajama pants, no underwear, and as I started running, my wang was slapping to and fro inside my pants! What a sight I must've been!"

George caught up with the thug (with those long legs of his) and managed to hold him till the police caught up, and the jerk was duly hauled away.

Another public incident involving George's brashness took place in a popular drugstore. George and Hal were waiting their turn in line to pay for their purchases when George spotted a little girl standing at the counter with her mother. The tot was digging her finger into a small pot of lip balm. George poked Hal. "Look at that," he said. He had assumed the child had taken the balm out of her mother's purse. Then he made another discovery that, in fact, the impish one had taken the lip balm out of the display of many lip balms on the countertop.

George was appalled, sure that it would be put right back into the box with all the other fresh balms. He just couldn't stand the disgusting thought of it and just had to speak up. He loudly said, "I beg your pardon!"

The crowded store and everyone waiting in line went silent. George spoke up again and said to the girl's mother, "That is diss-guss-ting! You don't know where that little girl's fingers have been!"

The child placed the balm on the counter, and mother and daughter then turned to leave. George immediately snatched the pot of balm off the counter and said to the saleslady, "And don't put it back in the display!" slamming the pot down. After having his say and grabbing the attention of all the customers in the place, George turned and gallantly walked away.

George sees something annoying and calls people out on it every time. It's what everyone else wants to say or do but is afraid to be so bold. Not George.

I've known George for years now and love him as much as I ever have, probably more. He's a wonderful friend, and through his brazen forwardness, there's a warm, funny, and friendly side that his close friends, including me, get to bask in.

A Visit and an Emergency

Stan and I had a few visitors throughout the years, and some such visitors were Serena and Ed, all the way from Grandville, USA. We had a fun-filled time that included showing them all the sights, going on road trips, and having a few too many along the way. Stan and Ed got along well, so all of us made a good group together. It was just a scream having the two of them there.

We were all enjoying our time, laughing, talking, drinking, and laughing some more until the phone rang, and it was Lexi. "Mom, I think you need to come home. Grandpa isn't doing well at all, and we may lose him."

I went into a complete panic mode. I needed to get home and fast! Dad had some heart problems but had been doing quite well for a few years; Mom took such good care of him. She had prepared all his food with little or no fat, absolutely no salt, and on top of that, she watched him like a hawk. She was doing everything she possibly could to keep him well and alive for as long as humanly possible. The whole family owed her a world of gratitude for keeping our awesome guy alive. No matter her efforts, Dad had taken a turn.

Too late that day to make any arrangements to fly to the States. I hardly slept at all that night, worrying and waiting for morning to come to get going home to my daddy for what may be the last time...

As soon as I awoke, I ran to the phone and learned I could leave that same night. Stan rushed me to the airport, and off I went, nowhere near fast enough. I landed at the airport late and got on the bus. Mom came to pick me up. Dad had improved. Thank God.

The following morning, Mom and I got into the car and headed to the hospital. Mom hadn't told Dad I was coming, not wanting to alarm him, making him guess how close he had come to death. As we entered Dad's room, Mom announced, "You have a visitor!"

I walked into the room behind Mom, and when Dad saw me, his face lit up and he said, "Oh, honey, I'm so happy to see you! I knew you'd come!"

Maybe he knew more than we thought he did. And I was never so happy to see my daddy's familiar face and sparkly blue eyes. He was still alive and hopefully would stay that way for quite a few more years. There was no way I was anywhere close to saying goodbye.

My Boss, My Friend, My Beau

The phone was ringing. It was Sarah, now ex-wife of Phil I had worked with years back; we had all worked with Beau. I was surprised to hear Sarah's voice because even though we had been friendly to each other in the past, she was the last person I would expect to hear from. She asked how I was and then said, "I thought I should call you. Beau has been killed."

The color drained from my face. All I could say was, "My Beau?" I asked Sarah what had happened, and she said that nobody seemed to know. The word had been passed around the store where we all had worked. Beau had been somehow mysteriously killed, and as it tends to happen, the story ends up all misconstrued.

It had been about a year since I had seen Beau in person. Stan and I had gone back home to the US to visit and had made plans to visit Beau. It turned out to be a bittersweet reunion for Beau and I. It was the first time Stan had met Beau, but Stan felt as if he already knew him for the many times I had talked about him.

When we arrived at Beau's neat vintage apartment, he and I were overjoyed at seeing each other. We sat in his sunroom and began talking and talking, just like the good old days. Suddenly, Beau began to cry, and the horrible story he had to tell couldn't be held back any longer. Beau's latest boyfriend had committed suicide a few weeks before. He had hung himself. Beau explained that his latest love had been a troubled soul. Crazy hilarious Beau was beside himself with grief. I had never seen him so dreadfully upset.

When he finally managed to calm down, we decided to go have something to eat at a nearby restaurant. As we sat there in the restaurant, Beau sat across the table from Stan and I; he seemed okay, and we were having a nice conversation. Beau remembered his companion again, and silent tears rolled down his face. I got out of my seat and sat next to him, putting my arms around him; it was all I could do.

Through the weekend, off and on, Beau would turn into himself, his usual funny full-of-it self, then the nightmare came back to mind, and he would fall to pieces again. Wonderful to see my old friend again, but so sad to see him struggling through his grief.

Back in the UK, and the next time I heard from Beau was on the phone when he told me he had been promoted and, as a result, landed a job in New York City! He was beyond excited and couldn't wait to go. I was delighted for him and thought, *Yes, Beau, cheer up and just start over.* Beau was very talented at what he did. He was very creative, and really, he should've been somewhere big and fabulous like New York years ago.

Since I knew when he'd be starting his new life in New York, I gave him a few days to settle in and then called him to see how it was going. When he answered the phone, all I said was, "Well?"

He practically shouted on the phone, "Oh, girl, it's FAB-U-LOUS!"

I couldn't have been happier for him. He was running around in the middle of it all, still trying to get set up in the big city, so he couldn't talk long, but he would for sure call back when things were calmer, if they ever would be. Little did I know that would be the last time I would ever speak to my treasured friend.

After I had the call from Sarah, my mind was racing. What had happened to Beau? I got on the Internet and started looking for atrocious traffic accidents that may have taken place in New York. It was a long shot, but I had to know. There was nobody I could contact for any information since I had long since left that job back in the States, and the people I had known at the store had since left or I had lost touch with them.

A few years after I got that unbelievable call from Sarah, we went back to America to visit again. Stan and I were out shopping with Mom at a popular discount store. As we looked around, I heard who I assumed to be the store manager being paged overhead. "Mr. Wilson, pick up line one, please."

It hit me—Dennis! Beau's old boyfriend from our days at the store together! I hadn't seen Dennis in years, but we always got along. I'd love to see him, and maybe he would and could give me some answers about Beau. What had really happened to Beau? I went to the cashier at the front of the store and asked her to page Mr. Wilson. She said, "Who should I tell him is here?"

I said, "Don't, it's a surprise."

As the cashier paged Dennis, I stood in the main aisle of the store and waited. I saw him come toward me from his office in the back of the building. He looked straight at me, and when he got close enough to recognize me, I saw a big grin appear on his face. He called out my name in amazement and ran the rest of the way to hug me. He had always been so sweet. We chatted for a few minutes, and he said we could meet the next day. He would tell me what he knew about Beau's death.

The next day, Dennis and I met for coffee and a chat. He knew all about what had happened to his ex-love and my good friend. And it was really bad and terrible, and more than anything, sad and pitiful beyond words.

Dennis had actually gone to Beau's funeral. I listened to the story of Beau's horrendous mishap, and it made me realize once again how short life is and when your number is called…

After getting settled in New York, Beau had been partying with some of his new neighbors (Beau was not shy). A party had been held in a banquet room of sorts on the ground floor. Beau loved to drink and party and was always the life of the party. As the bash dwindled down, Beau said goodnight, stating that he'd go to the roof to smoke before turning in (no smoking allowed in the building). He went to the roof, smoked his cigarette, and started down the stairs to his apartment. And he fell and broke his neck. *Oh, Beau.* That was it. His new exciting life, gone. Just like that, from falling down some stairs.

I was more shocked than before, hearing the awful truth. And now so many years later, I still have a hard time accepting it. Another special person in my life that I could never speak to or laugh with again. *Damn it, Beau.*

Looking for Me Mum

Every now and then, it drifted through my mind to find my birth mother, especially since I lived in England, and she most likely did too. Stan would gently prod me now and then to find her, but you can't do much without a name...

So I started back at square one. The info I had from the adoption agency years before was non-identifying information. No help at all without the all-important name. All I could do was to contact the agency again. I put in a call to them, and oh, they could search all right...for megabucks. No way. And this is why: If I gave them a pile of money, several months later, they'd get back to me and say, "Sorry, we couldn't find anyone." How do I know? I don't. They've got my megabucks, and I'm still none the wiser. So hell to the no on that.

The agency did, however, give me other ideas of where to begin. They told me to start at the courthouse in North Haven near to my old home in the USA and to request my birth certificate. The birth certificate I had always had only said "Baby girl" on it. It contained my adoptive parents' names and absolutely no clues about anything else.

Okay, go! I promptly called the courthouse, first being told that the building where older records had been kept had burnt down years ago. Are you kidding? Oh, sure, that would just be my luck. But there was another way. I was told I would need to write to the judge who presided over adoption matters, giving reasons for why I needed my certificate (This made me mad. It's mine to have!). So they did have my birth records somewhere... I'd just have to jump through hoops to get them.

The lady on the phone also suggested that I "lay it on thick," meaning to appeal to the judge using my health issues, for a start. In addition to that, I could convey my deep longing and tireless search I had been pursuing for years (really, I had thought about it hundreds of times, but I wasn't going to die if I didn't find out; I just needed to make it sound like that). If that's what had to be done, so be it, and I began drafting my letter. One last thing the woman from the courthouse told me that day—and get this—was that it would entirely depend upon the judge's mood the day he reviewed my case. She said, "If he doesn't think you need to know, he can say no, and that will be the end of it."

What the hell? Who is he? God? I'd better "lay it on thick" and pour my heart out in the letter I was going to send.

And lay it on thick as clotted cream I did. I kissed the letter, sealed it up, and sent it off. Now just how long would I have to wait?

A few weeks passed, and I noticed a pile of mail in the usual spot where Stan always put it. I leisurely went through the mail. Bill, bill, advertising, bill, bs-mail, and then an envelope with the official heading on it from the courthouse! I was almost afraid to open it, thinking it could be a letter of rejection. "Stan! Stan! Look what has come!" I shouted.

Stan said, "Open it, honey, open it!"

I tore it open quick, and there it was—my official birth certificate with my mother's name on it! And the next thing I noticed blew me away. She had given me her exact same name, first and last! To say I was floored doesn't even describe how I felt about the whole thing.

Of all things, she was from Liverpool! "Ferry Cross the Mersey," my favorite song from way back—the Mersey River is in Liverpool! Shocking and amazing. I was beyond bowled-over! I said to Stan, "If this is all I ever get or all I ever know, it will be enough just knowing my mother's name. And the fact that she's from Liverpool!" Over and over in my head, I repeated her name: Maxine. And to think that would've been my name too had my dear adoptive Mom and Dad not given me the name they had chosen.

In celebration, Stan said, "Let's go have a drink and talk it over down by the sea."

Good idea. I needed to absorb it all. When we got down to the sea, we found a nice pub with a patio overlooking the water. Stan went in to get us some drinks.

The sun was shining, the water was shimmering, people were happy, and overhead, there was music playing, and I now had my mother's name on the tip of my tongue to say aloud anytime I wished—a momentous and perfect day. Stan shortly returned, drinks in hand, and as soon as he sat down, I couldn't believe what happened next… Now this was totally unreal, and you can believe me or not, but "Ferry Cross the Mersey" began to play! I am solemnly telling the truth. They say things happen for a reason.

Okay, I was in England, and that is a very British song, but of all the songs that could've come on right at that very moment in time? It was truly the icing on the cake! What a momentous day through and through, and I really did feel a sense of coming together, being a whole person as I had never felt before.

Oh No, and How Did that Happen?

Something weird was happening. My vision had become very blurred off and on, and I was always so thirsty. I've never been one to drink a lot of liquids, and somehow, I just couldn't get enough. I thought I should perhaps have a chat with my doctor.

I must give credit where credit is due. My doctor, Dr. Simons, was the best doctor I've ever had before or since. He was unassuming, had a casual bed side manner, and was such a kind and caring man. He would listen with both ears and gave me his undivided attention. He had such a personal way of dealing with his patients. He was a human being and not holier than thou as some doctors would have you believe. I had been so lucky to find him and thought the world of him. He was hard to get an appointment with at times because just everyone wanted to be seen by him. My sister-in-law, when she found out I was going to Dr. Simons, told me a lady she had worked with once said of him, "Oh, I could just fall in love with him."

Telling him of my symptoms, Dr. Simons ordered some blood tests for me, one being just a simple finger prick. And the finger prick told it all. That was it: diabetes. Why me? I clearly pictured my dear mother giving herself shots with those big long needles as if it had been yesterday. What really baffled me was the fact that me and Mom didn't even have the same blood. It wasn't hereditary. I had been adopted. Yet, here I was with the same disease. How in the world did that happen?

The good thing was I had Type 2 diabetes that could be treated with pills, not insulin and those big long needles. "Watch the diet,"

Dr. Simons had said. "If the pills don't work, then you may have to go onto insulin."

I hoped not. And I stuck to my diet religiously. No more cake for me!

My Main Man, Stan

Everyone loves Stan, one of the most genuine people you'll ever know. He used to drive his coworkers crazy when they would moan to him about what a drag it was being at work. His reply, "It's a good day today!" Followed by groaning from his workmates, his next comment was, "Every day is a good day!" That's my Stan.

He's fair-minded and gives everyone a chance. Although I never met Stan's dad, I would imagine that's who Stan takes after. From what I've heard from all Stan's relatives and friends, his dad was known to be even-tempered and kind to everyone, just like Stan. I wish I could've met the man who had such an influence on making Stan who he is today, the Stan we all know and love.

Stan's mum, having had a sad childhood from neglect and being ignored in general, was very quiet and closed, at least when I knew her. Always sweet to me, she didn't offer any information about her past. I can't say I blame her. What it must've been like for her, I can't even imagine, growing up and not feeling loved. So sad for sweet Mum.

It was so completely different the way Stan was brought up compared to my experience. The biggest difference being mostly the era of not having much in England and having quite a lot in the US. Not that I came from a wealthy family because I did not; we ate beans and hotdogs for dinner and had a few hand-me-downs we weren't too good to wear. Most of the money my dad made probably went toward Mom's medical bills and medication. But we had an indoor bathroom, for heaven's sake.

Stan grew up using an outhouse and has told me tales of "doing his business" as quick as he could in the cold of winter. Stan and his sister also took baths in a tin tub in the living room in front of the fireplace. They were behind the times in comparison to the customs and conveniences we enjoyed in the US.

Stan has told me of saving all his pennies in stacks on the fireplace mantle, and to this day, he's a good saver of money—lesson learned from those times when money was scarce.

At Christmas time (and this is cute), when Father Christmas came, he left Stan's presents in a pillowcase at the foot of his bed. I'm sure there wasn't much in the pillowcase, but his most treasured present he ever got was for his tenth birthday: a new bicycle! And wasn't he proud. Even though it wasn't brand-new, he shined it up and rode it all around the neighborhood.

At age eleven, he had a mishap and drove his prized possession into a stone wall, flipped over, and bent the front forks of his treasured mode of transportation. But he had a worse episode with the bike when he was twelve. The bike, being a bit wobbly from the first accident, Stan wobbled out into the street one day, forgot to look both ways, and *bam!* He was hit by a car and ended up flying in the air, landing on the hood of the vehicle. He was knocked out and was rushed to the hospital, unconscious. It was touch and go, but Stan woke up, and as soon as his eyes opened, he requested a glass of milk. After telling me the story of his brush with death, he stated, "And I'm still alive to tell the tale." I'm ever so glad.

Back when Stan was a kid, they didn't have the medical knowledge they do now, and they had to get along as best they could. Stan had asthma, and fresh air was thought to be the cure for everything. His mother, not knowing any better, opened the window in Stan's bedroom each night—fresh air. Stan said it was freezing cold, and the bed he slept in had a deep gully in the middle which he burrowed into for any warmth he could get. He'd wrap up like a cocoon in whatever bedclothes were available, and by the time he finally got to sleep, ice cold and uncomfortable in his gully, his mom was calling up the stairs, "Stan, wake up! Time for school." Stan was always so tired every day at school.

Also, Stan made many trips to the doctor. Besides the asthma, Stan had other ailments. He didn't eat much as a child, and it was a concern to get him to put some weight on his small frame. Stan, his mom, and his sister would all board the city bus for Stan's doctor appointments. Stan couldn't tolerate the smell of the diesel fumes from the bus, and his mother would ask the bus driver to stop the bus, followed by Stan getting out to throw up at the curb. The bus would stop every so often to let Stan out and back on all the way to the doctor's office. Stan despises going to the doctor even now, and I have to beg and scold to get him moving. Those frequent visits as a kid, I guess, he felt then and still, would be enough to last a lifetime.

As Stan grew up and became a teenager, he loved soccer as does every young man in England (Soccer to Americans, known as football in the UK). As an older teenager, Stan attended football games with various friends, and when Stan told me about these outings, well, they were barbaric. And the rivalry and vicious fighting that goes on at these games is still taking place today. A few times after these games, he and his friends got into knockdown drag-out fights with fans from the opposing team. Stan got the hell beat out of him and came home one night worn-out, clothes torn, and blood everywhere. After that, Stan decided it wasn't fun at all going to these games, and he stopped going altogether. Honestly, it's so brutal he could've been killed. I find it shocking and appalling that anyone could get so worked up over a dumb game that they would turn into animals defending their favorite team. What fun! I say idiotic.

Stan and his group of friends also went to the latest greatest clubs. They saved their money, now having jobs, and they all had fancy hip suits made to measure. They really felt they were "in the groove" with these new duds. And they all loved American Motown music. All of them. With all the great music coming out of the UK we were listening to across the pond at the time, they were intrigued by R and B and soul coming from the US. It's funny, you always seem to want the latest music, trends, and fashion from somewhere else, especially when you're young.

Bowling at the age of twelve, Stan then went on to playing darts in the pub when he was of legal age to drink. After that, he began playing the English game of Skittles at the age of about twenty and played it for years and years after. Skittles is a bowling game of sorts that uses small wooden pins and a wooden ball, smaller than a bowling ball. It's played in an array of pubs on a bowling alley with no two alleys being the same measurements. Some alleys are longer or wider, have a hump, or veer to the left or to the right. You just have to remember the characteristics of each one before you start to bowl. Few women play the game. It's mostly men who partake in this sport, which is only played in the west of England. Stan had known all the same players for years, and I went with Stan to watch him play. I too got to know this funny and entertaining bunch and then knew why Stan loved to join these guys, his comrades who heckled, joked, and enjoyed the not-too-seriously-taken game.

Stan does have a serious side, and when he gets churned up, especially if he's already mad, don't piss him off (so much like my dad was). But both his loving and serious sides have pulled me through more times than I can mention. (Dad again—they say subconsciously you look for someone like your dad, which is a good thing for me). He's always there with understanding and love when I've faced any upset or dilemma that's come my/our way. Whether I've had difficulties at a particular job, health issues, or just been down in the dumps, Stan stands beside me, and I know in my heart he always will. And that's the main thing about having a good relationship. Having someone who will always back you up and love you for your faults and all.

Everyone loves Stan. Me too. And I love to share him with everyone for the kind, witty, and the one-of-a-kind person he truly is.

It Was Only a Dream

I was alone, and it was early morning, not quite light yet, the time between darkness and sunrise. I entered the dining room in our family home in Small Town. I was my current age in the present time. I heard a noise like the soft ting of a cymbal, and it seemed to come from outside. I crouched down just under the picture window that looked out onto the backyard and the woods beyond. Just my eyes were peering over the windowsill. I was afraid of what I might see in the half darkness.

Then what I saw was beautiful, huge, amazing, and terrifying all at once. Mostly amazing. Very slowly and gently lowering down from the sky was a whole futuristic glittering city. It looked to be made of glass and shiny metal, like the Emerald City, only more space age. Small sparkling orbs were pinging and exploding everywhere around the whole floating city. Silently it hovered for a few minutes over the middle of the yard and then lightly landed on the grass. The entire large yard was filled with the spaceship city from another planet. I wasn't feeling afraid anymore. I just sat there, mouth agape, in complete and utter awe.

I heard a knock on the door, and when I opened it, there stood a spaceman in uniform like you see in sci-fi movies. Nothing was said. Telepathically, he told me to come with him. There was no use refusing because I knew there was no escape; his powers were much greater than my earthly ones. And I was outnumbered. Who knew how many others like him were aboard the enormous craft? Another telepathic message was conveyed, and I understood that these aliens were taking human women to their planet to inseminate them in order to populate their realm.

I knew I had a very short time to say goodbye to my family and friends, and then I had to go, no questions asked. They had come for me, and that was it. In the early morning hours, I went to family and friend's doors to say I'd be leaving and goodbye forever. Nobody answered their doors.

Another Kind Soul, Gone

Once again, my old friend, Joy, called, bearing bad news. She's one of those people that must feel her day is not complete if she doesn't read the obituaries. I started calling her "the angel of death." This time, she informed me that my old boyfriend, Jimmy, had passed away. It hit me hard. He had died from leukemia, and I hope to God he didn't suffer. Oh, Jimmy. He was the one who had driven me crazy in the past with his detective work, but all in all, Jimmy was a loving and caring guy, and he had been there when I needed him most. He had been good to Lexi and I and had spoiled us in many ways.

After we moved to Grandville all those years past, I had always wished the best for him. More than anything, I hoped he would find a nice woman that would love him for the kind and generous man he was. The new, better woman never came. He had been alone since I decided years ago that he wasn't the one for me. Now he was gone. May Jimmy have all his heart desires and be given the love in return that he so freely gave here on earth.

My Baby, My Best Girl...Must I Give Her Away?

Lexi was getting married, and the time had come for me to give her away. OH NO! It's the natural order of things, but I didn't want to do it. She wasn't going anywhere, never to return again, but in my secret thoughts, that's what it felt like to me. It stemmed from all that time we had been together for so many years. And now it made me feel like I may not be as important to her. Stupid, I know, but we were also best friends. The good thing is we still are today.

Beyond beautiful, Lexi was married under a beautiful decorative arch in lush surroundings located on a well-manicured golf course. The wedding was lavish, to say the least. Lexi had originally wanted the wedding to take place at the serene setting of the lake house of her new in-laws but was reminded that because of the steep hill the house was perched on, it would be difficult for the old folks and Lexi's friend, wheelchair bound, to be transported up and down.

Stan and I made the trip over for the wedding of my "baby." I was a bit apprehensive that I would be in the company of her dad, my ex, and his whole family. They were making the trip down from Small Town. Did they care to see me? Did I care to see them? Probably not. AWK...WARD. *Let's make the best of this*, I thought to myself. It's *Lexi's day, not mine.*

It was a bit odd at first, seeing Roll after quite a few years had gone by, and all the rest of the clan. I got to walk Lexi down the aisle, which pleased me to no end. Age had made Roll's walking abilities steadily worse, and by now, he was having a hard time getting around, in general. His mother told me they had taken him in a wheelchair to find and purchase some suitable clothes for the wedding.

I delivered Lexi to the altar, and then the most unnerving thing of the day took place: I took my seat in the front row, right in between Stan and Roll! There I sat with my ex-husband on one side and my current husband on the other. Part of the arch where Lexi and her husband-to-be stood was blocking my view, so in order to see, I practically had to lay across Roll's lap! Oh, for the love of God. Then the minister asked, "Who gives this woman to this man?"

Roll spoke up clearly, "Her mother and I."

Really? It was just so uncomfortable sitting there next to Roll after the past was long gone, and here we were again, side by side. Just too weird.

The rest of the day and evening went on fine, and everyone got along. I really did enjoy conjuring up old memories with Roll's sister, my old pal, Freda, from high school. However, Lexi's friend had done the seating arrangement and had seated me right next to my ex-mother-in-law for dinner. We chatted pleasantly, but it was so odd to sit so close to her as if nothing had taken place in between divorcing her son and now. I was worn out from the whole ex-family event. The main thing of all was Lexi had a good day and was happy. And that made me happy too.

Me? I'm Going to Be a Grandma?

I couldn't believe it. Me, a grandma... Wait, I'm not old enough to be a grandma. In my mind, Grandma—stereotype for old. It took some time for it to sink in, and when it did, as a first-time grandma, I wanted to be with Lexi to help her and be one of the first to hold my new grandson.

Traveling to America a week before "our" new arrival was due, we anxiously awaited the birth. Lexi and I had some time together on our own before the eventful day, and it was so good to have that time—mother-daughter time. We went to stay for a few days at her in-law's lake house, and it remains one of my most treasured memories (one of the many), the time we had together up in the peaceful woods, just enjoying each other's company. We talked and laughed and reminisced as we leisurely floated along across the lake.

Our reflective, happy, and relaxing time together came to an end, and we headed back to her house in time for her doctor's checkup appointment the next day.

Lexi was going to go on her own to the doctor. I had planned that day to visit a friend. What am I doing? I needed to go with Lexi! At the doctor's office, we went into the examining room. The nurse came in and took Lexi's blood pressure. The nurse then commented that the blood pressure reading was high, saying she'd return in a few minutes to try it again. The reading was still too high. Then the doctor came in and told us that Lexi would stay put and have the baby right now! Lexi had preeclampsia, a serious condition that can be fatal to mother, child, or both if not addressed immediately.

As soon as the doctor left the room, Lexi looked at me with tears in her eyes and said, "Mom, I'm not ready!"

In my typical, motherly voice of reason, I said, "You're ready now, honey!" We had both assumed it would be a routine visit to the doctor, not the birth; not today, not right now.

Lexi's husband raced to get there and I could see he was churned up with the sudden reality that this was it, and the baby would be born right now, today!

What an ordeal Lexi went through for her first experience of giving birth. She was induced to get that baby out. Right now. It's the most awful thing to see your own child in pain and distress and to know there's not a darn thing you can do about it. After what seemed like an eternity, I was kicked out of the room for the actual birth, which is only right that the mother and father share that intimate and life-changing time together.

Oh, I paced, I tried to read, tried to sit still—the anticipation was more than I could bear. I was also nervous and fearful that everything would turn out the way it should, considering Lexi's condition with the preeclampsia.

And all was fine, and a new most adorable baby was born. His name was Perry. And it felt pretty good being a grandma. Just being there through the whole ordeal, I went back in time when I had gone through the rigorous rite of giving birth, remembering a feeling of utter joy, relief, and disbelief. You now have a tiny version of yourself looking back at you. It's a monumental day in your life. For any woman anywhere.

The Best Dad in the World

Dad was not well. When his heart failed, the doctors had asked Mom if she wanted them to keep Dad going or let him go. Previously, Mom and Dad had talked about it. If they should have to cross that bridge, Dad said to let him go. On the phone with me, Mom tearfully said she just couldn't let him go. That is beyond a major decision to make, and I know I would've done the same. How can you just say goodbye?

Dad was a bit confused when he came around after the trauma, and Mom calmly told him that his heart had just done a "flip-flop." She didn't want to upset him by telling him he had been on death's door again.

Stan and I flew home, willing the plane to go faster.

He was in good spirits, but the trauma Dad had been through left him weakened, and he went to stay in a nursing home for physical therapy. He was having a hard time walking and needed professional help to get around.

When Dad first got to the nursing home, he had a nice private room for a time. Then someone worse off needed the room, and they moved Dad to a different room. The only room available for Dad was in the Alzheimer's unit, even though Dad didn't have Alzheimer's.

Joe, a pal of Dad's, came to visit the day Dad moved to his new room. Dad got into a wheelchair, and as Joe pushed Dad down the long hallway, the thought occurred to me, what if Dad thinks he has Alzheimer's for real? I said, "Joe, stop the chair!" I squatted down in front of Dad and looked into his eyes and said, "Dad, you're going to the Alzheimer's unit, but you DON'T have Alzheimer's."

Dad looked directly back into my eyes and said, "What did you say your name was again?" That was totally Dad's sense of humor. What a guy.

Everyone loved Dad at the nursing home, and he was the "talk of the town" among the residents and nurses alike. He especially enjoyed the sing-along. Once, when the leader of the sing-along didn't show up, Dad led the residents in song, singing an array of patriotic and religious songs all the old-timers knew.

I also got Dad a small CD player and some CDs of his favorite old music—jazz and swing. When I was there alone with him one night, he thanked me again for the music and told me he listened to it each night before going to sleep. On purpose, I pretended not to know the tune and words of the songs and asked him, "How does this one (or that one) go?" I wanted to hear him sing in his quiet voice. He was actually quite a good singer. And to see that glazed look come over his face (like the same look his sister, Auntie Angel, got on her face when she had sung "Danke Schoen") was a sweet and treasured moment with my daddy. By now, all my dad's sisters had passed away, and he, being the baby of the family, was the only one left.

Sadly, so sadly, Dad didn't get any better, and his next stay was in hospice. Nobody knew how much time he had left. But as ever, he was good-natured, and we all kept asking him if he was in any pain. He said he wasn't, and for that, we were all so thankful. One day, our immediate family was there—Mom, me, Stan, Vance and family, and Lexi. Dad asked the nurse if he could just dangle his legs out the side of the bed. The nurse decided that wouldn't be a good idea and gave him a flat no. She left the room. When the door closed, I said, "Yeah, bs, come on, Dad." And we all helped him to a position so he could dangle his legs. That's all he wanted, for heaven's sake!

That same day was the Fourth of July. Dad was happy he could see the fireworks from his bed. As we sat together, just the two of us that night, we chatted a bit, and I told Dad that Stan and I were heading over to Serena and Ed's. I promised we would see him the next day. I said, "Goodnight, Dad, the best dad in the whole world," which I had said to him every day, wanting him to have that in his mind always. Then I said, "I love you so much."

He said in a sleepy voice, eyes half closed, "And I love you, my darling." I had always loved it when he called me darling. He didn't say the special word all the time, but from the time I was a child and for years to come, when he called me darling, I felt the most loved.

I was exhausted from the day at the hospice, exhausted from the thought of losing my dear sweet Dad. Stan and I headed out to Serena and Ed's place. Ed retired early, having to rise when the sun came up the next day, off to work. I couldn't stay awake a minute longer and I too went off to bed. Serena and Stan were in for the long haul and stayed up, having drinks and talking, which they both show great talent in doing.

Around 2:00 a.m., I awoke. I thought I could hear a phone ringing. I did hear a phone ringing! And then it hit me: This was it. I jumped out of bed, ran to the phone, and it was Vance on the other end. I said, "Is he gone?"

Vance then confirmed what I knew was true. Then Vance asked if I'd like to come and see Dad before they "took him away." I told Vance that I'd call him back. Did I want to see my best dad in the whole world, dead? No, I did not. The last snapshot I wanted in my head, till the end of time, was our last sweet time together, me and my daddy, when he had called me darling in his peaceful almost asleep voice. I called Vance back and said I would come but not to see Dad or what was left of him. I wanted my beautiful memory to hold, just the way it was.

Since Stan and Serena had been up for hours, neither one of them able to drive, forget them bringing me to be with Mom and Vance. I myself was perfectly fine to drive but had an expired driver's license, having lived for years by now in the UK. What to do? I got on the phone to my old pal, Mandy, and asked if she could come get me and bring me to Grandville. She didn't hesitate, saying, "Do not let either one of those two drive!" *I hear ya, Mandy.*

My dad, my rock, my mentor, my friend was now gone. The end of another chapter in my life. Mom cried and cried and was distraught. Vance crumbled and cried and crumbled again. Vance was the lost, abandoned, grown man-child. I cried too but was glad in myself to have no regrets where my dad was concerned. He knew how much I had loved him, and I knew he had loved me back in the special way only a father can. Knowing how much Dad had loved the Fourth of July, I thought to myself, how appropriate that Dad had "gone out with a bang." He couldn't have planned that better if he had a choice.

Stan had gone back to the UK, hoping he still had a job, and thought it best to go in person to tell his boss that he needed to go back again for the funeral. The worst thing for me, besides the obvious, was not having Stan there when I needed him the most, but he had to go.

A formal funeral was held in Grandville, then our immediate family taking two cars along with Dad's ashes headed north, a long drive back to North Haven where Dad now needed to be. It was planned that we would have a gathering at the family cemetery on the hill so that Dad's old friends could take part in his memory.

When we reached our destination, I recalled when our neighbor had sung at Mom's funeral years—a lifetime ago. I wondered if he'd sing again at the cemetery. I hadn't even seen or spoken to Martin for years. I gathered my courage and called him. After a few words between us had been exchanged, I asked him if he could sing for Dad this time. Martin replied, "I'm terribly sorry. I just don't do that anymore. I'm older now and wouldn't want to embarrass myself or anyone else." I thanked him for his honesty and hung up.

So many old familiar faces I saw that day at the cemetery. Dad would've been pleased to see all of his lifelong friends, relatives, and acquaintances there. We passed out printed sheets of words to familiar songs everyone could sing along to. Martin and his wife were there, and when the singing began, you could hear Martin's crystal clear voice taking the lead. He could still sing beautifully, and it was a true gift to all of us that day. As Martin led us in song to Dad's favorite hymns, Mom poked me in the side, and there at the edge of the woods, a fawn timidly walked out.

Just minutes after the fawn leaped and ran away, a rainbow appeared just overhead to everyone's disbelief. A sad and mournful day for everyone, but those two wonders of nature seemed to help in a small and graceful way. Wasn't that just perfect as we all paid tribute to Dad.

After the gathering, everyone was invited to the large and stunning lake house owned by Mom's cousins who lovingly agreed to lend it to us for a luncheon that day. It was a lovely sunny day, and everyone had a nice visit with friends and relatives, some we hadn't seen in years. Later in the afternoon when the last guests had left, it was then time to release Dad's ashes into the lake. Lexi had recorded one of Dad's all-time favorite songs to be played at this time—"Sentimental Journey"—a song that had special meaning to me, the song Dad used to sing to me as a child as he had tried his best to get me off to sleep. That song, perfect for a heartfelt send-off as we sprinkled Dad's remains into the lake, the lake he had loved so much. Goodbye, Daddy, I'll see you in my dreams.

It Was Only a Dream but Also a Visit

After Dad died, I had quite a few dreams about him. I welcome these with open arms because I truly believe these dreams are visits. Whether it be my dad or another person I've lost, it's their way of communicating from beyond since they're no longer able to do it in person.

Dad appeared to me as a much younger man as a janitor wearing a gray uniform. He was sweeping the floor. Not a word was said between us, but he knew me, and I knew him, and we smiled at each other.

In another dream, my dad stood before me with a pretty wrapped present in his hands offering it to me. Again, not a word was spoken between us as I took the package from him. Immediately, when I removed the top of the box, I could hear the sound of the ocean, whispering the melody of the tide.

Peering inside, I saw the most shimmering, pearlized, iridescent seashell. It was so exquisite it looked almost otherworldly. What a beautiful gift—first to see my dad again and then to get such a thoughtful magical present from him.

Three Visits from Dad

Within days, after my dear old dad had passed away, Mom started receiving sympathy cards in the mail, most with monetary gifts enclosed. Mom immediately wanted to send thank you cards in return (I think, in part, it was to keep herself busy and to distract herself from the deep sorrow she felt). She went to find some thank you notes she was sure she had in the bedroom closet. She returned holding the box of notes in her hand, crossing the room to sit next to me on the couch. The notes were a forest green color with gold lettering on the front: "Thank You."

Mom then took out the first note, opened it, ready to write. In in a near whisper, she said, "Oh my God, look." And there in Dad's handwriting (what we always called chicken scratch), he had simply signed "Love, Grayson."

Mom and I looked at each other in wonder. She then pulled another card from the box. Same thing: "Love, Grayson." Then one more. And it too had the same message from Dad. Three cards altogether were signed exactly the same. One for Mom, one for me, and one for Vance. How can it be? When would Dad have signed these cards? No other message, just his signature. Had his spirit come back and signed them? I was convinced it was a visit from Dad. There was no explanation, except for he was thanking us. No, thank you, Dad.

The next visit came when Mom was sitting quietly at home alone and heard a crashing noise that seemed to come from the bathroom. She went to investigate, and there on the bathroom floor was a small framed picture that had fallen off the wall. The picture was one I had sent to Dad from the UK a few years before.

I sent it to Dad because it was an unusual print made by an artist, a silhouette of a golfer with the sun rising in the background. The picture could've just fallen on its own for no reason; however, the nail was still firmly in the wall, and the wire on the back of the picture was still intact. And why that picture, of all the pictures in the house? Hi, Daddy!

The third visit (all of these happened within days of Dad's passing) happened when Mom and I were leaving to go somewhere. We were out in the garage in the car when Mom suddenly remembered a letter she had left on the kitchen table. "Honey," she said to me, "will you go in and get the letter on the table for me?"

I went into the house and retrieved the letter. I got back into the car, and Mom said, "Who was on the phone?"

I replied, "Mom, the phone wasn't ringing."

She was certain she had heard it.

"I know why you heard it, "I said, "and I know who it was. It was Dad calling. He got to where he was headed and was just letting us know he's okay and is still with us." And if anyone would have the power and the will to send messages from the afterlife, it would be my dad. No matter how much energy it took, he'd find a way. And he did.

Me? Grandma, Again?

Grandson number two: little Jack. As I was unable to make it back home for his arrival, Lexi kept me up-to-date, sending me pictures via the net, starting with her big belly phase up until the time of giving birth, sending newborn pictures taken in the hospital. Baby Jack looked so much like Lexi with his full head of dark hair and his button Lexi nose. I couldn't wait to get there sometime as soon as possible, to hold "my" Jack.

I always called both the grandsons "my" babies as if I was the one who had given birth to them. I think when you go beyond childbearing age, you relive the experience so much so that the new bundle seems to belong to you. At least in your mind.

As Jack grew, Lexi kept me up-to-date each month, sending me short videos of Jack doing all those miraculous tricks babies do in their new world. She sent more pictures through the mail, and of course, I took them to work to show off. I was really tickled one day when a woman at work, in her Scottish accent, after viewing the pictures, said, "Oh! Isn't he a bonny lad?"

A Man and His Dog in the Great Beyond

I answered the phone. It was Mom, and her first words were, "Roll died." It didn't sink in.

I asked, "What are you talking about?"

Mom repeated, "Roll died."

I asked her why, and she didn't know, but she had spoken to Lexi, and that's how she knew he was gone. I hung up with Mom and immediately called Lexi. "Lexi, are you okay, honey?"

Lexi was crying and said she wasn't okay. Lexi had gone through a phase in her early twenties of coming to terms with who her dad was. Roll never quit his drinking. Sometimes he worked, most of the time not. He had never paid a penny in child support, and Lexi knew it. She felt slighted, and the bottom line was she wanted a regular guy for a dad. When she did see Roll, not often since he still lived in Small Town, hundreds of miles away, they got along well, and Lexi knew that in his own way, he did love her. And she loved him too. He was her Dad. I think she was just disappointed that he never really did anything with himself. She so wished for a very different type of dad.

I asked Lexi that day on the phone what her Dad had died from, and she said the family wasn't going to have an autopsy done because he had never taken care of himself, kept drinking, and never even went to the doctor. Everyone put his death down to his years of drinking. Sad. And hopeless. Lexi also said she wasn't really that surprised that he was gone with all those years living a poor lifestyle.

It was a while ago that he died, but I think he passed away sometime between Thanksgiving and Christmas that year.

I had so many mixed feelings. I had loved Roll with all my heart all those years ago, especially when we lived in the big crazy house with Auntie Shirley. Our "worldview" was near enough the same, and we used to have some really good discussions in general. On the other hand, he drank too much, picked too many fights with me, and sometimes didn't work. I wondered what our life would've been like had I struggled through and stayed married to him. There's no way...

I forgot to mention that Roll had a handicap. As a child, he had been given a polio vaccine that his parents came to realize later had not worked. Did Roll get a bad batch of the serum? So his right leg had been affected and it appeared as a child's leg; very thin, no muscle, just bone with skin covering it. The first time we were intimate, I must admit I was a bit freaked out when I saw his small leg.

Roll never had properly fitting boots because his right foot was smaller. He would buy the correct size for his normal foot, but he always wore about three or four socks on his other foot to make up for the space in his boot. He walked with a severe limp and would use his hand to help his weak leg move. He constantly had perfect strangers ask him what had happened to him, and when he got sick of the prying questions, sometimes he'd make up a fantastical story and tell the nosey person that he had completely wiped out riding his Harley.

It didn't take long for me to not even notice his leg and his limp; it was just part of him. Because of his affliction, from the age of eight or nine, he was taunted by the mean kids in the neighborhood and at school. His mom and dad told him to be strong and stand up for himself. I think it became a mantra, and by the time Roll had grown and left school, by God, he wasn't going to let anyone give him any shit whatsoever. That's a good thing for anyone to live by, and you shouldn't take crap from anyone; however, I think it became so ingrained in Roll's head that it made him a bit of a bully, now doing what he did best—standing up for himself. I think it was part of the problem we had when we were together.

He had become so tough that he had a hard time being understanding with me. He had to be right, and according to him, he always was.

He wanted to fight for no apparent reason, but I really didn't want to fight and would tell him so. He actually asked me once, "Can't you just fight to fight?"

Why? If you're going to fight all the time, why be married?

All of these thoughts came back to me, reminiscing about our time together, thoughts whirling inside my head of how we began, of when our dear daughter was born, the good times, the bad, the terrible, and finally, the demise of our marriage. I never hated Roll. I guess in the end, after his death, all I was left with was that Roll had gone off the track and had never found his way back. Oh, for things that could've been and should've been. Now my ex-husband I had loved, despised at times, and had said goodbye to years ago had gone off to the great hereafter, doing what he loved best: sitting near a campfire out in the woods with his favorite dog, listening to some old jazz music, drinking a beer. And I hope he's happy doing just that.

After Roll died, Freda's husband sent me a DVD he had composed—old pictures of Roll in different stages of his life, a copy of the DVD shown at Roll's funeral. On New Year's Day, when Stan was out at work, I pondered, *Should I watch the DVD?* It was a good time while Stan was away. I'm sure he wouldn't have any real desire to view it himself. It was more of a personal thing for me. Not knowing if I really wanted to fall into the past, not feeling the way I once had for Roll, I got my head together and put the DVD in.

The first picture was of Roll as a teenager, a familiar picture I had seen before (No commentary, "You've Got a Friend" playing in the background). *So far, so good. I can do this…*

The next picture did it. There was Roll, holding Lexi as a newborn baby. I completely broke down. The tears fell and did not stop. I was crying and sobbing through the rest of the tribute of our past: Roll's, Lexi's, and mine. At the very end was a compilation of pictures of various old friends, some I hadn't seen in years. As I recognized each one, I spoke their names out loud and kept right on crying my heart out. I was completely wrung out when the heart-wrenching memorial ended. I have never ever watched it again.

About a half hour later, after I had sort of managed to pull myself together, the strangest thing happened. I was dumbfounded by it.

I had purchased a new calendar for the upcoming year at a pop-up shop downtown. The calendar had appealed to me because each month depicted poster art of France. I opened the first page, being January, of course, ready to hang it on the kitchen wall. The first picture I saw was intriguing. It showed old-fashioned women in big poofy old-fashioned dresses; they were riding in a hot air balloon, floating above a city. I studied the picture, and somehow, I thought the city below the floating women looked familiar. How could that be? I happened to notice a teeny sign on one of the buildings in the city. I got a magnifying glass. Maybe I could make out the message on the minute sign.

And I couldn't believe my eyes! It wasn't France at all. It was North Haven, the city I had grown up with my whole life, where I had gone shopping with Dad for my special dance, where I had worked at the bar and the pizza factory, and had attended the vocational school! North Haven! The city I had grown up knowing so well forever ago. The city that had played a significant part in my life was right in front of me on this day, miles and miles away from my past in America (The calendar had even been purchased in England!). The very same day I had been wiped out by my "blast from the past"—the DVD with all the pictures of bygone days and tender emotions. Astounding. Happy New Year.

Finally Found Me Mum

Everything was perking along as usual and as normally as ever. I still worked at the "La-La" department store. Shelby (now my boss after Barry had left for greener pastures) and I sat talking at lunch one day, and I told Shelby my adoption story and added that I would someday find my mother. Then Shelby said something that would change my life. He told me of a friend of his that worked for a TV show in London, tracked down missing persons, your birth parents or whomever you were looking for. He said he would look up the website that night at home and bring it to me the next day at work. Would something really happen this time? I said to myself, *Don't get your hopes up.*

"I have nothing to lose, I'll give it a whirl," I told Shelby as he handed me a note with the info he had promised. Stan had tried to help more recently, trying different sites on the net that said they could locate someone, but each time the feelers were put out, nothing came of it. It was nice of Stan to help, and at times, I think he was more keen to know than I was.

I got onto the site Shelby had recommended. I filled out the necessary requirements, which mostly asked how much I knew about the particular person I was searching for. Information? I had zip. I did have my mother's name now and knew my nationalities and where I had been born. I also had the basic information I had learned from the adoption agency years back.

I had a reply within a few days via e-mail, informing me that they had a backlog of cases they were working on, but in due time, someone would get back to me. Yeah, yeah, that's what they all say. The wind went out of my sails, but I had tried...

Two days later, I got a call from a woman with an American accent! Her name was Gina. She was from the TV show, and I told her what little information I had, hoping it would be enough that she would take me on. She thought my story interesting and said she would have to consult her boss; it may be a few days until she could get back to me. She was sincere, and I believed her when she said she would let me know what the decision was. Only two hours later, the phone rang, and it was Gina again with good news that her boss had approved my story. I was shocked and elated.

Gina and I then had a personal conversation, and besides both of us being American, there were lots of similarities between us, one being that she had also married a Brit, nice for going through the process I was about to embark on, having a new friend on the other end of the phone. Gina also told me that the expert searcher who worked with the show would be calling me soon to confirm my story.

Sure enough, a few days later, I got a call from a lady named Celeste who promised she would do all she could to help me find my mother or whomever she may be able to locate. She asked me questions about how I felt, if I was ready to know the truth whatever it may be, and warned me that my mother may not still be alive. In her kind and professional way, she assured me that she would do her very best. I believed every word of it. Celeste had been searching and helping people for years, reuniting them with their long-lost families.

Now I was getting somewhere. At last. The next part of the process was for the camera man and interviewer to come to our home and film for the show that would be aired on TV sometime in the near future. In the meantime, Celeste kept searching. A date had been set for the filming to take place in my living room! I had never cleaned the house so much in my life! I'd be damned if my living room was going to be on TV across the whole country of England, not looking near perfect!

The young woman and young man that came for the mind-blowing event showed up, and the woman fussed with the pillows and the throw on the sofa, rearranging them. I guess she was trying to make my home look as homey as possible. I was a bit annoyed and said to her, "Okay, don't portray me as an old granny."

She then decided she'd like to film and interview me sitting at the dining room table. The camera was switched on, and she began asking me deep questions (making it dramatic for TV, I'm sure). Little did she know that I was not as desperate as some people are on these types of shows: tears in their eyes, barely able to speak that they've thought about their long-lost person every waking moment of every waking day, and if they don't find their special person, then they will shrivel up and perish. As I've said, I wanted to know like every other adopted person on earth, but my life would go on, and I knew I wouldn't cease to exist if my mother, in my case, couldn't be found.

The interview went on, camera rolling. The young woman interviewer was trying every angle she knew to get me to cry. I don't recall what she finally said, but she got her moment for TV, and I began to cry. Not wail, but a few tears slid down my face. Shortly thereafter, they had what they wanted to capture on film and wished me luck and said goodbye. I felt rather foolish for succumbing to Miss Interviewer's psychological methods of getting me to cry but secretly thought to myself, *Good, that oughta get me on TV!* Hee-hee. Really, it had nothing to do with me being on TV. For me, I just wanted to locate any family members out there, somewhere out there in the big wide world.

At least a month went by, and I had a call from Celeste. She said she found someone who matched my mother's date of birth. Celeste explained that she had driven to the woman's house just outside of London. Celeste actually went and knocked on the woman's front door. Once inside, she informed the woman of the reason for her visit. Celeste asked the woman some pertinent questions, and the woman denied ever being in the US, ever. Celeste was just reporting to me on what she had discovered and told me she'd keep searching. I got straight on the phone after this latest news. I had to tell Mom back in the States what I had just heard. Mom and I were both convinced that the lady Celeste had paid a visit to was lying through her teeth and was not going to admit to being my birth mother for whatever reason. How could you not claim your own kid? How dare this unknown woman hide from the truth!

I thought perhaps that would be the end of my and Celeste's search. Never mind. I thought I would still be just fine going on with my life not ever knowing. I'd have to be. Oh, well, so close and yet so far away...

A few more weeks passed, and Celeste called to inform me that "the show must go on;" the show had gone into production. I was no longer to be on the show since she still had not located my mother or anyone else. Then she said something very generous. She said it wouldn't be fair for her to stop searching. Celeste normally charges a fee for her services when it's a search not connected with the TV show, but in this case, since I had waited patiently and she had already done work on my case, she said she would keep searching, at no charge. Celeste had no idea that she had given me one of the greatest gifts I had or have ever received. I thanked her a million times over. She didn't have to do that for me, but she did, and I feel she was put on this earth for the sole purpose of bringing lost people together.

Bless you, Celeste, wherever you are. I will never be able to thank you enough. I thought about her name: Celeste, as in celestial, which is a perfect name for her because she was one of the few angels I've come across in my lifetime.

A few weeks passed again, and THEN, I heard Celeste's voice on the other end of the phone line, and the whole thing came vaguely clear in ten minutes time. Her words were, "I found your mother."

I said, "You did? Really?"

Celeste replied, "Yes, but sadly, she's no longer with us, and your sister is gone too."

Oh no, I was too late to meet either one of them. But before I had a chance to absorb the sad news, going at a speed faster than lightning, Celeste blurted out the whole history about all the family I had never known. Good thing I can write faster than lightning because I scribbled down every word as she spoke. Names, dates, places, and a history of who was married to whom, and when, and last names I had never heard. Names of husbands, wives, their children, and everyone in between, starting from the roots, all the way through to the tips of the branches of my unknown family tree.

I have a sister. I have a sister (or did), kept playing over and over in my head. That bit of heartbreaking news that she was gone forever was devastating to me because all my life, I had longed for a sister and always felt that somehow, she had been missing more in my life than even the mother that had given birth to me. Celeste informed me that both my sister and mother had died from pancreatic cancer and that I would probably want to see my doctor to be on the safe side. I thanked Celeste for her warning, a serious warning I must heed.

Tangled up in all the dates, places, and history, I found out that my sister, Flora, and I had the same father (that rarely happens) who was American. He was married and had five children with his wife in America. Busy man, he was! He was in the armed services, and when he had been stationed in England, to put it politely, he and my mother, Maxine "got together" on at least two occasions... My sister had come before me, four years prior to my birth. When my mother became pregnant with me, it was agreed that my father would leave his wife. When that didn't take place, my mother then traveled to the US, gave birth to me, and returned to the UK. After that, Mother got involved with another American guy, moved to the States with my sister, and married. Again, it didn't work out, and back to England again. She was on her own for quite a few years before she met an Englishman this time. They got married in later life and were happy together until she died.

Whew! A lot to take in so quickly.

Finally (and this was why she talked so fast), Celeste gave me the number of my niece who was living in northern England and said, "You better hurry because your niece, Fern, is leaving in a few minutes for Spain." What? I had to gather myself within seconds if I wanted to talk to a real blood relative—my niece, my sister's daughter! What would I say? "Oh. hi, it's me, your Auntie!" Given no time to absorb all I had just taken in, I dialed the number Celeste had provided. The good thing was Celeste had already conversed with Fern, and she was expecting my call.

A young-sounding woman answered the phone. I said, "Fern?" Fern said, "Yes it's me."

I asked if she had been totally surprised when Celeste informed her that she had a new family member. Her reply was one I hadn't expected. Fern said, "No, I wasn't very surprised that you existed because my mom and Grandma were all over the place. They traveled everywhere together." But since Fern was on her way out the door, off to the airport, she promised that the minute she got home again, she would give me a call, and we could further discuss the whole saga.

I sat there, stunned after hanging up the phone, mind whirling, heart racing. Instantly, now I knew everything I had ever wondered and thought about since childhood. I read through my hastily written notes again, then rewrote them. I could actually understand what I had written in what looked a bit like hieroglyphics. Wow. I had some big, big news for Stan when he got home from work.

Back from her trip, Fern and I talked and talked on the phone. She filled me in on some of the other questions I had longed to ask. She told me that her mother (my sister) and her grandma (my mother) had traveled extensively; they had been stuck together like glue—inseparable. Would I have been the third wheel? Could I possibly have been pushed aside had mother kept me too? Maybe I would've been a nuisance and disrupted their bond. I then asked Fern the all-important question. "Did my mother tell anyone about me?"

She gave me an answer I didn't want to hear. "No," said Fern, "but my mother would've been over the moon had she known about you."

My mother had died before my sister. Now don't you think, perhaps on her deathbed, she might have said to my sister, "By the way…" I can't imagine keeping a huge secret like that till the day you die. Did my mother never ever tell a soul? Wouldn't you have a close friend who you could confide in and who would keep your secret safe, just for the asking? Evidently not. I asked myself all the normal questions: Did she think of me? Did she wonder where I was? Did she wonder if my parents had been good to me? I would never know. No one would ever know. Since I had never felt a pull toward my father (like I had with my mother and the idea of having a sister), I then asked if Fern knew where my father was. Was he still alive? Of course not. He was gone too. Everyone was gone.

Later that night, Stan and I were watching TV when it suddenly hit me. I said to Stan, "Everyone is dead."

Stan said, "Yeah, they are."

I said again, "They're all dead."

Stan said, "And?"

Getting a bit hysterical and nearly shouting, I exclaimed, "EVERYONE IS DEAD!"

I went through the list of those I had held near and dear: my sweet mom, wonderful dad, my birth mother, birth father, my sister, grandmas, grandpas, and a slew of aunts, uncles, and some really dear friends, not to mention my ex-husband and an important-at-the-time years ago boyfriend from the past. Do regular people experience this much death in their lifetime?

Fern and I both knew we would have to meet face-to-face as soon as it could be arranged. Since she lived in northern England, it would be a day's worth of driving for either one of us. Fern was married and had two kids and also had a brother, my nephew, Andrew (a few years younger than Fern, she now being in her mid-thirties). And my sister's husband, Tim, my brother-in-law, was still alive. He and Andrew both lived near Fern. So when at last I did get to meet Fern, I could also meet Andrew and Tim. It couldn't be soon enough. Stan said we could make the journey there to meet my other family at last. And soon.

Here Goes Nothin'

I decided I'd better go see Doctor Simons about the news of my mother and sister, both having died from pancreatic cancer, before I came to the same sorry end. I explained to Dr. Simons that I feared I would be next, meeting my mother and sister soon on the other side. He said he would send me for some tests just to be on the safe side, beginning with an endoscopy. Ick. Tube down the throat to see what could be seen. Ick. But it was a matter of life and death, so "Ick" it was.

The day came, and I went for the test. I was given a twilight drug which is the weirdest thing: awake but not awake. I swallowed and swallowed the long tube. Now and then, I could feel the tube snaking around in my innards. I remember howling out, "Owwww!" a few times, and when at last they pulled the tube out, oooooh, it felt like a snake being pulled out of my throat.

When I was good enough to leave the hospital, I stated with great conviction to Stan that I would like to go across the street to where George worked to say hello. George knew about the procedure and couldn't believe it when I came through the door. He laughed and laughed and told me I was acting loopy. I thought I was behaving perfectly normal.

The results came back from the endoscopy, and it hadn't shown much since the pancreas is behind some of your other guts—the sneaky pancreas…hiding in wait…to rear its ugly head…and kill you.

They do call pancreatic cancer "the silent killer" because you can feel just fine, and suddenly, it's too late. Scary stuff. So the next plan of action was to have a Whipple's Procedure done where the bad part of the pancreas would be removed. Okay. I had no choice, and the "show must go on (which is ironic for me to use that saying since the operating room in the UK is called a theater)."

Three Families Are Better than One

Within a few weeks, Stan and I were on the road at long last to meet my new family—my other family, my real blood relatives. I squirmed around in the car, I sang to the radio, I fidgeted, I fretted for about four hours straight till we finally pulled up in front of Fern's house. I practically ran to the door. I rang the bell, the door opened, and there she stood, my Fern. My niece. What an attractive young woman she was! Tall and blonde with a big, beautiful, wide smile. Instinctively, we hugged.

As Stan and I went into the house, there were several others there. Fern's husband, Mark, Fern's two kids, the oldest a little girl named Chelsea, and a little boy named Harry. Then another person I hadn't known would be there, Tim, my sister's husband, Fern's dad (my brother-in-law). Wow. Here they all were. Fern said that her brother, Andrew (my nephew), would be there soon.

We all sat down in Fern's kitchen, and she brought out the pictures. *Well, here we go...* This was the first time I would see my mother and my sister. The picture of my mother I stared at for a long time. I definitely saw similarities. We had the same eyes and face shape, so strange and wonderful at the same time looking at a picture of someone you resemble. I had never looked like anyone in my family before. Then I saw a picture of my sister; tears came to my eyes. All I could muster was, "Damn it, I really wanted to talk to her." She was pretty, short like me, but had dark hair, and though we looked dissimilar, I felt a strong bond between us. Then came a picture of my father. Nothing. I felt no connection whatsoever. Weird. He was dark-haired, where my sister's dark hair had come from. I remarked, "Yeah, there he is." I was so not interested in him.

As I looked through all the photos, I realized that especially when we were both younger, my mother and I looked very much alike. One picture showed my mother in a party setting with a silhouette of her face, mouth wide open, laughing. I couldn't believe it. I said with excitement, "Oh my God! It's me!" It is exactly how I look when I'm laughing hysterically.

There were pictures of my sister as a teenager, a real beauty, then a bit older with her beloved Tim and then holding my niece as a baby. A few years later still, a picture of my sis with both kids, Fern and Andrew.

Quite a few pictures were of my mom and sister together. It was true what Fern told me. They had been glued together. This made me feel even more that I would've been the little pest in the way of the closeness they obviously had together. Fern told me that Mom and sis liked crossword puzzles and were also interested in anything to do with words. Me too! They were best of friends, just like my mother and I had been and Lexi and I are. I didn't feel jealous. I just so wished I could've known them, even for a short while before they left.

One picture showed Mom and sis on a train, sitting at a table, having a drink. My mother had written on the back of the picture about what train it was, making a reference to James Bond probably being on that same train. My mother's handwriting!

A few years before my sister died, she went to visit my father's family in America. Flora, Tim, and Andrew made the trip to meet our half brothers and sisters (our mother and father both deceased at that time). There were a few pictures of that trip showing all five of our half brothers and sisters. I told Fern I decided I didn't look like any of them. "Except for this one here," I said, pointing at the photo. I had just, for the first time, seen pictures of my sister and hadn't even realized that the person I was pointing to was her!

Another of the pictures that struck me was of Mom, Flora, and Fern together shortly before Mom and sis had passed away, my niece, Fern, being in her early twenties.

In that particular picture, there's a strong similarity between my sister, Flora, and my Lexi; they both have dark hair and the same oval face. They definitely looked related.

Fern told her husband, Mark, to go find the movie of when they got married. Fern thought it would be nice for me to hear my mother's voice. She had given a short speech at the wedding. It was a bit muffled, but I got to see her alive and hear her voice. And I saw my sister alive too, though she didn't speak in the video. What a gift to see them both alive and happy and having a good time.

My mom had been married when she died, to a sweet old guy named Mac. He was still alive, and I said to Fern that I'd truly like to meet him one day. He didn't live far from where Stan and I lived. In fact, Mother (when she was still alive) and he lived there when I had first come to England. I just hadn't known then that she was a mere few miles away. Of anywhere in the whole country she could've lived, it was so nearby. Fern also told me that after Mom died, Mac had found my birth certificate all folded up in Mom's wallet. Mac tried to search for me himself but had no luck because, of course, I had a new name from my adoptive parents and I had also been way far away in the US. Good of him to try.

Fern then spoke about when her grandmother (my mother) and her dear mother (my sister) had passed away. Mother went first and had been sick for a time. By the time she was seen by a doctor, her time had run out. My sister had been a bit more proactive, but "the silent killer" had already done it's evil job, and it was too late for her. They died within a few years of each other. Mother had been seventy, and my sister was only in her forties. And then a shocking revelation: My sister had been cremated, and her ashes were sprinkled into the River Mersey as the song "Ferry Cross the Mersey" was played! Unbelievable but true. That wonderful song I had loved since I was a little girl had followed me through my whole life. This would be the last reference to my all-time favorite song to date. And how could that even be? I was and continue to be stunned by it.

Andrew (my nephew) and his girlfriend, Tina, showed up, and what a pleasure it was to meet them. What a handsome young man he was. I knew that all the girls and now women probably never left him alone. He was adorable and funny too.

It was almost time for dinner, and Fern said there was a pub just down the road we could go to. This is when I got a chance to get to know Tim a bit more. Tim is a few years my senior, and what a nice mellow guy. I can see why my sister fell for him. He's blonde and tall. Fern takes after him. I think Tim was a bit mesmerized by meeting me. For one, not knowing I even existed for all these years, and secondly, that I must have had similarities that he knew all too well, having been my sister's husband and my mother's son-in-law and having spent lots of time with both of them.

We all said goodbye, hugs and kisses all around. Tim gave me a big hug, and I saw tears in his eyes. He said how very glad he was to meet me and that he just couldn't get over it.

Stan and I went to our hotel, and I talked a mile a minute. He told me about his discussion with Tim. Stan said to Tim, "So what do you think?"

Tim replied, "Well, LaVonne is Maxine and Flora rolled into one. If I put LaVonne's American accent aside, even the tone of her voice is the same."

Poor Tim. It must've been like seeing a ghost. Two ghosts.

I decided to go outside for a smoke. Standing in the darkness just outside the hotel, I looked up into the night sky. I saw a Chinese lantern floating by. I said, "Hi, Mom." I thought, *Let's have another one for my sister.* Lo and behold, another lantern appeared. Then another one. *That's me,* I thought. And that was it, just three—Mother, my sister, and me. The three of us together at last up in the sky.

The Big Op or Is this the End?

I had to have some pre-op tests done, heart checked, etc., making sure all systems were go before anyone could cut me open and do their thing. Lovely...

Since it was nearing Christmas, several people told me that my operation wouldn't be done till after the holiday and that all the doctors and surgeons would be somewhere abroad, soaking up the sun. So I was quite surprised when the phone rang just days before Christmas. It was the hospital, checking to see if everything was on for me to come in the day after tomorrow for my operation. The woman on the phone said they had sent me a letter confirming the date, time, and other information about the surgery, which I never got. Well, it was probably better not to have more time to be nervous and freak out. Just go in and get it over with. That's not to say I wasn't afraid. I was.

Here I was in a foreign country, about to have a big operation, not even knowing how big it would really be... I was used to the hospitals in America, and at that, the few small operations I had in the US were not much to speak of compared to what I was about to face.

I spoke to Lexi quite a few times before the big day was to take place, and she said the smartest thing. "Mom, a surgeon is a surgeon is a surgeon. They know what they're doing, and it won't be their first operation."

Thank you, Lexi. That helped. So many people through the years would say that Lexi was beyond her years in wisdom, and they were all correct.

The day before the surgery, I was increasingly scared to death. I called George (Stan was at work). I told him I was freaking out and started to cry.

George said, "I'll be right there!" My longtime friend got on his bicycle and pedaled like a bat out of hell and was at my door within minutes. That's what you call a true friend. All six-foot-eight of him put his arms around me and assured me that all would be fine. Shortly, Stan arrived home and tried his best to comfort me, but that night, I hardly slept.

Early the next morning, I readied myself for the unknown, having calmed down somewhat because really, what could I do? Have the op or die—my two choices. *Think I'll live today.* My good friend, Fiona, wanted to come with Stan and I that morning to lend support and to give me a cuddle (hug as we Americans would say) before I went "under the knife." Did Fiona think it would possibly be the last time she'd ever see me? After all, her dear husband, Roger, had died from pancreatic cancer. Later, I thought that was very brave of her to be there for me when the love of her life had left her by no choice of his own. But she wanted to be there for me. She was so sweet, always.

I had to say "goodbye" to Stan and Fiona as they hauled me away to my fate... Someone walked me down to the operating room (the operating theater—is it like a stage play?). Just next to the "theater" was a small room where five nurses waited for me. They helped me dress into a surgical gown, and I think they washed my hands and face. I was so nervous by now it's hard for me to recall exactly what they did and why there were so many of them.

But the thing I remember and will never forget: In my petrified state, not knowing if I would ever see all my loved ones ever again, especially my Lexi and my Stan, I started to cry, feeling completely helpless and hopeless. The oldest of the nurses, short with a kind face, dark hair in a bun, came to me and gently put her arms around me, enfolding me with her compassion. She put her hand on the back of my head and gently rested my head on her shoulder. I don't think I've ever had such a comforting and meaningful hug like the one she so genuinely gave me as I did that day.

Many times, in the years after that day, I wondered if she was an angel. I'm truly convinced that she was. I've also thought if I had gone back to ask for her, someone at the hospital would inform me that there was no such person working there, proving my theory. So now I must thank this beautiful angel-woman for her utmost caring gesture of kindness at a time in my life when I needed it most.

*****

When I awoke, I was alone in what seemed to be a giant gymnasium-sized operating room. I could hear some old doo-wop music quietly playing in the background. *Strange. I must be alive because I don't think I'd be hearing old '50s music if I was dead.* A woman appeared out of nowhere and stated matter-of-factly, "Oh, you're awake then (like, oh, big deal)." It sure was a BIG deal to me.

I was wheeled on a gurney into an elevator up a few floors into a dark room where a young male nurse and female nurse transferred me to a regular bed. Wow, that hurt. And the thing that hurt the most was both of my arms. Why? They ached like I had swum the English Channel. The two nurses washed me and tried to make me comfortable. I remember being overwhelmingly thirsty. All I could picture in my mind was a giant glass of 7 Up filled to the top with ice.

It was two in the morning by the time I was settled. I had lost all sense of time. The male nurse looked up and said, "You have a visitor." Another thing I'll never forget: The vision of a dark silhouette coming closer and closer. It was my sweet, loving husband, Stan. As he came into focus, I was never so happy to see anyone in my life. He leaned over and gave me a kiss and said how happy he was to see me. We had a little chat for a short time. He said he would return the next day, telling me he loved me and that I had come through with flying colors. Thank God.

The young woman nurse left, and the young man, John, would be my caretaker. What a kind and calmly mannered guy. I could not have asked for a better person to care for me after the whole ordeal I had just been through. I asked him all sorts of questions, and he gave me clear and concise answers. I asked him, "Do I have a big cut?"

He replied, "Oh, it's a 'biggun'."

I also asked why my arms hurt so much, and he explained that my arms had been pinned over my head for the whole TWELVE hours I had been in the surgery. I really had been out for a long time.

The next day, having been moved to another room and having said goodbye to my pal, John, I was in extreme pain and was given morphine every few minutes. I remember begging for more, and I was moaning in pain as I had never experienced before. Suddenly, I began to shake violently, teeth chattering. Little did I realize I was overdosing on the morphine. Instantly, the room was filled with medical staff encircling the bed. One young woman seemed to be in charge, and I managed to say to her in total panic mode, "I can't breathe! I can't breathe!"

The answer I got has haunted me ever since. "Well, if you don't calm down, you're not going to breathe." UNREAL. Is that what you say to someone who thinks they're about to die? And that's what I believed was happening to me. A simple "Just relax, and you'll be fine" in a calm tone of voice would've been sufficient, thank you very much. But to say what was said in such a sarcastic way was not, in any case, the response I should've heard. One by one, everyone who had dashed into the room began to leave, abruptly leaving as fast as they had arrived. The first young man who dashed away had been at the left-hand foot of the bed. I truly thought he had disappeared because what use was it for him to hang around when I was going to die now? He wasn't needed anymore. I asked, "Where did he go?"

And the next shocking answer came. A young Irish nurse replied in her lilting accent, "Why? Do you fancy him?"

The remaining staff all chuckled. Not funny. And so inappropriate, especially considering I thought it was the end for me. Then the Irish Miss tried to distract me, asking me all kinds of questions about my personal life. I knew what she was doing, and I didn't appreciate it. Her demeanor and her accent irritated me. When they all left the room, I asked the attending nurse, "Am I all right now?"

She told me yes, that I was.

I then asked, "Do you promise?"

She gave me a flat, "Yes" and left the room.

Still not convinced, two young nurses entered the room and went behind the head of the bed and started whispering. Okay, that freaked me out all over again. Were they whispering about what to do now in preparation for my death? After a few more minutes had passed, and I was still coherent and breathing and thinking, I had to assume that I would live.

Could anyone, anyone, have given me an ounce of encouragement? Evidently not.

Again, I was moved to another ward in the hospital, which was dimly lit. I could hear a weird motorized noise nearby, some sort of contraption keeping someone alive, I assumed. It was creepy and irritating. Stan was sitting next to me, and I almost asked him what kind of little bugs were flying around the room. They were beautiful, small, flying insects—nothing scary. They looked like mayflies. I then came to realize: *Lavonne, it's the drugs. There are no bugs in this room.* Once I knew I was hallucinating, I rather enjoyed the graceful winged creatures floating around in the air.

Now average hospital rooms in England are not the hotel-like rooms of the hospitals in the US. No TV, no phone, and drill sergeant-type nurses on duty, day and night. And you share a room with other people. Thank goodness I had some lovely women in my room, and aside from the drill sergeants, a few of the nurses were some of the best. All in all, a very odd experience.

I was moved to a shared room. One of the surgeons came to see me and explained what they had done. After they had made the enormous incision, which one of the surgeons referred to as my "shark bite," they cut off the first part of the pancreas and sent it to the lab... bad. They cut off another piece and sent it to be examined...worse. The next part was even worse, so they removed the whole thing. And as long as they were in there, they removed the gall bladder. Now they had some "plumbing" work to do and had to reconnect things, guts and tubes leading from one thing to the next (my interpretation of what the doctor told me). So in the process, they had to remove part of the intestines and part of the stomach. No wonder it took twelve hours!

A few days later, my feeding tubes were removed, and ahhh…I had all sorts of visitors and became friends with my roommates. I remained in the hospital over Christmas, but I was alive. The main doctor in charge allowed me to go home for a few hours on Christmas day. I moaned all the way home every time Stan went over a bump. But it was worth it to be back in our own cozy home if only for a short time.

I must reminisce about the ladies I came to know in our shared room. I got to know them quite well during our stay, and what a memorable bunch they were. I had just had a giant operation, and I felt that all three of my roommates were way worse off than me.

The first one in the bed next to mine was named Maggie. She was jaundiced when she was admitted and also had dementia. She must've been a real beauty in her younger years. She was a stately, blonde, and a real sweetheart. Next, opposite from me, was Gertrude or Gertie, another sweet older lady, rather timid and so very sick. She was either throwing up or messing the bed, having no control of her bowels. The poor, poor woman. The last woman, over in the far corner, was named Ethel, only a few years older than me. And she could be feisty. She would tell the nurses off daily if something didn't go in her favor. However, I got along with her just fine, and I think her cantankerous ways came from the fact that she was very sick too and was totally miserable. I could sympathize.

Maggie, since she couldn't remember from one minute to the next, would repeat herself all day long. The minute she awoke each morning, she would start pestering the nurses for a sleeping pill. She wasn't even aware that it would be hours and hours till bedtime when she would at last get her precious pill. Every day, she would ask me where the bathroom was, even though she had been there many times each day. I would tell her that it was right across the hall but ended up taking her most of the time. Repeat, repeat, repeat—all day long. This seemed to irritate everyone else in our room and the nurses too, but I really didn't mind. She couldn't help that her memory was gone.

Once, around 2:00 a.m., she said, "LaVonne, are you awake?"

I replied, "I am now…" I didn't sleep well the whole time I was there as it was, and then, when I managed to drift off, Maggie would wake me up. It was amusing to me, and we would whisper in the middle of the night. The sad thing with Maggie was that hardly anyone ever came to visit her. I think once her family came (her still being there when I left) to visit, and they stayed for a short time like it was "putting them out" to do so.

I wanted to take her home with me. The day I left, Maggie said, "Goodbye. I will miss you."

I said, "I'll miss you too, Maggie."

Then she said, "I love you."

I told her that I loved her too. And I did.

Gertie had been taken off food and liquid for a few days. I guess they were trying to get her meds regulated because everything she ate or drank seemed to cause her trouble. A few family members came to visit one day, and they gave her a can of cold pop. She was in heaven with her cold refreshing drink. She begged the nurses for something to drink, and most of the time, due to her condition, was denied.

Wide awake as ever in the middle of the night, I was craving a nice cold fizzy drink. By luck, earlier that day, I had discovered a vending machine with nice cold fizzy drinks. I got out of bed and made a beeline for the machine of my dreams and brought enough money to get Gertie a drink too. When I got back to the room with the two prized cans, I found a straw, opened the can, and tiptoed over to Gertie's bed. I whispered, "Gertie, Gertie, look what I have for you."

Gertie opened her eyes, and the cutest thing happened. When she saw the can with the straw poking out, all she did was purse her lips. Not a word was said. I put the straw to her lips, and she drank, and her face lit up. She thanked me and thanked me. No thanks necessary. It was her sheer enjoyment that was more than thanks enough. Then the dear soul asked how much she owed me! I said that I supposed I could afford it. It's moments like these that make your life worth living. Again, something so simple. And before I left to go home, Gertie said she wished I were her daughter. She had never had any children. Ahh...I would've gladly been her daughter.

I could've exchanged phone numbers and/or addresses with Maggie, Gertie, and Ethel and kept in touch with these endearing friends I had made, but I didn't. No, what was done was done, and I now wanted to put the whole trying experience behind me. I wished them well, hugged them goodbye, and went home to finish recuperating.

Before I went in for the operation, I had wanted Lexi to come, but I also couldn't drag her away at Christmas from her two kids, my grandkids. So she came when I got home. It was so good to have her there. I felt pretty good when I came home, aside from having to sleep in an upright position, and climbing the stairs was a task, to say the least. While Lexi was there, Fern and her friend, Vick, came to visit, the first time Lexi and her cousin, Fern, would meet. And they got along like they had known each other forever. Vick had known my mother and sister for years and was now meeting the long-lost auntie. She made a comment that day that I even had the same posture and stance as my mother had. It had to be strange and neat for her, too, doing comparisons.

Another great thing when Lexi was there visiting was that she and Stan had some time together. I told them to go and see the sights one day. I'd be fine on my own. They went on a short road trip, Stan showing Lexi some of the local attractions. I wanted them to have some bonding time together, two of my favorite people.

After Lexi went back to the States, and I recovered a bit more, I returned to work.

A few weeks later, I had the thought that since my life had been spared, and I was still alive, I should like to move back to the US to be with my beloved Lexi and my two precious grandsons, Perry and Jack. I wondered what Stan would think of my big new idea, but I seemed to remember that he had expressed to me more than once that he would like to give it a whirl in that big country across the pond.

I broke it to him gently, and he wasn't opposed. Plans were made, and a few weeks later, I was on my way. Stan stayed behind to sort out all the legal immigration documents he needed to have before he could join me. I hoped it would be sooner rather than later…

I must say that I love the UK. It's a calm and beautiful place to live. It never felt chaotic or rushed or insane the way it can in the US. I would gladly live there again, and it could happen… Who knows?

But for now, I'm back "home" with my Stan, my Lexi, my awesome grandkids, along with the rest of my family and friends. As much as I love my immediate family, I also love my extended family in England and my newfound family too. And I will forever feel that I have one foot there and one foot here, my heart reaching miles across the water to both shores.

And Flora Wrote a Book Too

I was amazed once again when Fern told me that Flora (her mother, my sister) had written her life story, something I had always talked about doing, even before I found out about my whole new grand finale. I also would've liked to compare notes with Flora of how we grew up, our similarities, differences, and dreams. I find her story to be as close as I can ever get to having an idea of who she was.

Unfortunately, Flora's life ended too soon, and she didn't get to finish her story. I've picked out some interesting and humorous bits to share with the world since she never could.

Lower House Lane, Liverpool

This was the first house I can physically remember living in. It was situated in the district of West Derby and was virtually in the first row of houses in Liverpool that you reached if approaching from Manchester. The house belonged to (or more likely was rented by) my grandparents.

My grandmother had died just before our return from America. I only know that I had been to America because there are photographs in existence of me as a very young child eating a big American ice cream in front of a big American car.[1]

---

[1] Your faithful author here: I think this part was where I entered the picture and was placed for adoption. My sister was four years old when I was born.

My granddad was actually known as Charlie. No one, including his two daughters, ever knew why. He was very short at just over five feet, the sole survivor of triplets. He was of uncertain age, but Mum believes him to have been in his late seventies when he died, which was quite an achievement considering his lifestyle. He liked nothing better than a "nice bit of ham" that one of his dubious friends had "provided" (stolen) which could last him for weeks. He drank his tea with condensed milk, and I, for one, never saw a piece of fruit or a fresh vegetable in his house. He would rinse pans and plates out under cold water with no detergent, and if mum hadn't changed his bedclothes for him, it would've never, ever been done. He chain-smoked Woodbine cigarettes, which have always been strong, and drank as much as he could, relying on the generosity of customers as he got older and became a pot man (a collector of empty glasses) in a local pub.

He was always a bit of a scoundrel from what I've been told, in and out of work but generally quite happy about it. The family were as poor as everybody else in the street (apart from Mrs. Quinn who my mum and Aunty were forbidden to speak to as she had "gentlemen callers"). Grandad liked to be liked and when he was in work, he would make his family despair by giving money to other kids in the street and buying more than his fair share of drinks in the pub. I knew nothing of this and was very fond of Charlie, not least because of his knack of tell-

---

This would explain why only looking at pictures did she know she had been to America. At four years old, would you realize your mother was pregnant? Or would Flora have thought Mum was just fat?

ing tales which I realise now were probably figments of his imagination. Later on, I would ride for miles on my bike to visit him when he was a security man on the docks. If truth be known, he probably pilfered more from the warehouse than he protected. When he died, they found nearly twenty brand-new shirts still in their wrapping.

Burnard Crescent, Kirkby

Mum and I then lived with Aunty Jo and Uncle Barrick and their three children—a girl and two boys. The houses in the area were like dream homes to most of the pioneers, particularly those who had never had a front garden (yard), let alone a rear one as well and especially an inside bathroom. Strangely though, the majority of houses still had open fires, and the running joke was that the more simple-minded thought the bath was to keep their coal in. Although we had the four-bedroomed house, it was very small, two doubles (bedrooms that would fit a double bed) and two box rooms (bedrooms that would fit a single bed). Mum and I shared the front double, Aunty Jo and Uncle Barrick the other.

My cousin, Jayne, was in one tiny room, and the two boys in the other.

Through child's eyes, I thought ours was the nicest room in the house. Everything secondhand or homemade, of course, but Mum has always had some style and could make something out of nothing.

We mostly ate as a family in the tiny dining room with the adults at one end and the children at the other. I don't know if it was deliberate or not, but the salt, pepper, and any other condiments were always placed at the adult end and never offered to the children. As a result, I have never developed a taste for them. Apart from meal times, I felt an isolation from my extended family. Mum and I were the original team. I'd spend many hours toward the evening, kneeling up on my bed, looking down the street, waiting for Mum to come home from work.

I got to take ballet lessons that were very amateurish in a converted Nissen hut![2] Mum made me a tutu by hand for a show the class was staging. In fact, now I can't remember wearing anything apart from my school uniform that wasn't handmade by my mother.

Everything she made for me was quite out of the ordinary and commented on. I hope I was as grateful for that then as I am now.

I also joined the Brownies, St. Chad's first pack. They were an adventurous lot. If it wasn't raining, Brown Owl would take us around and about, foraging through the woods, fishing in the ponds behind the church, sitting in a field, singing Brownie songs. When I was nine, I wrote a poem for the *Liverpool Echo* newspaper, children's page, which got published. It earned me ten shillings and sixpence with which I paid for Mum and me to get a bus into Liverpool, get into the cinema, have an ice cream each, and get the bus home. When I was older, I had to leave the Brownies and join the Girl-Guides. I went twice. All they wanted you to do was sit in a draughty old hall and knit.

---

[2] I had to look this up: A Nissen hut is a prefabricated steel structure for military use made from a half-cylindrical skin of corrugated steel, designed during the First World War. In America, it's called a Quonset hut.

Now in the early 1960s in England, and fashion was everything. No teenage girl worth her salt was going to be seen dead outside school with a hem that was any less than three inches below where her underwear finished, pan-stick on the lips, and great streaks of eyeliner anywhere it would go without being too obvious. Hence a group of us would get just far enough into the park to avoid any teachers and hitch our skirts up to the required length. The ties would get loosened, and hats would be perched as far back on the head as possible, or in the case of a beret, stuffed into pockets. These measures needed to be quickly rearrangeable in case of an unexpected sighting of a teacher or a far more dreaded prefect, which were the girls who stayed on at school to study even more on their way to bigger and better things. They could give out detentions to the "lower" school for the slightest things.

We appreciated living in Belem Tower, me and Mum on our own again. The grounds were well tended, and things were fixed quickly. Everyone who lived there was proud too. I get quite incensed nowadays when I hear disparaging remarks about high-rise blocks. I can only assume the people who live there aren't trying hard enough.

New Year's Eve was a fine occasion when the residents who wanted to would leave their front doors open and have snacks and drinks ready for anyone who called. There would be a conga up and down the stairways, and just before midnight, we would gather on the balconies to hear the ships foghorns sounding on the River Mersey to herald in the new year. The flats were also ultra-modern. Fitted cupboards in the kitchen, glass interior doors, and at last a gas fire. We were so happy there that when Mum met her husband-to-be rather than move to just about any house she fancied, she chose to transfer to a bigger flat in Belem Tower when one became available.

His name was Bob, and he came from Alabama. He was eighteen years older than my mother and completely grey but very nice-looking and extremely pleasant. Over the course of a year, though only a few visits to Liverpool, he produced an engagement ring, which we still refer to as "the rock." Bob and Mum got married, and Bob went back to sea. Everything was wonderful.

Almost immediately, we started to travel. Thankfully, it was the period before schoolwork got serious, and it wasn't unusual for me to take a few days off school every couple of months to meet Bob's ship at various ports around Europe. We especially got to know our way around Belgium, Holland, and Germany, staying at lovely hotels, eating foreign foods in wonderful restaurants, and generally having the time of our lives. It is amazing how quickly you can adapt to a completely different lifestyle. We became jet-setters with the greatest of ease.

I was fifteen when we went to Alabama. I spent the first week or so being carted round to various relatives and places of interest in what seemed to be the biggest car in the world on the widest roads in the world, and all I could do was gawk, open-mouthed at these huge houses, and assume everyone who lived in them was wealthy beyond belief.

Talk about being a novelty. At sixteen, we had a stream of visitors who had just come to look at me. I don't think they were disappointed—as pale as a sheet, full sixties makeup, and the inevitable miniskirt. Everybody wanted to know what the Beatles were like in real life.

Back in England again, and I was interviewed and accepted by the Wallasey College of Art to take a diploma of Art and Design over three years. Wallasey is a largish town situated on the Wirral, which is a peninsula on the other side of the River Mersey. Not quite seventeen, I wasn't quite old enough to drive at that time, so for the first few months, myself and the only other two students in the college to live on the Liverpool side of the river would take the ferry back and forth. "The Ferry Cross the Mersey" was a song made very famous in the '60s, and there was a certain something to sing about.

Mum had met a new friend named Hilda, and they met with a circle of friends at a pub called The Merebrook. The landlord mentioned to Hilda that he needed a barmaid, and Hilda volunteered my services without asking me, and the very next evening, there I was. I was soon asked out by a chap named Peter. He had this idea that he had reached some sort of career pinnacle at a tender age. He was so satisfied with his achievements that I took to calling him "life at the top." In fairness, he was quite a pleasant chap and said all the right things to Mum. Problem was that I was far more interested in his work colleague, and poor old "life at the top" was unaware that he was taking me to parties and other occasions where my sole intention was to seek out Tim.

Tim was the one with the mohair suit, nice line in ties and, shame on me, a Triumph TR5 sports car. We eventually got to talking at a party and ended up sitting in his car to carry on the conversation. Poor daft Peter actually knocked on the window to ask if I was ready to go home. I really, really hope Peter's career was all he wished because he didn't come up to much in the romance stakes.

It was at this time that life with Bob had become unbearable. It was so easy to forget he existed as he was at sea for such long periods. The problem was that when he did arrive home, each homecoming became a little more fraught than the last. Just moodiness at first, then general irritability, and finally, bad temper. His behavior became bizarre. He would accuse us of making a fool of him and say that we were talking about him behind his back. He made up ludicrous stories about Mum's friends to make her distrust them. Finally, one evening culminated in the smashing of an expensive glass in the fireplace and the telephone wires being ripped from the wall. Eventually, things calmed down, and he was all apologies and promising the world as he always did, and we said we would give him another chance, but we didn't.

He went back to sea within the week. We waved him off at the Manchester airport, and no sooner had we arrived home, we got a call from him. He had landed in Ireland to board his ship, but the ship was being repaired, and he was on his way home. A few phone calls later, and much hurried packing, we found ourselves taking refuge at Hilda's daughter's house, the whereabouts not known to Bob.

Eventually, he had to return to his ship, and we moved back into the house for just long enough for me to get married and Mum to form an everlasting friendship with Mac.

In a nutshell, what then happened to mum was that Mac had left his overbearing wife and was staying in a bed and breakfast. He arranged for a room for Mum at the same place. Bob had gone back to Alabama and reneged on any maintenance payments, so Mum got a job. However, in the fullness of time, she did get half the profits on the sale of the house, which weren't that great as we hadn't lived there for long, but the amount was almost exactly the same amount Mac's father had left when he died, and together, they had a tidy deposit for their home together.

Flat 4, 25 Warwick Drive, Wallasey

Apart from our bed, cooker, coffee table and the odd gift, Tim and I furnished our first home with secondhand bits and pieces and acquired everything else we needed along the way.

We didn't have a traditional wedding, preferring a simple civil ceremony with immediate family and a few close friends. We were married at 10:45 in the morning. It turned out to be the perfect day for us. After the ceremony, we went home because nowhere else was open, and consequently, we were drinking champagne before noon. We had our lunch at the Dibbinsdale, which is a hotel in a picturesque setting by a lake. We finished our lunch to get to the Merebrook before closing time at 3:00 p.m. where the wedding party got a little bigger and louder. By the time we got to the rugby club, things were very merry indeed. By 7:00 p.m., we called it a day and left to spend the first night in our own little flat.

Being January, it was cold and dark, and as we let ourselves in through the front door, it soon became obvious that we had neither light nor heat. The flat was dependent on electricity, and this was not available, even though we had arranged for the supply. We found out on the following Monday that the meters were collectively housed in one of the downstairs flats, and the tenant had not moved in to provide access. Tim was unthwarted. He had been a Queens Scout for many years of his youth and had moved his scouting equipment into the flat, unbeknown to me. He soon had his Tilley lamp set up and prepared to light it.

He can't have been aware of how much he had drunk over the course of the day because the minute it was lit, the mantle fell off and set fire to the coffee table that was awash with methylated spirits. We relished the heat for some minutes before dousing the flames. The next day, we were back at my mother's house to be fed and thawed out.

The house we lived in was very close to the promenade, and from our first-floor flat, we had uninterrupted views of the river. We were so close that we could watch The Royal Iris, which was a pleasure boat/ship that took day-trippers to the Isle of Man and back. We would watch the river for hours, especially in the summer, leaving the TV and light off until bedtime.

Still living happily in the flat, our daughter, Fern, arrived. It was a very happy time, and her being born in the first week of June meant that walks along the promenade became an everyday pleasure.

Sometimes we would walk all the way to New Brighton, which was a proper, though declining, seaside resort. There would often be a band playing in the park, and we could get an ice cream to eat on the way back. Tim had to give up his TR5 and got an MGB GT, which was still a two-seater sports car, but it had a shelf at the back which would accommodate the baby's carry cot. Poor Tim.

Before long, Tim was getting bored with his job at the Metal Box Factory.[3] We contacted a few breweries and eventually got an interview to assess our suitability regarding the tenancy of a pub. We were then interviewed by Mr. Guest. We renamed him Aunty Guest as he was elderly, fussy, but a kindly chap. He explained that breweries did not consider young couples with no experience but that there was a pub available that had been neglected, then shut down. As the ingoing was cheap and North Wales held no mysteries for us, we decided to view it.

The Cross Keys Inn was certainly in a dilapidated state but small enough to renovate quickly. Upstairs, there was a cosy sitting room leading to a good-sized kitchen. We had two bedrooms and a near-bathroom, no basin. This was rectified later when the brewery fitted one in our bedroom. Meanwhile, we used the one in the "ladies'" downstairs.

In the small Welsh village, in which we lived, you could count thirteen pubs and thirteen chapels. It was hopelessly old-fashioned, and

---

[3] Me again, no idea.

walking down the high street (main street) was like being in a time warp with little funny shops selling the merchandise they probably sold thirty years ago, men wearing brown or grey mackintoshes (raincoats), women spending whole days talking in Welsh to neighbours on the doorstep.

*****

That was as far as my dear unknown sister got with her story. I kept the spelling the same for the English charm factor. Thank you, Fern, for giving me permission to use excerpts of your Mum's writings to complete mine.

You Can't Live Forever but You Can Try

Death is an odd occurrence, and not to be morbid, but death has been woven like a sad tapestry of loss upon loss throughout my life.

You can cry, question, and grieve till you can't grieve anymore, but the conclusion I always come to is this: There's not a damn thing you can do about it. The person is gone.

Where have they gone? Heaven? Hell? The Great Beyond? Maybe he or she is just dead, and that's it. No, there's more. There's a second life or an everlasting joyous place you go to, providing you've been good here on earth as you've always been told.

I like to think that you're reunited with all those who've gone before you. That gives me great comfort, feeling that the joyous reunion will be my final reward. Wouldn't it be the greatest gift you could ever receive just to kiss your mother again, to talk to an old friend, to hold your child, or to hug your grandpa?

I also truly believe that people can give you signs or signals from wherever they go. I've witnessed it and heard some miraculous stories on the subject. Most people don't notice the signs and pass them off as coincidence, but the subtle visits are there right in front of you. When you dream, you may see a loved one or even speak to that person. It's a gift, a visit.

Each of us have our own way of grieving. Some cry for days, months, even years. Some shut themselves away from the world. And some of us, including me, sit back and remember just how special and wonderful the person was. I mostly feel grateful that I had the privilege of knowing my loved one, whoever it may be, of loving them even if our time together was cut short. I'm always thankful for being graced with his or her presence.

You can never replace the one you've lost; you can't have them back. But you can send out a prayer, you can kiss their picture as you pass by it, or you can hope they're standing beside you, sharing a beautiful painting, a breathtaking sunrise, or a moving piece of music you're experiencing for the first time. And if you believe it, then all of them, those you loved so much, are always with you. They're cheering you on, they're sharing your dreams, they're feeling your pain. That's what love is. It's all about love. And love is forever.

Dear Grandpa Ed,
    I hope you're happy typing away
in Heaven. Wish I would've had
more time to know you.

Dear Grandma Inga,
    Oh thank you so much for the
love, the fun, your glamour, and
your quirky ways. Thank you for
choosing me that morning at the lake.

Dear Grandpa Sam,
    What a kind and gentle man you
were. I loved you a lot, mine papa.

My cute little Grama Lil,
    I was your precious, precious and
you in turn, were so very precious to me.

Dear Grandpa Henrik,
    You loved me as your own grand-
daughter and for that, I'm forever grateful. Thank you for your humor and
your rousing rendition of Turkey In The
Straw.

To my dear Mom,
    My biggest fan and my best friend-
you loved me unconditionally. I can't
find the words to thank you enough,
for being the most beautiful person
and the perfect example of the mother
you were to me. I love you always.
And I have so much to tell you.

Jim,

You nearly made it ... I'm so sorry you weren't strong enough to overcome your demons. You were such a good person — the drugs got the best of you. Have fun at the "big party in the sky." NO DRUGS this time!

Dear Auntie Sylvia,

I didn't know you well, you lived too far away — when I did see you, I always felt loved by you with your quiet and gentle ways.

Dear Auntie LaVerne,

Such a sweet lady you were. I loved your shining eyes and your genuine smile. I wish I could've seen you one more time, at least.

Dear Uncle Charles,

You were the most lovable devil I've ever known. Thank you for your uniqueness and the love that radiated from your face. And also for your wonderful laugh.

My lovely Auntie Angel,

You were always one of my favorites. From head to toe, you were an amazing woman. You had an aura of warmness about you. I think of you often, remembering your kindness and your love of Danke Schoen.

Joe-Joe,
I hope you found what you were looking for and are reunited with your soul mate. Thank you my friend, for everything.
All is groovy now.

Oh, Roll...
I mostly thank you for helping to create our wonderful daughter. I really loved you with all my heart, way back when. Wish you would've figured it out but I hope you're happy and at peace doing what you loved most: sitting next to a campfire with your dog.

My hilarious and also wise friend, Beau. What a guy. An amazing, awesome guy. If you wouldn't have been gay, I would've married you in a heart-beat. I love you and miss you.

Dearest Mum,
So happy and thankful that you accepted me with open arms. Thank you for raising a lovely son I'm glad every day to call my husband. Hope you're sitting comfortably with a nice cuppa. Cheerio, Mum.

My dear loving Dad,
How I miss you. You were the kindest, fairest, funniest Dad anyone could wish for. Thank you for hanging in there as long as you could - for all of us. (especially me). Love you "muches" forever.

My dear Mama-Nina,
    I would've gladly had you as my mother
had I not had a perfect one already. You
were my "second Mom" and I loved you more
than you knew. We'll have one of our hours-
long chats when we see each other again.
Thank you for being you.

My funny Uncle Chum,
    Loved your cleverness, your wit, and
your artistic talent — the talent that
could've made you a celebrated artist —
loved you. Thank you for the special
bond we shared. Unspoken, but I always felt it.

Dear Mother-Maxine
            and sister-Flora,
    Even though we never met, I feel such
a connection to you both. I love that you
are a part of me and I am a part of you.
So many things I'd like to say. So many
things I'd like to ask. There will come
a day...

These two I didn't know personally but their
passing really made me sad.

Dear Purple One,
    You were amazing. Thanks for the dance,
the music, the sex, and the romance.

Gorgeous George,
One of the most effortless voices I've ever heard. Smoothness personified. I could listen to you all day long - and often times do. Thank you for your many musical moods and for being so gorgeous.

Now retired, I must thank Gerry Marsden (of Gerry and the Pacemakers)! You have made my life complete with the gift of your song, Ferry Cross the Mersey! Sometimes I feel as if you wrote it just for me. Many, many thanks, Gerry.

Just before this book was finished, Gerry passed away. He'll always be remembered for the music and the joy he bestowed on the world.

328

CPSIA information can be obtained
at www.ICGtesting.com
Printed in the USA
LVHW092128280721
694009LV00009B/56

9 781648 019388